Tumulus Cemetry of Hagios Basileios

Tumulus Cemetery of Mesonisi

Macedonian Tomb IV

Church of Hagios Dimitrios

Macedonian Tomb V

Northern Cemetery

Church of Hagia Paraskevi

● CITY OF DION

N ▶

Satellite map. From left to right: Mount Olympus, the Pierian plain, and the Thermaikos Gulf.

GODS AND MORTALS AT OLYMPUS

ANCIENT DION, CITY OF ZEUS

EDITED BY DIMITRIOS PANDERMALIS

HELLENIC REPUBLIC
Ministry of Culture and Sports

Onassis
Foundation (USA)

This catalogue is issued on the occasion of the exhibition *Gods and Mortals at Olympus: Ancient Dion, City of Zeus*, held at the Onassis Cultural Center, New York, March 24–June 18, 2016. The exhibition is organized by the Onassis Foundation (USA) and the Dion Excavations, in collaboration with the Hellenic Ministry of Culture and Sports—Ephorate of Antiquities of Pieria.

EXHIBITION

Curator
Dimitrios Pandermalis

Exhibition Manager
Roberta Casagrande-Kim

General Assistant
Niki Dollis

Conservators
Dimitrios Maraziotis
Costas Vasiliadis
Marguerita Benaki

Exhibition Designer
Daniel Kershaw

Graphic Designer
Sophia Geronimus

Lighting Designer
David Clinard

CATALOGUE

Scientific Editor
Dimitrios Pandermalis

Managing Editor
Roberta Casagrande-Kim

Copy Editor
Mary Cason

Translator
Valerie Nunn

Designer
Sophia Geronimus

Photographer
Orestis Kourakis

Image Editing
Yannis Stavrinos

Color separation and Printing
Register-Petros Kalamatianos

CONCEPT AND DIRECTION
Amalia Cosmetatou

Published by the Onassis Foundation (USA)
Olympic Tower
645 Fifth Avenue
New York, NY 10022
www.onassisusa.org

ISBN 978-0-9906142-2-7
Printed in Greece

Front cover: Cult Statue of Zeus Hypsistos (detail of cat. no. 6).
Page 2: Boissonnas Frederick, 1913. *Sous le sommet Mitka.*
Page 6: View of the Mytikas and Stefani Peaks (2015).
Page 8: Boissonnas Frederick, 1913. *Untitled* (View of the Mytikas and Stefani Peaks).

7   FOREWORD
Aristides Baltas
Minister of Culture and Sports of the Hellenic Republic,
Ministry of Culture and Sports

9   FOREWORD
Anthony S. Papadimitriou
President, Alexander S. Onassis Public Benefit Foundation

10   PREFACE
Dimitrios Pandermalis
President, Acropolis Museum, Athens; Director, Dion Excavations

12   Satellite maps

ESSAYS

19   ANCIENT DION: A CHRONICLE OF THE EXCAVATIONS
Dimitrios Pandermalis
President, Acropolis Museum, Athens; Director, Dion Excavations

31   THE CULT OF DEMETER AT DION
Semeli Pingiatoglou
Professor of Classical Archaeology, Department of Archaeology,
Aristotle University of Thessaloniki

41   FROM THE KINGDOM OF MACEDONIA
TO THE COLONY OF DION: THE USE AND
FUNCTION OF COINAGE
Sophia Kremydi
Senior Researcher, Institute of Historical Research,
National Hellenic Research Foundation, Athens

49   SNIPPETS OF EVERYDAY LIFE IN ROMAN DION
Angelos Chaniotis
Ancient History and Classics Professor, School of Historical Studies,
Institute for Advanced Study, Princeton

57   GREEK MYTHS AT DION: DIVINE FAMILY IN
A HUMAN LANDSCAPE
Richard P. Martin
Antony and Isabelle Raubitschek Professor in Classics,
Department of Classics, Stanford University

67   ZEUS OLYMPIOS AND HIS CULT IN GREECE
Fritz Graf
Distinguished University Professor, Director of Epigraphy,
Department of Classics, Ohio State University

75   MOUNT OLYMPUS AND ITS NATURAL WEALTH
Katerina Boli
Archaeologist, Department of Exhibitions, Communication
and Education, The Goulandris Natural History Museum-Greek
Biotope/Wetland Centre, Kifisia

Maria Katsakiori
Environmental Scientist, Head of Department of Exhibitions,
Communication and Education, The Goulandris Natural History
Museum-Greek Biotope/Wetland Centre, Kifisia

CATALOGUE

90   THE SANCTUARY OF ZEUS OLYMPIOS
Maria Iatrou
Archaeologist, Department of Archaeology,
Aristotle University of Thessaloniki

94   THE SANCTUARY OF ZEUS HYPSISTOS
Maria Iatrou
Archaeologist, Department of Archaeology,
Aristotle University of Thessaloniki

99   THE SANCTUARY OF DEMETER
Semeli Pingiatoglou
Professor of Classical Archaeology, Department of
Archaeology, Aristotle University of Thessaloniki

108   THE SANCTUARY OF ISIS
Maria Iatrou
Archaeologist, Department of Archaeology,
Aristotle University of Thessaloniki

114   THE VILLA OF DIONYSUS
Dimitrios Pandermalis
President, Acropolis Museum, Athens;
Director, Dion Excavations

124   THE GREAT BATHS
Maria Iatrou
Archaeologist, Department of Archaeology,
Aristotle University of Thessaloniki

129   FINDS FROM THE CITY AND
THE NECROPOLIS
Maria Iatrou
Archaeologist, Department of Archaeology,
Aristotle University of Thessaloniki

151   BIBLIOGRAPHY

159   Drawings and Photography Credits

Associated with the cult of Zeus Olympios and the Muses, Dion is a unique archaeological site with a life-span from the Archaic period to the Roman era and located on the slopes of Olympus, the Mountain of the Greek Gods, in a remarkable natural setting blessed with impressive environmental wealth.

The exhibition *Gods and Mortals at Olympus* is a significant effort designed to present a glimpse of the scientific work—including excavations, conservation, restoration, and promotion—carried out at Dion from the early twentieth century to the present day. The main goal of the exhibition is to shed light on the interplay among daily life, art, and cult practices in one of the most important religious centers of the ancient world.

The focus of the exhibition—exploring human life on the slopes of an awe-inspiring mountain identified as the seat of the gods through the centuries—invites us to reflect upon the relationship between the sacred and the profane, the ordinary and the sublime in human societies. The objects selected for the exhibition include breathtaking artworks, such as sculptures and mosaics, as well as artifacts from the daily and ritual life of the city.

The catalogue accompanying the exhibition is a beautifully designed publication containing essays covering the chronicle of the excavations, cults, everyday life, and the natural environment of the area. Through these essays, ancient Dion comes alive to the eyes and mind of the contemporary viewer.

It is from this perspective that I would like to express my gratitude to the organizers of the exhibition for their efforts to create a strong synergy aimed at highlighting the significance of a sensational archaeological site. I am certain that the New York public will appreciate and enjoy the exhibition.

Aristides Baltas, Professor
Minister of Culture and Sports of the Hellenic Republic

Ἠὼς μὲν κροκόπεπλος ἐκίδνατο πᾶσαν ἐπ᾽ αἶαν,
Ζεὺς δὲ θεῶν ἀγορὴν ποιήσατο τερπικέραυνος
ἀκροτάτῃ κορυφῇ πολυδειράδος Οὐλύμποιο·
αὐτὸς δέ σφ᾽ ἀγόρευε, θεοὶ δ᾽ ὑπὸ πάντες ἄκουον·

Dawn wearing her golden-orange peplum covered all earth
when Zeus, carrying lightning, called for an assembly of the gods
on the topmost summit of Mount Olympus with the many crags
and forests. He spoke to them, and they were listening....

(Homer, *Iliad*, 8.1-4. Translated by A. S. Papadimitriou)

There is always a reason why a city is built in a specific location or why a specific place takes on a special meaning as a center of religion, art, and education. Certain cities have risen to fame, and soon they were destroyed and faded into insignificance. Others have maintained their resilient claim over the millennia embodying, so to speak, a specific idea. Mount Olympus is such a place. There are other sacred places in Greece graced by nature and the gods, such as Delphi, Olympia, Delos, Dodoni, and many other smaller sites. None, however, was elected to be the abode of the gods. It is not just that it is the highest mountain in the Balkans. As anyone who has been there can attest, this mountain is special.

Living beneath such a legend in the city of Dion can be awe inspiring. How can you hold your agora in the shadow of the place where the gods were called to assemble in a protodemocratic but very characteristic forum? How can you daily gaze at the same "Dawn covered by her golden-orange peplum" that the gods behold? Nevertheless the citizens of Dion, from Paleolithic times to the Byzantine era and beyond, managed to do that without converting their polis into a theocratic state. Of course, religion is everywhere but not more so in Dion than in Athens, for example, or Sparta or Corinth.

Dion was not a major city from a historical perspective. However, as this exhibition attests, one citizen living in Dion had four sculptures (now headless) of philosophers chatting and a magnificent mosaic of the retinue of Dionysus on the floor of his dining hall. You can judge for yourself the religious quality, or lack thereof, of this fantastic mosaic: a god who is not a god, nor man, but something in between.

In this exhibition, as in the past, we seek to provide the viewer with a challenge: What is it to live in the shadow of Olympus? What was it to live in a mid-sized post-Classical Greek city? Thanks to the efforts and wise choices of Professor Pandermalis, we strive not just to give an exhibition of wonderful artifacts. This is only the beginning. We strive to recreate a space and its feeling. Its natural surroundings. Its atmosphere. We cannot recreate a capsule in time and space, but we can try to give to the sentient visitor the opportunity to glimpse what might have been.

It has been said that history is what we think is correct, from what we understand and from the historical evidence that has survived. We offer this exhibition as a living example of this motto. As to the rest, each of us carries his own gods and reaches for his own holy mountain.

My special thanks to the Minister of Culture and Sports, Professor Aristides Baltas, and the Secretary General of the Ministry of Culture, Dr. Maria Andreadaki Vlazaki. A warm thank you to the authors of this catalogue for their instrumental contributions to the understanding of Dion, its relevance, and its complex ties, ancient and modern, to the majestic Mount Olympus. Last but not least, I wish to thank the staff of the Onassis Foundation (USA) for their hard work, dedication, and enthusiasm in organizing this exhibition as well as the full inaugural season of the renovated Cultural Center in New York.

Indeed, this major exhibition marks the reopening of the gallery spaces at the Onassis Cultural Center NY after three years of renovation. We are eager to welcome American and international visitors to our new space and are ready to host a new series of art exhibitions that, following in the established tradition of the Onassis Cultural Center NY, will continue to explore and present the Hellenic heritage while challenging preconceived stereotypes of ancient societies and their cultures.

Dr. Anthony S. Papadimitriou
President, Alexander S. Onassis Public Benefit Foundation

When I first arrived at Dion in 1970 to supervise the archaeological excavation organized by the University of Thessaloniki, I could not imagine that I would remain bound to this site for the next forty-five years of my life. Three years later, following the retirement of Professor George Bakalakis, I became the director of the archaeological excavation. Dion was then a land that was almost unknown in the archaeological landscape. Through large-scale excavation, the area of the sanctuaries outside the city walls was revealed along with a good portion of the city itself. The conditions under which the excavations on the eastern side of the archaeological site were realized were particularly difficult. The entire area was submerged under water that was constantly renewed by hundreds of natural springs that drew to the surface the abundant underground water supply supported by the gorges of Mount Olympus. Ironically, the great benefit of this disadvantage was that on many occasions—as for the excavation of the Sanctuary of Isis—the finds had remained intact, as they must have been on the day when they were ultimately covered by the alluvia strata carried by the torrid floods of that era. Indeed, some of the statues still stood erect on their bases.

At the excavations of Dion, we found works that had been restored in antiquity, such as the statue of Aphrodite Hypolympidia, which had been damaged, repaired, and then mounted on a new base. Other sculptures and inscriptions were found incorporated as construction material in the city walls. Some statues, damaged through earthquakes, had been shifted to other locations, as was the case with the portrait head of Herennianus. Finally, many inscriptions were found in the Sanctuary of Zeus Olympios discarded in large pits.

During these forty-five years of work, not only were we able to locate ancient buildings and portable finds but also to chart the adventures of many individuals throughout the centuries. Beyond the multitude of statues, mosaics, ceramics, and coins, the excavations brought to light ancient inscriptions that allowed us to glean information about the persons and personalities who were central figures in the history of Dion. Reference to the kings Kassandros, Antigonos, Philip V, and Perseus testify to royal presence in Dion during the Hellenistic Period and thus the significance of the city. From these inscriptions, we learned also of the Macedonian nobles Epigenes, Agasicles, and Pyrilambes as well as of common people such as Theotimos, son of Parmenon; Aristotima, daughter of Sosos; Eukleia, daughter of Hegisandros; and Sosandros, son of Apollonios.

The exhibition *Gods and Mortals at Olympus: Ancient Dion, City of Zeus* at the Onassis Cultural Center in New York aims to provide visitors with a sense of Dion through the presentation of some of its most significant finds, as well as to introduce the wonder of the natural environment that inspired the ancients to develop a sacred center at the foothills of Olympus, the mountain of the Greek Gods.

For the decisions and support that made this exhibition possible, I would like to thank Professor Aristides Baltas, Minister of Culture; Maria Andreadaki-Blazaki, General Secretary of the Ministry of Culture; Suzanna Houlia-Kapeloni; Head of the Directorate of Museums; and Natasha Balaska, Archaeologist with the Directorate. I am also grateful to Eleni Papastavrou, Director of the Ephorate of Antiquities of Pieria, as well as Eva Alvanou, archaeologist, and Maria Papathanasiou, conservator, both of the Ephorate.

I warmly thank the President of the Onassis Foundation, Dr. Anthony S. Papadimitriou, and the members of the Foundation's Board of Directors in Athens and New York, who generously supported the exhibition as the first to take place in the renovated galleries in New York. The Board of Directors also adopted the historic project of the conservation and display of the Dionysus Mosaic at Dion. The Foundation's Executive Director, Amalia Cosmetatou, as always, provided enthusiasm and momentum for our collaboration, ably supported by Roberta Casagrande-Kim, Assistant Manager of Exhibitions and Publications, while the design of the exhibition was artfully executed by Daniel Kershaw. Of course, I must also thank Ambassador Loucas Tsilas for his role in the initial discussions that led to this exhibition.

For their highly skilled work in remounting the exhibits, I particularly wish to thank the conservators of the Acropolis Museum, Dimitrios Maraziotis and Costas Vasiliadis. Special thanks also to Marguerita Benaki for her supervision of the delicate task of the removal, restoration, and display of the Dionysus Mosaic with the assistance of her entire team.

To Semeli Pingiatoglou and archaeologist Maria Iatrou, my thanks for their work in preparing the documentation of the exhibits for the catalogue. I am grateful to my longstanding colleague archaeologist Korinna Vastelli for coordinating preparation of the exhibits. In Athens, I thank Niki Dollis, director of my office, for her work coordinating our efforts with the New York office of the Foundation.

To the authors who contributed their excellent essays to this catalogue, I thank in order of their presentation, Semeli Pingiatoglou, Aristotle University of Thessaloniki; Sophia Kremydi, National Hellenic Research Foundation, Athens; Angelos Chaniotis, Institute for Advanced Study, Princeton; Richard P. Martin, Stanford University; Fritz Graf, Ohio State University; and Maria Katsakiori with Katerina Boli, Goulandri Natural History Museum.

I close with the hope that this exhibition provides a successful start to the new generation of exhibitions in the renovated gallery spaces of the Onassis Foundation in New York, and that it will be the first of many pleasures therein for its visitors.

Dimitrios Pandermalis
Director, Acropolis Museum; Director, Dion Excavations

Early Christian Basilica

Villa of Dionysus, Mosaic Room

Water Organ sector

Macellum

Baths of the Agora

Agora

House of Leda

House of Zosas

Odeon

South Gate

N

Satellite map, Dion: Detail of the city center.

Great Baths

South Gate ▼

Sanctuary of Demeter

Sanctuary of Zeus Hypsistos

Sanctuary of Isis

Satellite map. Dion: area of the sanctuary
complexes outside the South Gate.

ESSAYS

ANCIENT DION:
A CHRONICLE OF THE EXCAVATIONS

THE CULT OF DEMETER AT DION

FROM THE KINGDOM OF MACEDONIA
TO THE COLONY OF DION: THE USE
AND FUNCTION OF COINAGE

SNIPPETS OF EVERYDAY LIFE
IN ROMAN DION

GREEK MYTHS AT DION: DIVINE
FAMILY IN A HUMAN LANDSCAPE

ZEUS OLYMPIOS AND HIS CULT
IN GREECE

MOUNT OLYMPUS AND ITS
NATURAL WEALTH

ANCIENT DION: A CHRONICLE OF THE EXCAVATIONS

DIMITRIOS PANDERMALIS

Acropolis Museum

As the gateway to ancient Macedonia and a sacred center for the cult of Zeus Olympios and the Muses, Dion first appears in history in the fifth century BC through the words of Thucydides (4.78) and Diodoros (17.16). The earliest finds unearthed by the excavation also belong to the same century. The importance of Dion lies in the sacred nature of the site and in the reorganization of the great festival of Zeus and the Muses by Archelaos, King of Macedon (413–399 BC), who increased its duration to nine days and added athletic and theatrical contests.

Responsibility for organizing the majestic rituals and the contests in honor of Zeus lay with the royal court at Pella. The kings themselves entertained friends and foreign visitors there, held banquets, hosted lavish meals, and presented gold and silver wine goblets to their guests. Philip II himself crowned the winning actors of the theatrical contests at one such banquet, while Alexander erected a royal tent with a hundred couches and addressed himself personally to his companions and other officers, managing to alleviate their gloomy mood and rouse their enthusiasm for undertaking a great campaign in the east. It was at Dion that Alexander dedicated the first great monument to his triumphs in battle. Twenty-five bronze horsemen, equestrian statues of the king's companions who had fallen in the first clash with the Persians in the Battle of the Granikos in 334 BC, were set up in the sanctuary of Zeus Olympios. This sculptural group by the celebrated sculptor Lysippus earned great fame. When in 148 BC the Roman praetor L. Caecilius Metellus won a decisive victory over the Macedonians, he removed this sculpture from Dion and placed it in the Campus Martius in Rome in front of the temple of Zeus and Hera as a symbol of his victory (Vitr. 3.2.5). Following the end of the Hellenistic world—traditionally associated with the naval battle at Actium in 31 BC—Octavian designated Dion a colony (Colonia Julia Augusta Diensis), exempt from taxes and entitled to self-government. Thus began a new period of prosperity and flourishing for Dion that culminated between the second and the first half of the third century AD, the period of the philhellene emperors. Afterward, Dion experienced a rapid decline due to the Ostrogoth attacks on Macedonia, when the city walls were repaired to withstand the threat of the barbarians. Subsequently, in the fourth century AD, there was a short-lived resurgence: in the center of the shrunken city, an impressive Christian basilica was built along the paved way that led to Mount Olympus.

During the Middle Ages, Dion was abandoned and forgotten. It was only in 1806 that the British military officer and traveler William Martin Leake (1777–1860) discovered and identified the ruins of Dion amid the dense vegetation and rushing waters near Melathria, a small village of farmers and herdsmen.[1] He recognized in two earthen mounds a theater and a stadium and, in nearby bushes, the fortified walls of the ancient city. Nothing changed until 1855, when the first archaeologist, Léon Heuzey (1731–1822), visited Dion. He mapped the perimeter of the city walls, identified some of its towers, and recorded a number of inscriptions from ancient funerary stelae. As soon as Macedonia was liberated from the Ottoman Empire in 1912, lively interest was shown in Dion. The archaeologist G. P. Oikonomos collected and then published all the inscriptions he had found in the vicinity of Dion. In 1928 the University of Thessaloniki finally commenced excavations to uncover the ancient city. In June of that year, George Soteriades, the rector of the university and professor of archaeology and history, began excavating, initially with the primary aim of discovering the great sanctuary of Zeus Olympios.[2] He explored many of the tumuli scattered around the site and dug deep trenches that revealed massive dressed stones and heaps of ancient bricks. The first extensive search was carried out on the largest of the tumuli, within the walls of the city, revealing an Early Christian basilica with two building phases. The notion that under this building there was an ancient temple drove the excavator to go down more than 5 m, but in vain. Soteriades continued looking for the famous sanctuary of Zeus Olympios: he dug exploratory trenches both inside and outside the walls, and in 1929 he excavated a low tumulus on the western side of the site, which concealed a magnificent vaulted Macedonian tomb with a Doric facade

Fig. 1. Villa of Dionysus. Discovery of two statues of enthroned philosophers.

and an Ionic antechamber dated to the end of the fourth century BC. The marble doors had been broken down and were lying on the floor of the antechamber, and the vault had been broken by ancient tomb robbers who had entered the burial chamber to plunder the tomb. Several pieces of a frieze with Persian-style lions had been preserved on the vaulted roof of the tomb, while a depiction of a cavalry battle was found on the far side of a marble funerary couch (fig. 2).

In 1955 the Ephor of Antiquities, Charalambos Makaronas, found and excavated the second Macedonian tomb, which contained a stone couch and had a colored pebble floor. A third tomb, with a masonry couch and three pedestals, was excavated a year later. In 1979 the fourth Macedonian tomb, closed by marble doors and containing a funerary couch decorated in ivory inlays (cat. no. 61), was discovered under a tall tumulus to the northeast (fig. 3). The fifth and last such tomb came to light in 1988. Among the excavators' finds were a plate inscribed ΕΠΙΓΕΝΗΣ ("Epigenes," cat. no. 66) and a silver tetradrachm of Alexander the Great (cat. no. 65).[3]

In 1962 the topographical mapping of the entire area containing the ancient ruins led to the discovery of a large section of city walls with towers on the south side of the site, while a second theater, dated to the Roman Imperial period, was revealed to the southeast of the Hellenistic theater. Excavations had halted in 1931 and only resumed thirty years later under the direction of George Bakalakis, a professor at the University of Thessaloniki.[4] Despite his persistent search, Bakalakis's exploratory trenches did not lead to the discovery of the sanctuary of Zeus Olympios. However, during this same period, the Byzantinist Stylianos Pelekanidis completed the excavation of the city's Early Christian basilica.

In the summer of 1973, Dimitrios Pandermalis, of the University of Thessaloniki, assumed direction of the excavations. The main objective was the exploration of two buildings with stone socles that were visible on the outside of the city's south walls. After the first few days of work, it became clear that they were two flanking temples with accesses from the east. The excavation finds (e.g., sculptures, small objects, and pottery) suggested that the two temples were dedicated to the goddesses Demeter and Kore.

Fig. 2. Macedonian Tomb I. Marble funerary bed after restoration and reconstruction.

Fig. 3. Macedonian Tomb IV. Facade of the tomb during excavations.

This theory was confirmed by an engraved dedicatory inscription on a fragment of a fourth-century-BC skyphos that bore the name of Demeter, to whom the vessel had been dedicated. The exploration of this sanctuary was later taken over by Semeli Pingiatoglou, who also published the excavation finds.[5] That same summer, a small temple was discovered and excavated. It had an entrance on the south side and finds associated with the cult of Asclepius, Hygeia, and Telesphoros. Finally, the excavation of the central paved road led to the discovery of a monument over 37 m long and decorated with relief panels representing cuirasses and shields.

In the sanctuaries sector outside the city of Dion is the great horseshoe-shaped mound of the theater. The *scaenae frons* was identified from the initial exploratory trench that was dug in 1970. Subsequently, excavations revealed the orchestra and its *cavea*. This theater is dated to the Hellenistic period; the fifth-century-BC theater in which Euripides staged the *Bacchae* in the presence of the Macedonian reformer king Archelaos would probably have stood on the same site.[6] Bakalakis identified and excavated an impressive Roman theater contiguous with the sanctuary of Zeus Olympios.

A second large mound proved to be the stadium of Dion, where the "athletic contests" of the Dion Olympics were held. In 1995, in the exceptionally careful excavations carried out under the supervision of George Karadedos, the track was found along with several of the audience seating rows that were built of bricks laid upon terraces dug into the mound. It was in this stadium, in the second century AD, that Lucian read an oration on the work of Herodotus or Aetios in front of a large audience.

Toward the end of the fourth century BC—when Dion was already well-known thanks to the presence there at one time of Archelaos, and later Philip II and Alexander the Great—King Kassandros embellished the city with great public buildings and marvelous city walls. The new city, roughly half of a square kilometer in size, was almost square; it had monumental gates on each side, and fortified towers every 33 m along the walls. The excavations of the city walls began in 1928 under Soteriades and ended in 1998, when they were published by Theodosia Stefanidou-Tiveriou.[7]

Some 4 km to the west of Dion is a large, sloping area cut into by deep and strikingly wide dry riverbeds. During periods of torrential rain, large quantities of water rush down from the mountain, carrying with them massive amounts of pebbles and rocks. The largest stream, the Ourlias, comes to an end at the northwest corner of the city walls, where a stratum of alluvial silt rises to over 7 m. As far back as 1928, Soteriades had found on the north bank of the Ourlias (at Hagios Basileios) round heaps of stones that he believed to be the remains of ancient huts. In 1980 excavations at the site revealed that many of these mounds, built in large pebbles, concealed graves: sometimes one or two, sometimes more—up to, in one case, twenty-two (fig. 4).

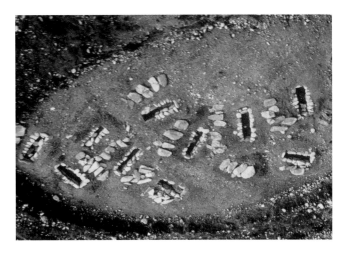

Fig. 4. Hagios Basileios. Discovery of the graves under a tumulus.

Fig. 5. Mesonisi. Excavation of one of the graves of the cemetery.

The excavations continued on the wide plateau on the south bank of the stream, at Mesonisi (fig. 5).[8] Most of the graves were simple pits, built of stone and informally arranged around the center of the tumulus. In several instances, a large grave, perhaps that of the head of the family, was found at the center. In female graves, buckles and brooches (cat. no. 57) for fastening clothes were found, together with spiral bangles (cat. no. 58), earrings, and coiled tubes (cat. no. 59) for fixing to a headdress of some sort, along with necklaces of carnelian and faience. Male graves were simpler; sometimes an iron knife was found. Clay vessels in both burials were predominantly oinochoes with the backs cut away, cantharuses (cat. no. 56), skyphoi, miniature craters, and

Fig. 6. Great Baths, Frigidarium. Statue of Dionysus at the time of discovery.

cups (i.e., drinking goblets). The pottery was usually unpainted; however, a number of vessels displayed a dark-colored geometric decoration in hasty, careless brushstrokes. The grave goods from the tumuli to the west of Dion, which are comparable to similar finds from all the tumulus cemeteries at the eastern foothills of Olympus, are precious evidence of the otherwise little-known period from the tenth to the sixth century BC, toward the end of which the Argead dynasty emerged in the plains of lower Macedonia with its capital at Aegae and its religious center at Dion.

One of the largest heaps of ruins was at the southern edge of the ancient city. Some large cornerstones remained standing, and polychrome tesserae were found in the rubble. A new excavation sector was established there in the summer of 1976, and it was soon apparent that the area was a large complex of public baths (figs. 6).[9] The picture emerging from the ruins was impressive, and the conditions of a mosaic depicting a sea bull, discovered in the area of the frigidarium, suggested that the building's destruction had been brought about by a powerful earthquake that happened already in antiquity. Indeed, this mosaic had been cut in two, one of the two halves being sunken 50 cm lower than the other. The walls of this room had also been split in two. On the

north side of the baths, excavations discovered a space containing a large, marble basin and many broken sculptures, which when restored revealed six statues identifiable by the inscriptions on their bases as Aegle (cat. no. 45), Akeso, Hygeia, Machaon, Panacaea, and Podaleirius (cat. no. 44)—the six children of Asclepius, a divinity who was a favorite of visitors to the baths. Interestingly, the right calf of Podaleirius was found outside the building where the rubble had been thrown when a part of the baths was being cleared by the ancients, sometime after the earthquake. During the investigations of the baths, the inscribed, headless herm of the philosopher Herennianus (cat. no. 43) was also found. Its head was eventually found in the Villa of Dionysus, where it had been brought after the earthquake. Excavations at the Great Baths continued up to 1984 and provided a wealth of finds from the sculptural decoration and the architecture of the building.

Dion's luxuriant vegetation and its isolation from the road network gave the site an exotic character up to the end of the 1960s. However, the abundance of fresh water had created many shallow lakes and marshes that urgently required drainage and sanitation work. As the Baphyras, the ancient river of Dion, had silted up over the centuries, it was necessary to dig a channel to provide an outlet for the water. In the digging work of 1951, the body of a statue had been discovered, pulled from the mud, and transferred to the museum of the Dion excavations. In the summer of 1978, digging began on the spot where this statue was said to have been found twenty-seven years earlier. The whole area had been covered by a stratum of 2 m of mud that had probably been created by alluvium from the floods that are frequent occurrences at the site. The excavations unearthed the first architectural remains right below this thick layer of mud; within a few days, it was clear that the entrance to a temple set on a podium had been discovered (figs. 7, 8).[10] Two small piers, topped by marble slabs with a pair of scooped-out footprints (cat. no. 26), were identified on top of some marble steps. Known as *bemata*, they were inscribed with dedications to Isis Lochia, the goddess who assisted mothers in childbirth and the difficult time

Fig. 7. Sanctuary of Isis. Aerial view of the complex.

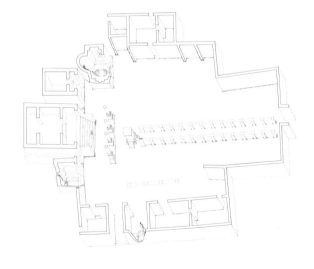

Fig. 8. Sanctuary of Isis. Axonometric drawing of the complex.

immediately thereafter. In addition, there was a relief depicting Isis that had fallen from the facade of the temple to the ground and was dedicated to the Egyptian triad of Serapis, Isis, and Anubis (cat. no. 25). The excavations, which continued until 1984, were carried out in unusually adverse conditions. Water gushed from springs throughout the area, and from time to time the entire dig was full of mud, causing the collapse of the trenches' interfaces. The search was carried out to a large extent by hand, probing the mud to locate finds. A circular dam was built on the site to drain the water, allowing drawing and photography to take place before each of the artifacts was pulled from its findspot. The overall picture of the excavation confirmed the initial conjecture that the sanctuary had suffered damage in a powerful earthquake. There was an attempt to repair the buildings, as can be seen from the tidy piles of architectural elements, part of which still remains on the ground. However, a great flood subsequently inundated the sanctuary, which was then abandoned. The sculptural dedications were found either standing on their pedestals or fallen in a stratum of mud 30 to 40 cm deep. When the excavation continued in the small temple to the north of the first temple, there were some surprises in store. This building did not have a proper floor: the room was largely occupied by a shallow receptacle for water. The water entered the room from the west, passed under the pedestal of the cult statue, filled the receptacle, and continued its course through an underground conduit into an open channel leading from the entrance to the sanctuary to the temple's altar. The inscription on the pedestal of the statue attests that the temple was dedicated to Aphrodite Hypolympidia—the Aphrodite of the foothills of Mount Olympus. Near the opening of the entrance through which the water flowed into the small temple was found a fallen female head, which fitted the body of the statue that had been discovered earlier when the channel had been dug. Unsurprisingly, the plinth of the statue slotted into the corresponding pedestal base. The cult statue was reassembled, and the identity of the Aphrodite of Dion was revealed (cat. no. 29). Two more small temples flanked the main one to the south. The second of these two was of special interest: its cult statue was found upright on its pedestal within a semicircular niche (fig. 9). In its left hand, the female figure holds a cornucopia, while the inscription on the altar that stands in front of the temple names the goddess as Isis Tyche. The base of the statue had been reused on a number of occasions. Originally it was the pedestal of the royal statue of Kassandros of Macedon, providing confirmation to the words of Polybius (4.62), who mentions the attack by the Aetolian general Skopas in 219 BC during which his men overturned the images of the kings when they plundered the sacred city. In the raised sides of the open channel to the east of the main altar, several small sculptures were found, including a statuette of Aphrodite. It seems likely that this channel was an "architectural substitute" for the Nile, the presence of which was important in a temple of Isis. In the left wing of the sanctuary, three pedestals were found for statues to its founders. The statue of Julia Phrougiane Alexandra was still standing on one of them, just as it must have stood in antiquity (fig. 10). Near the open channel was found a

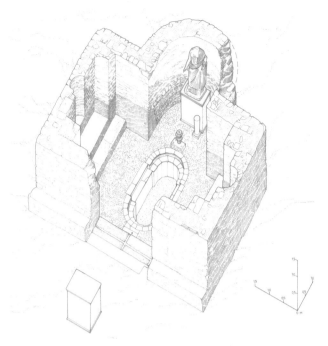

Fig. 9. Sanctuary of Isis. Axonometric drawing of the temple of Isis Tyche.

Fig. 10. Sanctuary of Isis. Statue of Julia Phrougiane Alexandra at the time of discovery.

small Hellenistic statue of a woman in the Archaic style with a pair of torches in her hand, probably a depiction of Artemis Eileithyia (cat. no. 28), the traditional goddess of childbirth, and likely the predecessor of Isis Lochia on this sacred site. Finally, it is worth noting the important role played in this sanctuary by water and by the receptacles that were meant to contain it. In the main temple, there was a built "Nile;" in the small temple of Aphrodite Hypolympidia, a shallow receptacle was on the floor in front of the cult statue; in the third temple, a masonry basin stood in front of the entrance; and in the tiny shrine of Isis Tyche, the masonry basin at the center was left bottomless as it sat over abundant flowing water that arose through the earth to fill it.

During a campaign of systematic investigations that took place at Dion in the early 1970s, it was observed that all the buildings located to the east side of the city were below a level of water. In order to explore the area archaeologically, it was absolutely essential to drain the water and channel it into the bed of the river that flowed nearby. It was decided to begin by excavating the paved roads that led to the river, taking advantage of the practice of the Romans, whose urban road system facilitated the discharge of most of the rainwater. In 1982, when the excavation of the roads had been successfully completed, archaeological explorations continued on a large building whose facade had been preserved to a reasonable height and that stretched some distance along the road. At first a series of shops came to light along with an entrance into the spaces behind them. It was soon ascertained that these rooms belonged to a relatively small bathhouse, a complex that could be accessed not just from the road but also from an adjacent building on the north side. A narrow passageway led to this building, ending in a tetrastyle atrium with a wellhead set on a stylobate.

The excavation then uncovered a second, more spacious tetrastyle atrium with a mosaic pavement, followed by a series of rooms. The last of these was a longitudinal hall with an apse at the east end, in front of which, buried by the debris, was found a fallen statue of Dionysus holding a drinking horn for wine (rhyton) in his left hand and raising his right, in which he probably originally held an oinochoe. In the middle of the hall, under the rubble, a mosaic panel was discovered depicting an enthroned Dionysus, crowned with ivy and holding a scepter in his right hand in the style of a ruler. This room was probably intended to be used for worship of the god as part of this large built complex. Between the two atria were found fragments of a statue depicting the well-known type of the Berlin Nike, with straps crossed over her chest and a gorgoneion at the point where they intersect. Of particular interest was the semicircular base of the sculpture, which depicts the sky. The Nike's feet scarcely touch the base, and the statue was fixed in place by using a strong wooden tenon under her draperies. The sculpture's head (cat. no. 40) was found in an adjoining room to the north, which gives onto a third atrium. Next to the Nike's head was discovered a marble head of Faustina the Younger, wife of Marcus Aurelius, and a short distance away was a head of Agrippina the Elder (cat. no. 39), the domineering mother of Nero. The third atrium—which was the most magnificent, with a marble wellhead in the center—was discovered after five years of excavations in this built complex, which by then had been conclusively identified as an urban villa with several atria, a shrine, and baths (fig. 11).

In June 1987, excavation of a large space east of the atrium commenced, and a splendid mosaic that covered the whole floor of the room, 100 square m in area, began to be revealed (fig. 12).[11]

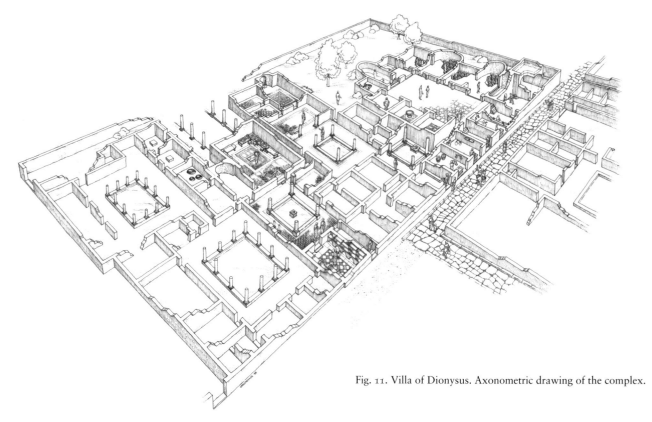

Fig. 11. Villa of Dionysus. Axonometric drawing of the complex.

Fig. 12. Villa of Dionysus. Discovery of the mosaic with the epiphany of Dionysus.

In the center, a large *emblema* shows Dionysus standing in his chariot in a triumphal epiphany (cat. no. 30). He holds a drinking horn (rhyton) and his thyrsos or ritual staff, decorated with ivy leaves and ribbons. Next to the god stands an elderly Silenus (Papposilenus) wearing a shaggy chiton and purple himation, not so much a charioteer as the god's supporter. The chariot, which emerges from a watery landscape, is drawn by two panthers, each with the tail of a sea monster, while two sea centaurs are in the driver's seat, holding the reins of the sea panthers. One of the centaurs is a mature, bearded man and carries a calyx crater on his shoulder to transport the wine needed for feasting. The other centaur carries on his shoulder a closed vessel, which probably contained the secret symbols of the Dionysus cult. In the lower part of the scene can be discerned the waves from which the coiled bodies of the sea monsters spring. The white background strongly emphasizes the figure of the god who manifests himself. The mosaicist used tesserae of various sizes and many dozens of shades to depict the details and to render the plasticity of the figures. Thus he managed to give a decidedly painterly character to his work, which was undoubtedly inspired by an important Hellenistic painting. Equally high is the quality of the mosaic in the six theatrical masks that frame the central *emblema*, three to the east and three to the west. Five of the masks have closed mouths, perhaps an indication that they are masks for pantomime actors. The central mask on the eastern side probably depicts Dionysus, with long locks and a hairstyle more suited to a woman. The mask immediately to its left depicts a mature satyr with a snub nose, pointed ears, and a drum (cat. no. 32). The mask to the right is unusual in that it depicts a bearded man with the face of a barbarian (cat. no. 33). His beard ends in a peak, his moustache is excessively long, and his hair is cut rather short and untidily. His eyes dominate the face, and his gaze is fixed on the ground. It is probably meant to be the mask of Lycurgus, King of Thrace and enemy of Dionysus. He pursued the young god, who fled to the sea and Thetis to save himself. Lycurgus's punishment for this impiety was to be driven mad: he kills his son and his wife, and ultimately is torn apart by wild horses. This myth was narrated in details in the satyr drama *Lykourgos* by Aeschylus. Located to the west of the central *emblema* are three other masks. The southernmost depicts a young satyr with pointed ears, while the mask at the north end represents a striking elderly Silenus with a white beard, sparse hair, fleshy lips, and large, expressive eyes (cat. no. 31). The central mask is that of a woman with loose and wavy hair, a small mouth, and a pale face. Her blue eyeballs are an uncommon feature and may be a reference to the water from which Dionysus emerges in the central scene, in which case the mask may depict the sea nymph Thetis.

There were few finds in this room, which seems likely to have been a splendid banqueting hall or triclinium, but they are significant: copper-alloy decorative elements with horses' heads from two supports from a couch, a satyr, a Heracles dressed as Omphale, and four statues of philosophers that were lined up along the north wall (fig. 1, cat. nos. 34–37). Three of the heads from these statues were found in the atrium outside the room, where the four philosophers, seated on thrones, had probably once stood. These types of statues recall similar sculptures of philosophers of the Epicurean School. The first statue on the east side seems to have been the most senior figure in the group, to judge by the open papyrus scroll he holds, and by his more elaborate throne. The statues were reused in the villa, and the facial features of the second and fourth philosophers were changed. In the north portico of the atrium, there was an aedicule from which parts of the Corinthian columns have been preserved, undoubtedly a second household shrine. To the north of the formal triclinium was found a mosaic that had fallen through from the upper floor. Its central medallion depicts the head of Medusa. The Villa of Dionysus is a splendid example of the highly developed style of urban life in a Greek city that was traditional but at the same time reflected the modernizing trends typical of the middle years of the Roman Empire. Immediately opposite the villa to the west, a unique find came to light: an ancient copper-alloy hydraulic organ, the earliest known to date (see p. 53, fig. 7).

In the area to the north of the Roman theater, two stray inscriptions mention that they were to be erected in the sanctuary of Zeus Olympios. It was this area that in 1973 had been proposed as the site of the most important sanctuary of Zeus: this was the location where great royal sacrifices were made to the father of the gods, and here statues of the kings of Macedon, including the already mentioned sculptural group of Lysippus, were set up.[12] In 1991 systematic excavations in search of the sacred complex and its finds began. By 2000 the precinct of the sanctuary had been discovered, including several important buildings, the great altar, and many of the copper-alloy straps used for tethering the animals sacrificed in the royal hecatombs. It seems that the damage caused by the army of the Aetolian Skopas in 219 BC was immense. Inscriptions that had been put up in the sanctuary were found as the fill of deep pits, while architectural members from earlier structures were discovered immured in the foundations of the great buildings. The inscriptions form an interesting group (cat. nos. 1–5), as they comprise the "published" versions of royal letters, the texts of treaties of alliance, and rulings on boundary disputes between cities. From them we learn not only of the existence of an epistates (royal representative) in Dion, but also of the *peleiganes* (a sort of local council). An inscription on the pediment of a marble stele refers to the alliance between King Perseus and the Boeotians. This alliance is mentioned by Livy (42.44) who says that its text was carved in three marble copies, one of which was intended for Thebes and another for the great sanctuary at Delphi. The destination of the third has hitherto remained unknown, as the name is now illegible in the manuscript that preserves this information. However, with this find, it is now certain that the third copy was meant for Dion and that the highly venerated and celebrated sanctuary mentioned in the text is that of Zeus Olympios. Among other finds was part of a copper-alloy shield bearing the star ornament of the royal house and the name Demetrius Poliorcetes, who was proclaimed King of Macedon in 294 BC. Among the bases of the royal statues, the pedestal of the Kassandros statue was found reused in the temple of Isis Tyche and, in an unrecorded location, that of the statue of Perseus, son of Philip IV of Macedon (d. 297 BC).

One of the most recent natural disasters to afflict Dion was the flood of 2002, which inundated the archaeological site and filled the large excavated area of the sanctuary of Isis with water, leaving the ruins of the ancient buildings buried under a thick layer of mud and silt once the water had drained away. To protect the sanctuary, it was decided to divert the course of the adjacent river Baphyras a few meters to the west and significantly widen the bed of the river so that future floodwaters would bypass the site. In the course of carrying out flood-defense works, a stylobate with parts of its columns was discovered in situ.[13] In the subsequent excavation, a colonette made of green marble, an Ionic capital in white marble, and a marble eagle with its wings spread were unearthed. These three finds, now

Fig. 13. Sanctuary of Zeus Hypsistos. Aerial view of the complex.

reassembled, were part of the same monument (cat. no. 9). On the body of the colonette was carved the inscription: Διί Υψίστω / Λ. Τρέβιος / Λέων / ευξάμενος (To Zeus Hypsistos / [from] L. Trevius / Leon / in fulfilment of a vow), leaving no doubt of the discovery of a sanctuary dedicated to Zeus Hypsistos (i.e., Almighty Zeus), whose cult was popular in Macedonia in the Hellenistic and Roman period (fig. 13). This identification was confirmed by the next find, a gabled marble pediment with the relief depiction of an eagle and a dedicatory inscription to Zeus Hypsistos. Excavations continued to the north, where the first discovery was the entrance to the precinct, followed by the altar, and finally the temple of the great god. Between the temple and the altar, more marble eagles were found. In front of the temple, and

on a continuation of its longitudinal axis, two small piers with reliefs of eagles were found in situ along with bucrania and sacrificial vessels. Contiguous with the north wall of the cella, there was a built structure, probably the base of the cult statue. A marble slab found fallen in front of this structure seems likely to have once been part of the revetment of this base. On the face of this slab are inscribed the names of the *dochai*, elected officials who were in charge of organizing the monthly feasts in honor of the god (cat. no. 10). Each of the twelve names of these appointees corresponds to one of the months of the Macedonian calendar, beginning with Xandikos. The inscription includes the date of the monument: the Roman imperial year 283, in ancient Greek ΓΠΣ. The imperial years were counted from the victory of Augustus at

Fig. 14. Sanctuary of Zeus Hypsistos. Cult Statue of Zeus Hypsistos at the time of discovery.

Actium: thus, 283 would correspond to 251/252 AD. Pieces of another inscription, probably from the same marble cladding of the base, refer to buildings associated with the sanctuary and to a list of names of devotees of Zeus Hypsistos. Zeus Hypsistos coexisted at Dion with Zeus Olympios, the god of Mount Olympus. Zeus Hypsistos was the god of the heavens, and when Dion was a Roman colony, he was also worshiped as Jupiter Optimus Maximus.

On July 6, 2003, as the excavation of the temple was approaching completion, the god's cult statue was dug out. Zeus Hypsistos was found lying against the east wall ((fig. 14, cat. no. 6). The enthroned statue, with a scepter in his left hand and a thunderbolt in his right, wore a himation folded back over the left shoulder, leaving bare the chest of the almighty god. This type of enthroned Zeus traces its distant origins back to Phidias's chef d'oeuvre at Olympia. The Dion copy, a work of high quality, can be dated to the second century AD and is based on creations from the Hellenistic period that drew from the same archetype.

The excavation revealed the whole of the sanctuary of Zeus Hypsistos. It is dominated by the southward-oriented temple that stands at its heart. To the west, contiguous with the west wing of the temple's pteron, is a water cistern, which seems to have played a part in the cult. To the north and west of the sanctuary, colonnaded porticoes (stoas) include rooms that apparently housed the *dochai* or monthly feasts held at the shrine. It was not possible to explore the east side, as it lies under the riverbed.

From 2007 onward, directed by Semeli Pingiatoglou, excavations were undertaken to find the earliest construction phases at Dion; a program was devised for the conservation of the ruins of the ancient agora; and studies were carried out on the excavation finds.[14] In October 2015, extensive work began under the supervision of Dimitrios Pandermalis and with generous funding from the Onassis Foundation, to detach, transport, restore, and display the large mosaic from the triclinium in the Villa of Dionysus in the Archaiotheke, an on-site conservation laboratory and interim display space for current finds in the Museum of Dion (fig. 15).

Fig. 15. Villa of Dionysus. Removal of the mosaic with the epiphany of Dionysus.

1 Leake 1967: 407ff.; Heuzey and Daumet 1876: 267ff.
2 Soteriades 1928: 59ff.; Soteriades 1929: 69ff.; Soteriades 1930: 36ff.; Soteriades 1931: 43
3 Pandermalis 1985: 9ff.
4 Bakalakis 1964, Bakalakis 1966: 347; Bakalakis 1968: 346; Bakalakis 1969: 341; Bakalakis 1971: 340
5 See chapter 2 in this volume. See also Pingiatoglou 2015.
6 Karadedos 1983: 235ff.; Karadedos 1991: 157ff.
7 Stephanidou-Tiveriou 1998.
8 Pandermalis 1981; Pandermalis 1984a; Poulaki-Pandermali 2013: 67ff.
9 Pandermalis 1985: 9ff.
10 Pandermalis 1982.
11 Pandermalis 1987; Pandermalis 1989b.
12 Pandermalis 1973; Pandermalis 1997b; Pandermalis 1998; Pandermalis 1999a; Pandermalis 2002; Pandermalis 2009.
13 Pandermalis 2003b; Pandermalis 2009.
14 Pingiatoglou et al. 2009.

THE CULT OF DEMETER AT DION

SEMELI PINGIATOGLOU

Aristotle University of Thessaloniki

Ancient Greek literature has preserved a wealth of information on the cult of Demeter in general and on the place the goddess occupied in the Greek pantheon. The evidence from written sources is supplemented by archaeological finds, not just in Greece but in the colonies of Magna Graecia and along the coast of Asia Minor. Originally worshiped as an earth goddess who protected the crops and ensured fruitfulness, like the earlier Gaia, Demeter would go on to become the goddess who promised posthumous bliss to those initiated into the mysteries of her cult.[1]

Unlike other sanctuaries, the cult of Demeter at Dion lacks references in the ancient literature, and thus reconstruction must be based exclusively on archaeological evidence and comparisons with the archaeological and documentary evidence from other sanctuaries.[2] The sanctuary of Demeter at Dion (fig. 2) is situated outside the walls, to the south of the ancient settlement, in the area occupied by the other sanctuaries. Specifically, it is located west of the sanctuaries of Isis and of Zeus Hypsistos, north of the sanctuaries of Asclepius and Zeus Olympios, and northeast of the Hellenistic theater. It occupies a pivotal point east of the main route leading from the ancient city to the area around the sanctuary of Zeus Olympios and the Roman theater.

Fig. 2. Sanctuary of Demeter. Aerial view of the complex and the southern limits of the city from the east.

Fig. 1. Sanctuary of Demeter. Aerial view of the northern section of the complex from the south.

The excavation of the sanctuary of Demeter at Dion began in 1973 and continued, with some interruptions, until 2003. During this period, an extensive sanctuary was uncovered (fig. 3), with many buildings and thousands of small finds. The excavation discovered two megaron-type Late Archaic–Classical temples (fig. 5); their two Hellenistic successors, which each had a pronaos and cella (fig. 4); a Hellenistic stoa; four temples and the remains of two stoas from the Imperial period (fig. 1); some areas of unspecified use from the Imperial period; and three kilns from workshops that must have been established there in the Early Christian period. There were also a series of altars, east of the temples, which had been set up in various periods.[3]

The discovery in the very first year of the excavation of a marble female head, covered with a himation and reminiscent of the Demeter of Knidos type, led to speculation that the goddess of agriculture was worshiped at the site (fig. 6, cat. no. 11). This theory was confirmed by a carved votive inscription on a fragment of a fourth-century-BC red-figure skyphos that preserves the name of the goddess in the dative: ΔΗΜΗΤΡΙ (to Demeter).

The most important characteristic of the cult of the goddess in Dion, during all phases of the temple's life, is the existence of two completely or virtually identical temples. It is worth noting that the beginning of the cult is also marked by the existence of two wells.

Fig. 3.
Sanctuary of Demeter.
Aerial view of the complex from the southeast.

Fig. 4.
Sanctuary of Demeter.
Aerial view of the Hellenistic temples, separated by a modern bridge for visitors.

This duplication of masonry structures reflects the worship of a pair of divinities. In other words, the two temples corresponded to two deities, probably Demeter and her daughter Kore/Persephone, whose cult at this particular sanctuary must have been combined with that of Aphrodite. This hypothesis is based on the archaeological evidence: the head of the marble cult statue of Demeter, mentioned above, was found in the southern Hellenistic temple, while a marble statue of Aphrodite was excavated from the northern temple. In one of the temples dated to the Roman Imperial period, a votive altar from the Imperial period and dedicated to Aphrodite was found along with a marble statuette depicting that same goddess (fig. 7).

Fig. 6. Sanctuary of Demeter. Head of the statue of Demeter at the time of discovery.

Fig. 7. Sanctuary of Demeter. Votive altar to Aphrodite pertinent to the Roman imperial phase of the sanctuary.

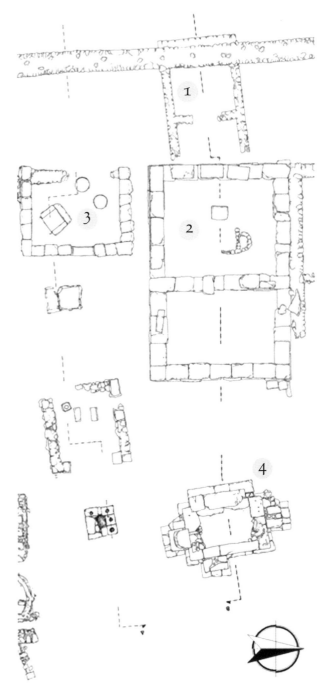

Fig. 5.
Sanctuary of Demeter. Plan.
(1) southern megaron
(2) southern Hellenistic temple
(3) precinct with wells
(4) altar

There is no evidence from the finds of any cult of a male god. The only head from a clay figurine that takes the form of a bearded male might depict Pluto, but other identifications are also possible. Moreover, a marble statuette of Asclepius attests to the close relationship between Demeter and Asclepius, with the healer god being worshiped in a neighboring temple, as was the case in other parts of the ancient Greek world.

There is evidence that a number of deities with related characteristics were worshiped in the sanctuary, a very frequent phenomenon at other ancient Greek sanctuaries. This can be deduced from archaeological evidence and is confirmed by epigraphic finds. The many altars suggest that multiple cults coexisted in the sanctuary; built altars, pits (known as *escharas*), wells, perforated libation stones, and tables for bloodless sacrifices, all attest to intensive cult activity at the sanctuary (fig. 8). The large number of altars combined with other evidence, such as inscriptions and statuary, offers further proof of the worship of two or more deities in tandem. There are many indications that Aphrodite was worshiped at this sanctuary, as noted above. Statues from the Hellenistic period depicting the goddess have been found, in addition to a votive inscription from the Imperial period. The dominant characteristic of Aphrodite as amalgamated with Persephone was her chthonic nature. In general, the relationship of Aphrodite with the Eleusinian deities, and above all with the maiden Kore, is reflected in myth—for example, that of Adonis. This is also attested in cult practices, either by the juxtaposition of their temples or by their joint depiction on votive offerings. Archaeological finds confirm this link at many sites, not just in Magna Graecia but also in Macedonia, at Pella, for example.

A horizontal offering table, found in secondary use and with a dedicatory inscription to Baubo,[4] can securely be associated with the sanctuary of Demeter. Indeed, this demonic figure of an elderly woman belongs to the Eleusinian cycle and in fact originates in the Orphic myth of the goddess. It should be emphasized that the inscription from the offering table, which reads Μενεκρίτη Θεοδώρου ιερητεύσασα Βαβοῖ (Menekrite daughter of Theodoros [who] served Baubo), provides the first indication that Baubo had her own priestesses, as it is more likely that the priestess of the inscription was offering her sacrifice to the goddess whom she served than to Demeter, the main deity of the sanctuary. In the case of votive inscriptions from other sites such as Paros and Naxos, Baubo is one of several goddesses together with Demeter, Kore, and Zeus Eubouleus (of Good Counsel) to whom sacrifice is made.

From some clay figurines and marble statuettes of boys, we can deduce that the cult at the sanctuary was connected with a goddess who protected children, as emerges from a statue base with a votive inscription addressed to the Kourotrophos (Child Nurturer). That Demeter shared the sanctuary with child-nurturing goddesses is accounted for by the similar qualities of the Eleusinian deities themselves, as can be inferred from epigraphic evidence.

An inscription found on a fragmentarily preserved statue base preserves the name of Eileithyia, the goddess of childbirth, in the second line. This goddess's connection with fertility would account for her being worshiped together with the chthonic goddesses, although the possibility of this inscription having been moved from the neighboring temple of Isis cannot be excluded. There is evidence in the latter of the worship of goddesses who protected women in childbirth and confinement, both Artemis Eileithyia and Isis Lochia.[5]

One Late Archaic clay figurine depicting Artemis is not enough to support the claim that this goddess was also worshiped at the sanctuary. However, the finding of two legs clad in high boots, one marble and the other clay, which could have come from a figure of Artemis, as well as a gold plaque with a depiction of Artemis holding a torch in each of her hands, and above all the discovery of a votive stele dedicated to Apollo and Artemis, all point to this conclusion. Further, in other sanctuaries, a shared cult of Demeter and Artemis based on the version of the myth in which the latter was the daughter of the former is attested in the written sources, by archaeological finds, and by iconography. For example, the sculptures from the sanctuary of Demeter in ancient Lete have provided us not only with statuary types of Demeter and Kore but also of Artemis, a probable indication of their having been worshiped together at that sanctuary.

As for the existence of the cults of other deities at the sanctuary, the presence of individual figurines depicting them does not necessarily mean that they too were generally worshiped there. But the dedication of a clay figurine of Cybele cannot be considered entirely fortuitous. Cybele was a Phrygian goddess, an exemplary mother like Demeter, and a mother goddess identified with the Mother of the Gods. There is also evidence elsewhere for the coexistence of these two related goddesses, Demeter and Cybele. In addition, although the dedication of a copper-alloy statuette of Hermes does not mean that he and Demeter shared a cult, it may owe something to the memory of the power this god exercised among the chthonic forces. The linking of these two deities is not unknown: an Imperial-period votive stele from ancient Kyrrhos, now in the Pella Museum, has an inscription below the pediment that names both Demeter and Hermes as the figures emerging in relief from the background.[6] In addition, a copper-alloy signet ring, dedicated as an offering in the sanctuary at Dion, refers to the potent fertility of Hermes and his connection with nature, depicting him as a hermaic stele, his most iconic image, standing amid plants with his favored animals, a he-goat and a kid.

If the fragment of a marble statue of Nemesis found in the sanctuary belonged there from the outset, it would constitute the first piece of evidence for worship of this goddess alongside Demeter. This possibility cannot be excluded, but it is more likely that the statue came from the neighboring sanctuary of Zeus Hypsistos, with whom she had a connection, as can be deduced from an inscription on a second- or third-century-AD

Fig. 8. Sanctuary of Demeter. Aerial view of two altars.

relief from Thessaloniki. Another likely provenance is the area of the Roman theater, as the relationship of Nemesis with such contests is well-known.

The close connection between Demeter and Asclepius, which has been pointed out with respect to many other sites, is also in evidence at Dion. An Asclepeion was established in an area that was adjacent to the sanctuary of Demeter, which, if we consider the conditions in which Asclepius's sanctuary in Athens was founded, could theoretically have once belonged to the sanctuary of Demeter. Gradually, his cult grew in strength, especially during the Imperial period, as the archaeological evidence found to date indicates, and his sanctuary expanded to the north and took over part of the sanctuary of Demeter.

According to the extant inscriptions, the priestly office in the sanctuary was served by a series of women. Verenike Korragou and Menekrite Theodorou in the Hellenistic period, and Mestria Nemesis in the Imperial age, left offerings in the sanctuary at the end of their terms of office. The first of them dedicated a statue; the second, a table for offerings; and the third gave an altar. Likewise, all the evidence suggests that in the Dion sanctuary the goddess was worshiped mainly by women.

An essential prerequisite for worship in the Dion sanctuary was purification with water, as can be deduced not only from the existence of two wells but also from the large number of water-carrier figurines (*hydriaphoroi*), hydrias, and kernoi, ring-shaped vessels with miniature hydrias attached to them. This ritual act was commonplace in almost all the sanctuaries of Demeter, and the above-mentioned finds are those most typical from sanctuaries of this goddess. Because water was required for purification in the preparatory rituals and in the sacrifices themselves, but primarily because water is the foremost fertility-enhancing power of the earth, sanctuaries of Demeter were established in places with plenty of water, as can be seen both from archaeological finds and documentary sources. It was the duty of the priestesses of Demeter to bring clear water from the holy spring. After the purification rituals, in which water played an important role, the cult involved a series of other religious rites. Blood sacrifices were offered up on the great masonry altars, and bloodless sacrifices—consisting of things such as fruit and other crops—were made on the cult tables, while libations were poured into the holes in the stones set on the altars and incense was burned in censers. At the same time, various offerings were made to the sanctuary (fig. 9). The discovery of tableware and cooking vessels indicates that ritual meals took place at the sanctuary after the sacrifices. Although no archaeological evidence survives that might categorically identify any particular areas as the places where they were held, the meals probably took place in the stoas and/or in temporary structures.

The Roman colony founded in Dion by Octavius Augustus after 30 BC was granted the right to mint coinage. On coins without the emperor's portrait from the reign of Nero, the obverse shows the bust of a horse, while the reverse has a hanging pot and a sickle. Sophia Kremydi,[7] who published the coins struck in the Dion mint, has suggested that the sickle on the coin referred to an offering made or a prize awarded at certain agrarian festivals held in Dion in honor of Demeter. This conclusion is based on the facts that the sickle is an agricultural implement, that it served as a prize at games held in honor of fertility goddesses (e.g., Artemis Orthia at Sparta), that at Ermioni it was the instrument of sacrifice in honor of Demeter Chthonia (Paus. 2.35.5), and moreover that Demeter was called the Drepanophoros (sickle carrier) (Nonnos, *Dionysiaca* 6. 104, 41.23). In view of the image on the obverse of the coins, Kremydi also suggested that these festivals may have included horse races. Indeed, there is evidence from some sanctuaries that such contests were held in honor of Demeter. There is no doubt that this was the case at Knossos, and it seems highly likely that the same was true at the sanctuaries of Demeter in Lete, Mykalessos, and Athens. Games (*ludi*) in honor of Ceres, the Roman goddess of the harvest and grain crops, the Cerealia, were held as far back as the Archaic period. The existence of theater-shaped buildings in sanctuaries of Demeter—for example, at Acrocorinth, Pergamum, and Syracuse as well as at the sanctuary of Despoina at Lykosoura, where Demeter played an important role—is an indication that such activities took place. It is worth noting that a considerable number of theatrical figurines were found in Lipara in a sanctuary that is likely linked with Demeter and Kore. Luigi Polacco has noted the connection between theaters in Sicily and chthonic cults of non-Dionysiac nature.[8] Hesychios speaks of a contest in Lakonia made in honor of Demeter.

Because offerings are the most tangible remains of cult practices, their types, the materials of which they are made, and their number provide a wealth of information to modern-day scholars regarding the nature of the deity worshiped there and the type of worship they received as well as the gender, social status, and financial circumstances of the people making the offerings. Any item, whether utilitarian or made specifically as an offering, could be offered up to the gods. Usually the offerings were accompanied by a plea or a vote of thanks from mortals to a deity, but they might on occasion also be instruments of self-promotion or propaganda.

The most common offerings in the sanctuary of Demeter at Dion in the Classical and Hellenistic periods were clay figurines (cat. nos. 20–23) and lamps (cat. nos. 14–18).[9] Equally common offerings, especially in the Classical period, were the many ritual vessels, kernoi, jewelry (above all copper-alloy buckles and glass necklaces; cat. no. 24), and miniature vessels (for the most part earthenware, such as Corinthian skyphoi and miniature hydrias, but also some lead examples, e.g., an olpe and a *lebes*). The custom of dedicating clay figurines to the sanctuary declined with the end of the Hellenistic world. This can be deduced from studying the material from other ancient sanctuaries that continued to operate in the Imperial age, such as the sanctuary of Demeter at Acrocorinth. By contrast, the custom of dedicating lamps continued into Late Antiquity.

The observation that the number of lamps found in sanctuaries of Demeter is greater than in the sanctuaries of other deities is confirmed at Dion. Indeed, the number of lamps from the Hellenistic and Imperial periods found in the sanctuary of Demeter at Dion is much greater than the number of lamps from the same period found in the sanctuary of Isis. In the sanctuaries, lamps served practical purposes as lighting apparatus, as well as religious purposes as offerings or ritual objects. In sanctuaries of Demeter, there are many more examples because they were not simply offerings but also ritual objects, since they served the specific cult of Demeter, which involved both vigils and initiation rituals. Lamps played an important part in both of these activities. However, it is also highly likely that lamps, together with torches, were a basic part of the reenactments of the myth of Demeter and Kore/Persephone. Moreover, in the initiation rituals, the act of lighting a lamp must have symbolized resurrection or rebirth. It emerges from the archaeological evidence, documentary sources, and inscriptions that lamps were also used in preparatory purification rituals, sacrifices, and lamp divination (*lychnomanteia*). In other words, lamps were widely used in the ritual practices of the cult, thus accounting for their increased numbers in Late Antiquity. For a large part of the population, they were the most accessible offerings because they were items of little value.

In addition to commonplace, cheaper offerings, there are others that stand out, by virtue of the materials from which they are made and their high quality, as examples of the more expensive

Fig. 9. Sanctuary of Demeter. Reconstruction of the Hellenistic twin temples and their altars.

equipment and extravagant offerings of the sanctuary, most of which are now lost. One impressive find is a Mycenaean seal of the late fifteenth to early fourteenth century BC incised with a schematically rendered lion standing proudly in front of a tree (cat. no. 13). The seal probably comes from one of the Mycenaean cemeteries on Olympus and entered the donor's possession by chance, following the looting of a Mycenaean tomb. This offering is important, not just because it is an antique, but because it shows the relationship the inhabitants of Dion had with their distant past and with those who had previously settled in the region. Rare finds include a fourth-century-BC glass phiale with leaf-shaped

decoration and a copper-alloy lamp in the form of an African's head (cat. no. 19), the latter an example of the copperware of the Early Imperial period.[10]

As to where offerings were placed, it has been observed in the Dion sanctuary that clusters of them were next to the wall inside the southern Late Archaic–Classical temple. Many more offerings were found outside the same temple, to the left and right of the pronaos, among rough-hewn stones. Thus it seems that offerings would have been kept on shelves or in cupboards inside the temple, or stored in a masonry table-like construction next to the entrance. The benches in the cella of the northern Hellenistic temple would have been used as platforms for statues, given that next to the bench on the south wall a statue of Aphrodite with Eros clambering over her shoulder was found fallen facedown.

As noted above, the offerings are a basic source of information not just about how and in what manner the goddess was worshiped but also about her nature. Even the earliest finds, mainly clay figurines, lamps, and jewelry, suggest a deity worshiped mainly by women, one who was connected with fertility and whose cult also involved mystic rites. These sorts of offerings are typical for Demeter across the Greek world, in Southern Greece, Thessaly, the islands, and Magna Graecia. Demeter is a chthonic goddess of fertility everywhere, a protector of agriculture, and a fruitful Mother Earth.

A marble relief depicting two ears is of particular interest, since if it were a dedication to Demeter, it would reveal another aspect of the form she took at Dion, that is, as a healer. The dedication of parts of the body was customary in the case of healer gods or those with the cognomen *epikoos* (listener), and thus one's first thought is that the relief might have been moved from the sanctuary of a healer god such as Asclepius, or from the sanctuary of a local "listener god" such as Isis, where similar finds have been discovered. However, this is not necessarily the case, as there is evidence from other sanctuaries that in some instances Demeter too had healing powers, although they are not among the goddess's primary characteristics.

The two goddesses, and above all the existence of a special cult and priesthood of Baubo, link the deities worshiped there with the Eleusinian cult. That sanctuaries dedicated to Eleusinian Demeter were set up in many cities is known from documentary sources.

The location in which it was decided to accommodate an earth goddess at Dion was not fortuitous. Demeter had a place in her element, that is, the fields outside the walls, which also served to ensure the secrecy necessary for the mysteries.[11] Spring waters—which are still abundant in the area and literally flood the site of the sanctuary—together with the consequently fertile soil must have been natural signs that prompted establishment of the cult on this spot. Two circular wells were the oldest structures in the sanctuary. Circular or rectangular ditches, often found in sanctuaries of Demeter, are usually interpreted as *megara*, pits

into which dismembered pigs were thrown, probably during the Skira festival in the summer, from whence their remains were drawn back up by the Antletries (water drawers) in the fertility rituals of the Thesmophoria. During this three-day autumn festival, Demeter was worshiped under the name of Thesmophoros as protector of the fertility of the earth and of women. There is no clear evidence for a similar interpretation of the trenches in the sanctuary of Demeter at Dion, given that the silt with which they are filled shows no trace of bones or the ritual gifts, mainly effigies of pigs, that generally accompanied the dedications. It seems likely that they were wells from which water could be drawn and thus were the initial reason for building the sanctuary on this spot. Gifts to the goddess from earlier worshipers (in the form of Archaic clay busts) lay scattered around them. In the Hellenistic period, the holy site was endowed with a larger well including a square, stone wellhead that replaced earlier ones and was enclosed within a built structure.

This sacred precinct, one of the oldest in Dion, must have played a decisive role in the formation of other sanctuaries in the area. The worship of Demeter as goddess of agriculture in Northern Greece, following ritual practices similar to those in the south, seems to have begun in Dion in the late sixth or early fifth century BC. Influence from Southern Greece was the result of trade and cultural relations, in the development of which an important role was played by the colonies of the littoral. The emphasis on the status of Dion as the sacred city of the Macedonians by King Archelaos at the end of the fifth century BC and by Philip II and Alexander III in the second half of the fourth century BC, and the recognition of its strategic position by Kassandros expressed in the building of its walls at the end of that century, resulted in more general changes to the whole city.[12] Dion's increased importance was also communicated, in a more monumental fashion, in the sanctuary of Demeter. The goddess's cult remained active even after a Roman colony was established at Dion. But when people in the city gradually began to worship other deities, such as Asclepius, Isis, and Zeus Hypsistos, the cult of Demeter must have declined and the sanctuary shrunk. Nevertheless it survived up to the end of the fourth century AD. However, when Christianity became predominant, workshops producing building materials to meet the requirements of the now Christian population of the city sprang up in the convenient precincts of the sanctuary.

1 On the cult of Demeter: Nilsson 1955: 461ff.; Burkert 1993: 338ff.; Clinton 1992 passim; Simon 1996: 97–121.

2 On the sanctuary of Demeter at Dion: Pandermalis 1999a: 60ff. On the cult of Demeter at Dion: Pingiatoglou 2010b: 209ff. On publication of the sanctuary: Pingiatoglou 2015: 16ff. (with bibliography relevant to the subjects discussed in this essay), 177ff.

3 Pingiatoglou 2015: 17ff.

4 Pandermalis 1977: 335ff., fig. 4; Karaghiorga-Stathakopoulou 1986: 88; Pingiatoglou 2015: 164.

5 Pandermalis 1984b: 273ff. On the sanctuary of Isis: Pandermalis 1999a: 88ff.; Giuman 1999b: 427–46. On goddesses who provided protection in childbirth: Pingiatoglou 1981.

6 Chrysostomou 2003: 143ff., fig. 3.

7 Kremydi 1996: 96ff.

8 Polacco 1989: 55–57; Polacco 1990: 155.

9 For the publication of the lamps from the sanctuary of Demeter: Pingiatoglou 2005; Pingiatoglou 2015: 111ff.

10 Pingiatoglou 2005: 85ff.; Pingiatoglou 2015: 114ff.

11 On the preferred locations for sanctuaries of Demeter and the extramural sites, as at Dion: Pingiatoglou 1999: 916ff.

12 See Stephanidou-Tiveriou 1998: 134ff.

FROM THE KINGDOM OF MACEDONIA TO THE COLONY OF DION: THE USE AND FUNCTION OF COINAGE

SOPHIA KREMYDI

National Hellenic Research Foundation, Athens

THE INTRODUCTION OF COINAGE IN NORTHERN GREECE

In Northern Greece, coinage was introduced as an exchange medium at an early date. The existence of important precious-metal mines in areas around the Mount Pangaeon and in the peninsula of the Chalcidice was certainly a decisive factor for this development. By the end of the sixth century BC, coinage was being produced by various Thracian tribes that occupied inland territories east of the Strymon River and in the Chalcidice, as well as by colonies of Euboean, Ionian, or Cycladic cities situated on the northern Aegean coast. In the first half of the fifth century BC, not long after the withdrawal of the Persians in 480 BC, Alexander I introduced the use of coinage in the Macedonian kingdom.[1]

Although some very rare, obscure, and early monetary issues—probably coming from the area east of the Strymon—were struck in electrum, silver was by far the dominant metal. Silver was struck mainly in the form of heavy, large-value coins that found their way east through the taxation system of the Persian Empire, as attested by many fifth-century-BC hoards found in the Levant, Mesopotamia, and Egypt. Although the need to pay taxes to the Persians was one of the important motives for the production of coins, the existence of smaller denominations shows that it was not the *only* motive. These coins scarcely survive since they were small in size and rarely deposited in hoards because of their lesser value. Coins of smaller denominations, however, gradually are coming to light: the recent publication of a hoard containing late-sixth-century-BC hemiobols of Abdera is, in this sense, revealing.[2] Since coins of lower value were not intended for export, their existence shows that the use of coined money for everyday monetary transactions and local trade must have been more important in the region than originally believed.

THE MONETARY POLICY OF THE MACEDONIAN KINGDOM[3]

Once Alexander I was able to expand his kingdom to the east, he gained control of the silver mines between Lake Prasias and the Dysoron mountains, situated in what is now the region of Philippi,[4] from where he obtained one talent of silver per day (Hdt. 5.17.2). This has been considered a crucial factor for the inauguration of coinage by the Macedonian king. The coinage of the Macedonian kingdom was originally struck on a local standard, usually called the "Thracomacedonian" standard. Large denominations of pure silver alloy were produced during periods when the metal was available, either through control of the mines or through trading with the Athenians. Otherwise, the coinage was restricted to smaller denominations or issues of poor alloy. The introduction of a double-currency system, coins of better metal for export, and coins of lower weight for internal circulation was an innovation introduced already in the fifth century BC. By the end of the century, fiduciary bronze coinage for everyday use had gradually replaced the smaller silver denominations, making Macedonia one of the first regions where the use of bronze coinage was established.

The permanent expansion of the Macedonian state under Philip II led to the creation of a "larger Macedonia" that included areas with mixed populations and that was gradually incorporated into the Macedonian state through the adoption of Macedonian institutions. The permanent control of the silver mines east of the Strymon was established under Philip's reign and was accompanied by important innovations for the Macedonian coinage. A second royal mint was created near the mining area, probably at Amphipolis. This mint facilitated production and distribution of coinage within the enlarged kingdom,

Fig. 1. Coin of Septimius Severus. Reverse: Asclepius standing within a temple. See fig. 11 for obverse.

and brought about the introduction of an important gold coinage that imitated that of the Chalcidians. The new gold coinage was struck on the international Attic standard and became the most important gold currency of the Greek world. Under Philip, gold and silver were struck on a completely different scale in order to account for military and administrative needs, as well as for the extensive construction projects that were taken on during this period. The Attic standard, introduced by Philip for the gold coinage, expanded to the silver coinage under his son Alexander. The coinage of Alexander was not limited to Macedonia, but became the international coinage of the Hellenistic world and was continuously struck by various minting authorities until the arrival of the Romans in the eastern Mediterranean.[5] Under Alexander's empire, the enormous deposits of precious metals hoarded by the Persians were put into circulation in the form of an international currency that dominated the markets of the Hellenistic world.

THE INTRODUCTION OF ROMAN CURRENCY AND THE TRANSFORMATION OF LOCAL ISSUES

Alexander's production, with the exception of currencies produced in the Black Sea, where circulation remained local, was interrupted in the first decades of the second century BC. The Hellenistic kingdoms that had been striking his currency gradually declined, and the autonomous cities turned to other types of silver coinage, often produced to meet the needs of the Romans.[6] In parallel with the local coinages, the denarius gradually made its appearance in the markets through the military activities of the Roman army and the trading activities of Roman merchants.

The end of the Roman civil wars and the establishment of the Roman Empire imposed a new status quo. The production of gold was thereafter the exclusive privilege of Rome, and the aureus was the only gold coin in circulation. It was used for long-distance trade and for payments to high officials of the Roman state. The denarius, on the other hand, was imposed as the strong international silver currency, and the production of local silver was severely reduced. In Macedonia and Achaia, silver was abandoned, and local production was subsequently limited to bronze. In Asia Minor, Syria, and Egypt, local silver continued in certain cases, but its circulation was limited and its production controlled by the Roman administration.[7]

Thereafter, the numerous provincial cities of the eastern part of the empire limited their monetary production to bronze coins of low value that were used for everyday transactions. Under Augustus an important innovation was introduced: just like the coins struck in Rome, the provincial issues, with very few exceptions, bore the portrait of the emperor on their obverse, providing for the first time a uniform appearance to the various local coinages throughout the empire. In the west and in the Balkans, these bronzes were immediately adapted to the Roman system of denominations.

In the eastern part of the empire, however, local denominations continued down to the second century AD. Studies of numismatic circulation have shown that provincial coins did not move far from their place of issue, and that they were used mostly within the territory of the city where they were produced and in the neighboring regions, where their value was recognized.

THE MACEDONIAN MINTS

In Macedonia, eight cities as well as the Koinon struck coins in the period between Augustus (r. 27 BC–14 AD) and Gallienus (r. 253–268 AD).[8] The mints with the largest production were those of Thessaloniki, an important administrative and trade center, and Amphipolis.[9] Both had been given the privileged status of *civitates liberae*, free cities with a significant degree of autonomy and exemption from paying taxes to the Romans. Edessa, a smaller city with a less privileged status, struck coins sporadically.[10] In addition to these cities, the four Roman colonies of Pella, Dion, Cassandreia, and Philippi also produced bronze coins.[11] All of these centers had been Macedonian cities with a long history. The Romans chose them for settling colonists mainly because of the available lands in their territory, suitable for cultivation and for their location on strategic routes. Unlike the cities of Thessaloniki, Amphipolis, and Edessa, the colonies struck coins with legends in Latin and with reference to the Roman magistrates. The eighth city to strike coins in Macedonia was Stoboi, situated in the upper Axios valley, a city that received the honorary status of a municipium (a community with the status of a Roman city but without colonists) under the Flavians.[12]

NUMISMATIC ICONOGRAPHY AND RELIGIOUS IDENTITIES AT THE ROMAN COLONY OF DION

Dion, situated in the foothills of Mount Olympus, on the main road that united Macedonia with the south, had a long history before the arrival of the Romans. It was the sacred city of the Macedonians, the place where they assembled to worship their gods and celebrate festivals. The temples, stadium, and theater were situated in a vast area outside the city walls, and among them was the well-known sanctuary of the supreme god Zeus Olympios, where important public inscriptions had been erected.

Like all cities of the Macedonian kingdom, Dion did not strike coins under the kings. Its citizens used the royal coins that were legal tender in the city and that have been found in large numbers on the excavated site. Neither did it strike coins in the period between the battle of Pydna (168 BC) and the reign of Augustus, as did the larger cities of Amphipolis, Thessaloniki, and Pella.

The city began to produce bronze issues only after the creation of the Roman colony during the reign of Augustus. Such coins have been found in large numbers in the excavated city: new unknown types have been discovered, and new evidence on their dating has come to light from the abundant archaeological evidence.

Coins were a medium of exchange—in this case a medium for small everyday payments—but they were also objects that circulated widely in the hands of people and, therefore, were a convenient medium for sending messages and reclaiming identities. In the provincial cities of the Roman Empire, civic coinage was managed by the local elites, who decided, organized, but also financed its production. Once the permission to strike coins was provided by the central authority, imperial interference was rare and exceptional. The city's ruling class established the timing for striking coins, the quantity of production, and the types of coinage according to their needs and interests.

Numismatic iconography of the provincial coinages followed the Roman tradition of using a variety of coin types as a medium to convey messages to their users. The presence of a portrait of the reigning emperor, or of a member of his family, on most obverses of the city coinages reflects a change that must have occurred after a regulation imposed by the Roman government. However, the choice of the reverse types was made by the locals and was seen as a means to deliver messages concerning civic identity through references to local cults, festivals, or buildings.[13]

The iconography of the coins of the Roman colony of Dion, as of all the Macedonian mints of this period, is rather limited.[14] Coin types refer almost exclusively to divinities worshiped in the city and thus offer valuable information on the city's religious life. Legends, when they exist, may be revealing. The first coins of the colony struck under Augustus (r. 27 BC–14 AD) bear the type of Athena on the reverse (fig. 2).[15] The goddess is depicted standing in a severe posture wearing a long peplos and a helmet, leaning on a scepter, and offering a libation. The type is reproduced, practically unaltered, on issues of the city until the reign of Gallienus. On issues dated to the time of Nero (r. 54–68 AD), the goddess is standing on a base, indicating that the coin type reproduced a cult statue that must have existed in the city (fig. 3).[16] In fact, Athena remained the only divinity depicted on the coins of Dion until the reign of Hadrian (r. 117–138 AD) and remained popular also in later coinage (fig. 4).[17] The insistence on the depiction of Athena on the coins of the colony shows that her cult was considered important. Which Athena is this, and why was she chosen as the main coin type by the new settlers?

We have evidence that Athena was worshiped at Dion since Hellenistic times. A votive inscription of the second century BC indicates her presence in the pantheon of the city. The continued importance of her cult in Roman times is testified not only through coins, but also through an inscription in honor of a priestess of Athena for whom the city erected a statue.[18] Although evidence is lacking, it is highly probable that the worship of Athena at Dion, as in many other Macedonian cities, had begun earlier than the second century BC. Emmanuel Voutiras convincingly argued that Macedonian cities had venerated a peaceful version of Athena Polias since at least the fourth century BC, and these cults had survived and were perhaps even reinforced after the fall of the monarchy in 168 BC.[19] It is this local version of Athena that the

Roman colonists chose as the protector of their city when they arrived at Dion, a century and a half after the conquest. Whether the local Athena could have been assimilated with a Roman Minerva brought over by the new settlers is something for which we have no evidence.

Fig 2. Coin of Augustus. Obverse: portrait of the emperor. Reverse: standing Athena.

Fig. 3. Coin of Nero. Obverse: portrait of the emperor. Reverse: Athena standing on a base.

Fig. 4. Coin of Philip I. Obverse: portrait of the emperor. Reverse: standing Athena with snake at her feet.

In some cases, provincial coins bear interesting inscriptions that offer important information on matters of cult. Coins of small denomination without the imperial portrait, the *hemiassaria*, were struck at Dion in parallel with the larger *assaria*, which bore the image of the emperor. Instead of the imperial portrait these smaller coins depicted a plough on the obverse, a symbol of the city's colonial status, of which its inhabitants were certainly proud. On the reverse, we find the image of Artemis in a short chiton, with a quiver and a bow, running to the right (fig. 5).[20] This is a very common iconographic type that appears on coins, reliefs, and sculptures in the round. The legend *Diana Baphyra* inscribed on the reverse reveals the identity of the divinity. Baphyra was the name of the river that flowed around the city walls: it sprang from Mount Olympus, reappeared in the plain near the city of Dion, and flowed from the east wall of the city down to the sea in a navigable form. The legend on the coin is in Latin, and the name of the goddess is therefore given in the Latin form, but the epiclesis Baphyria is clearly local and connects the worship of Diana with the local river. The cult of Artemis that already existed in Hellenistic Dion continued to have a special importance for the colony, as can be seen both by the coins and by the base of a statue erected by Anthestia Iucunda, a wealthy freedwoman of the city, who dedicated the statue to "Diana and the colonists."[21]

The discovery of a sanctuary outside the city walls, not far from the ancient coastline and near the river as it flows today, should certainly be related to the divinity mentioned on the coins. The cult statue that has survived nearly intact in the main chamber of the temple shows Artemis walking with a long chiton. The goddess must have originally held a bow and arrows in her hands, now broken off. The same type is reflected on an early and somewhat crude reverse of a coin, which has been dated to the first century AD, probably to the reign of Claudius (r. 41–54 AD). The more elegant depiction of Artemis, in the type of *kynegetis*, a different type from that of the cult statue, was introduced on the coins of the second-century-AD issues.

Evidence for the worship of Artemis before the arrival of the Roman colonists is ample at Dion. Just outside the Roman sanctuary mentioned above, a Hellenistic votive inscription was discovered bearing a dedication to Ἀρτέμιδι Σωτείρᾳ, Artemis the Savior.[22] Other Hellenistic inscriptions mentioning Artemis Eileithyia and Artemis Lochia, both protectors of women giving birth, have been discovered in the Sanctuary of Isis, just outside the city walls, which probably replaced a sanctuary of Artemis in the second century BC.

Another interesting example of a reference to a local cult, and of the way it was used on coins in the Roman period, is that of Zeus. The city of Dion was named after the supreme god of the Greek pantheon, Zeus, worshiped on Mount Olympus, seat of the gods according to Greek mythology. The sanctuary of Zeus Olympios was the major sanctuary of Dion, the place where public inscriptions were erected, and Zeus Olympios was a divinity of special importance for the Macedonian kings. "Olympia" had been celebrated at Dion since the time of Archelaos.[23] Festivals in honor of the god were held by the kings after important victories, and Zeus Olympios was chosen as a coin type by Philip II and by his son Alexander. It can easily be understood why the Romans avoided depicting this god on the early coins of the Roman colony and preferred Athena, in the form of Polias, a divinity connected to the autonomy of the city and not to its Macedonian background.

However, Zeus appeared on the coins of Dion under the reign of Hadrian. He was depicted standing in a long himation that left the torso partially uncovered, offering a libation from a patera held in his right hand, and leaning his left on a scepter. At his feet is his sacred bird, the eagle (figs. 6, 7).[24] On the obverse of the Hadrianic coins with Zeus Olympios, a portrait of the emperor is accompanied by the legend *Hadriano Olympio*. Hadrian is known to have achieved the construction of the temple of Zeus Olympios at Athens, where he was worshiped alongside the supreme god. Many cities dedicated statues in honor of Hadrian Olympios at Athens, and among them were the citizens of Dion. The inscribed base of a votive statue that has not survived bears a Latin inscription and is dated to 132/133 AD, as are most of the dedications of cities from all over the empire erected at the Olympieion. The year 132 AD was that of the inauguration of the Panhellenion, an institution created by Hadrian that included cities that shared a common Greek past and received special privileges from the emperor.

The dedication of a statue in honor of Hadrian Olympios at Athens, the legend *Hadriano Olympio* on the city's coins, and the introduction of the type of Zeus on the reverse of the colonial issues are certainly connected. In this context, the standing Zeus on the coins of Dion should be understood as a reference to Zeus Olympios. The standing Zeus continued to appear on the reverse of the city's coins, whereas a new type with Zeus standing alongside Athena was introduced in the late second century AD, on coins of Marcus Aurelius (fig. 8).[25] In the mid-third century AD, under the reign of Gallienus, another type is encountered: Zeus seated on a throne with Athena standing in front of him

Fig. 5. Coin of Antoninus Pius. Obverse: plough, inscribed COL[onia] DIENSIS.
Reverse: Artemis kynegetis, inscribed DIANA BAPHYRA.

Fig. 6. Coin of Faustina the Younger. Obverse: portrait of the
empress Faustina. Reverse: standing Zeus Olympios with
an eagle at his feet.

Fig. 7. Coin of Elagabalus. Obverse: portrait of the emperor.
Reverse: standing Zeus Olympios with an eagle at his feet.

Fig. 8. Coin of Commodus. Obverse: portrait of the emperor.
Reverse: standing Athena and Zeus.

(fig. 9).[26] The seated Zeus is closer to the classical image of Zeus Olympios as we know him from the cult statue at Olympia and the coins of Alexander III. Whether the statue that must have existed at Dion depicted Zeus seated, as at Olympia, or standing, as on the coins, is not known. In either instance, chances that the memory of this statue could have survived in the second century AD are slim at best. The standing Zeus with the eagle at his feet fits the image of Zeus Hypsistos, a cult introduced by the Romans, as we know him from Dion and other cities in Macedonia.

Finally, another divinity introduced on the iconography of the coins of Dion is Asclepius. The god is depicted in two very common types, standing and leaning on his rod, around which a snake coils (fig. 10),[27] or standing in the same posture inside a temple (reverse: fig. 1; obverse: fig. 11).[28] The worship of Asclepius at Dion is attested through archaeological evidence at least since the fourth century BC. A small shrine has come to light east of the theater, in which fragments of sculptures and inscriptions identifying the divinity have been discovered.[29] Asclepius appeared on the coins of the colony in the early third century AD, only under the reign of Septimius Severus and his son Caracalla. Types related to Asclepius are very frequent on Roman coins under the Severans, due to the special honors paid by Caracalla to the god of healing. The choice to depict Asclepius at Dion under the Severans could perhaps be seen as a tribute to the reigning emperor.

Archaeological and epigraphic sources for the religious life at Dion are abundant. Systematic excavations over a number of decades have brought to light evidence for the worship of numerous gods and goddesses such as Demeter, Kore, Asclepius and his family, Athena, Poseidon, Isis, Anubis, Harpocrates, Heracles, Dionysus, Zeus Olympios, Zeus Hypsistos, Aphrodite, and Artemis, as well as other minor divinities. Continuity of cult is also attested since the cults of the Macedonian city were often adopted by the Roman colonists, who gradually mixed with the local population. While few of these divinities feature on the coins, the deliberate choices made by local elites reflect the messages they intended to convey to their audience. Our interest today is to attempt to decipher these messages.

Fig. 9. Coin of Gallienus. Obverse: portrait of the emperor. Reverse: Zeus seated on a throne and standing Athena.

Fig. 10. Coin of Gordian III. Obverse: portrait of the emperor. Reverse: Asclepius leaning on a rod with a star at his feet.

Fig. 11. Coin of Septimius Severus. Obverse: portrait of the emperor. See fig. 1 for reverse.

1 Picard 2006.
2 Kagan 2006.
3 For a recent overview of the monetary policy of the Macedonian kingdom and relevant bibliography: Kremydi 2011.
4 Farraguna 1998.
5 For an overview of the Alexanders in the Hellenistic world: Kremydi and Marcellesi forthcoming.
6 Picard 2010; de Callataÿ 2011.
7 *RPC* I: 26–30.
8 For an overview of the provincial issues of the Macedonian cities: *RPC* I: 286–310 (Augustus to Nerva); *RPC* II: 70–75 (the Flavians); *RPC* III: 74–84 (Nerva, Trajan, Hadrian). See also Kremydi 2002.
9 The coinage of Thessaloniki has been studied by Touratsoglou 1988.
10 For the coinage of Edessa: Papaefthymiou 2002.
11 For the coinage of Dion: Kremydi-Sicilianou 1996. For Philippi: Amandry 1998; Amandry 2015. Kremydi 2002.
12 Josifovski 2001.

13 Howgego, Heuchert, and Burnett 2005.
14 Kremydi-Sicilianou 1996: 87–98.
15 Museum of Dion, inv. no. 5436. Kremydi 1996: 171.1.
16 Museum of Dion, inv. no. 1956. Kremydi 1996: 176.1.
17 Museum of Dion, inv. no. 5394. Kremydi 1996: 237.1.
18 Pandermalis 1977: 333–34.
19 Voutiras 1998.
20 Museum of Dion, inv. no. 3890. Kremydi 1996: 254.10.
21 For this interesting inscription: Pandermalis 1997a: 337.
22 On the sanctuary, statue, and inscription: Pandermalis 1999a: 272–79.
23 Mari 1988; Mari 2002: 51–60.
24 Coin of Faustina the Younger: Museum of Dion, inv. no. 2940. Kremydi 1996: 196.16. Coin of Elagabalus: previously unpublished.
25 Museum of Dion, inv. no. 1189. Kremydi 1996: 201.36.
26 Museum of Dion, inv. no. 70. Kremydi 1996: 246.50.
27 Museum of Dion, Kremydi 1996: 235.12.
28 Museum of Dion, inv. no. 6568. Kremydi 1996: 203.19.
29 Pandermalis 1999a: 85–87.

SNIPPETS OF EVERYDAY LIFE IN ROMAN DION

ANGELOS CHANIOTIS

Institute for Advanced Study, Princeton

WHAT IS ROMAN IN ROMAN DION?

"What have the Romans ever done for us?" This is the question asked by a member of the so-called People's Front of Judea in the film *Monty Python's Life of Brian*. A rhetorical question, one might think. The other members of the group, however, present an impressive list: the Romans have built streets, baths, aqueducts; they have brought sanitation, irrigation, education, wine, security, and peace. The brilliant makers of the *Life of Brian* put their finger on one of the most important questions asked by historians of society and culture in the Roman provinces, east and west. What difference did the Roman Empire make in the life of Dion, one of the most important Macedonian religious and urban centers?

The defeat of King Perseus in Pydna and the abolition of the Macedonian kingdom in 167 BC marked a turning point in the history of Macedonia. The royal and civic elites were decimated, either falling on the battlefield or leaving the kingdom. Twenty years after the battle of Pydna, the Romans defeated Andriskos, who attempted to reestablish the kingdom, and Macedonia became the first Roman province in the east. The Romans introduced provincial administration and, consequently, Roman legal institutions. Italian entrepreneurs began settling in this area and brought new cults, social customs, economic practices, rituals, and attitudes. A century later, in 30 BC, Octavian (later known as Augustus) ended the civil wars of the late Roman Republic, defeating Marc Antony and Cleopatra. Apart from establishing a new form of monarchical government, Augustus reorganized the eastern provinces. One of his measures was the foundation of colonies—self-governed settlements of Roman citizens, mostly army veterans. The Augustan colonies were founded in important urban centers and at sites with traditional symbolic significance, such as Corinth in the Peloponnese, Knossos on Crete, and the Macedonian royal capital Pella. Dion, the most important religious center in Macedonia, was selected by Augustus for the settlement of veterans.

The colonies were miniatures of Rome. Their political organization copied Roman institutions, and the religious offices were typically Roman. The citizens (*coloni*) had the full rights of Roman citizens and were exempt from the payment of tribute. They worshiped the gods of Rome, and for centuries after the establishment of a colony, Latin was used not only for the administration of colonial affairs, but also as the common language of private communication. The organization of civic space was also Roman. Two avenues that crossed each other, the *cardo* and the *decumanus*, dominated the city plan (fig. 1). The foundation of a Roman colony on Greek soil had an impact on the local culture and society as profound as the foundation of Greek cities in Asia Minor, the Near East, and central Asia after the conquest of Alexander the Great. Admittedly, there is a significant difference between the Greek colonization of Asia and the Italian migration to Macedonia. In Macedonia the Italian settlers arrived at an area with a long tradition of self-government, advanced political structures, refined culture, and widespread literacy, fully integrated into the *koine*—the common culture of the Hellenistic world. The result of the Italian migration in Greece was nonetheless comparable to that of the Greek colonization of Asia: an intense exchange between the local population and the newcomers, one that was not free of tensions or conflicts. This exchange gradually produced a new cultural and social profile.

Dion is such a city, where Italian and Roman traditions mingled with the traditions of the local population, which primarily lived in the vast territory of Dion, in villages and small settlements. At least during the first century of the colony, the majority of the urban population, the *coloni*, was of Italian origin: army veterans and other settlers from Italy who possessed Roman citizenship.[1] The migration of Italians continued in the first and second centuries AD. The population in the countryside, the *incolae* or *paroikoi*, consisted of the local Greek population; to judge from a few Thracian names that continued to be used in Roman Dion,[2] the population of the countryside was of diverse origins but fully Hellenized.

Fig. 1.
Dion. Aerial view of the *cardo maximus* from the south.
Top center: remains of the south gate. Top right: area of the Great Baths.

The city was governed by a council of *decuriones*, two "mayors" (*duoviri*), two supervisors of public space (*aediles*), and a board of six men (*seviri*). Additional officials included the *augur*, responsible for divination on behalf of the colony.[3] Sometimes the colony appointed the emperor himself to the office of mayor; in those cases, he was represented by a *praefectus Caesaris quinquennalis*, a prefect of the emperor who served without a colleague and for a period of five years. This extraordinary honor was reserved for individuals with wealth and prominence, such as a certain Caius Mestrius, a benefactor and constructor of public works.[4]

The cults of the colony were Roman, although the Roman gods always had their Greek counterpart: Jupiter Optimus Maximus (Zeus), Minerva (Athena), Liber Pater (Dionysus), and Diana (Artemis). However, traditional cults, such as those of Demeter and Asclepius, continued in the same sanctuaries.[5] The primarily Roman identity of the civic population is clearly expressed by a dedication made by a veteran of the third Scythian legion to the "Guardian spirit of the Roman senate and the Roman people" (*Genius senatus populusque Romanus*).[6] Of course, the Roman population of Dion interacted economically and socially with the population that lived in the countryside and with the Greek cities in this area.

INTERPERSONAL RELATIONS AND LIFE STORIES IN THE MONUMENTS FOR THE DEAD

Paradoxically, it is mainly through monuments dedicated to the dead that we learn things about the living. For instance, the epitaph (second–third century AD) set up by Dometia for her son Paulus— both mother and child had Roman names—is decorated with the representation of a seated dog, probably the child's pet (fig. 2).[7] *Moulion* (the mule-driver), the Greek transliteration of the Latin *mulio*, is written with small letters above the dog's head. Is it the dog's name or the name of a game that Paulus played with the dog, making it pull a cart, like a mule, and assuming the part of the mule driver? Whatever the case might be, this monument presupposes wit and affection. The mother wanted her son to be reminded in death of his favorite pet; by commemorating this playful relation between child and dog, she has given us a hint to family life. This grave monument was set up by Dometia, and not the child's father. Was she a widow? Was she an unmarried woman or a slave? We do not know her status, but she certainly had enough property to employ a sculptor for the construction of a grave monument that captured a happy memory in the short life of her child.

Another epitaph (ca. 150 AD), this time with a short Latin text and a Greek epigram, expresses grief for the death of Marcus Domitius Pyrilampes, twenty-three years old: in his short life he had found joy in hunting, and he died without causing pain to anyone.[8]

Interpersonal relations are a common theme in grave inscriptions, thus revealing life stories and experiences. One of the most interesting texts of this kind is the early second-century-AD epitaph that a woman, Philippe, set up for Leon. She had been his foster child, possibly an orphan or an exposed infant, found and raised as a slave by Leon.[9] The grave inscription presents the deceased man speaking from the grave and acknowledging that his foster daughter had fulfilled her duties: "To me, Leon who raised her, Philippe, set up this altar, returning a small favor with a large gift." Of course, it is not the dead Leon who is speaking, but Philippe, who puts in the mouth of her foster father the praise that she hopes to receive. She has her foster father say that to raise her was only a "small favor" (*anti mikron polla*) as compared to the favor she did by setting up his grave. Could this possibly reflect tensions between foster child and foster father?

Sidelights into the life of an ordinary individual are provided by the dedication, noted above, of the army veteran Lucius Castanius.[10] After serving in the Roman army, he died childless, leaving his property to two local people who must have been his friends: Caius Mestrius Priscus and Priscus's freedman Caius Mestrius Placidus. The different social backgrounds of these three

Fig. 2. Dion. Funerary Stele from Domitia to Paulus. Second-third century AD.

men, free and slaves, was not an obstacle to their friendship. Before his death Castanius requested that his heirs make a dedication. The recipient of the dedication was the "Guardian spirit of the Roman senate and the Roman people." Even after death, Castanius wanted to be remembered for his loyalty to Rome, the imperial power that he had served as a soldier.

Another short epitaph (ca. 150–200 AD) documents the friendship and affection between two women who were raised together without being related: "Claudia for Amareine, together with whom she was raised, for memory's sake." The two women possibly were exposed children, found and raised as slaves in a private household.[11] On occasion even the names recorded in an epitaph reveal human stories: "Lykos, son of Epiktas, and Aelia Hymnis, for Adymos, their child, in memory's sake" (second–third century AD).[12] Since the mother, Hymnis, was a Roman citizen—she has the Roman name Aelia— but the father, Lykos, and the child, Adymos, were not, we are probably dealing with people from the lower strata: the manumitted slave Aelia Hymnis who married a Greek of humble position. Another interesting life story that can be reconstructed through the study of personal names is that of Eros and Rhome, whom we know from the epitaph of their daughter Therine and their own epitaph.[13] In Latin their names were Amor and Roma (the palindrome of Amor). It seems that these individuals were the slaves of a Roman, who gave them names that wittily highlighted their connection. The short but affectionate epitaph that a former slave erected for her husband is a nice public expression of sentiment:[14] "Tertia Fannia, the freed slave of Fannia, set this up at her own expense for her own lover (*erastes*), who became her husband for a short time." Legitimate marriage was denied to Tertia as long as she was a slave. Her manumission—and that of her anonymous lover—made a marriage possible. With bitterness Tertia refers to her husband's loss shortly after their marriage.

With texts such as these, we approach individual lives and experiences in a city that shared the main features of social and cultural life found in most urban centers of Roman Greece. The perennial division between the poor and the wealthy continued to exist, and most of the buildings, works of sculpture, and objects of everyday life were connected with the life of the elite, its sophisticated pleasures, and the media of its self-representation. An important location for male members of the elite was the gymnasium, a genuinely Greek institution in a city with Roman municipal institutions. Accessible only to men of leisure, it was the place where they could train the body, engage in discussions about current public affairs, exchange gossip, and listen to lectures by intellectuals, orators, and philosophers. The gymnasium was usually associated with bath complexes, such as those excavated in Dion (figs. 3, 4), where a hermaic stele (late second–early third century AD) with a portrait of the philosopher Herennianus, which

Fig. 3.
Great Baths. Axonometric reconstruction of the complex from the northeast.

Fig. 4.
Great Baths. Aerial view of the complex from the north.

decorated one of the rooms of the baths, gives us a vague impression of the lectures and discussions that must have taken place in this area (cat. no. 43).[15] Unfortunately, we cannot determine to which philosophical school Herennianus belonged. Bathing and water were associated with health and healing, which explains the presence in the baths of the late-second-century-AD statue of Podaleirius, a son of Asclepius and a healing god himself (fig. 5, cat. no. 44).[16]

Fig. 5. Great Baths. Statue of Podaleirius at the time of discovery.

The wealthy elite, which owed its fortunes mostly to the ownership of large estates, monopolized public life. Only its members had access to public offices, since only they could afford the expenses connected with service. Only they made proposals in the council. This high position was accompanied by the obligation to serve the community. The *honoratiores*, or "first citizens," felt the moral obligation to make donations and benefactions, thus winning the acceptance of the other citizens. For instance, the *duovir* (one of the two chief magistrates or "mayors" of the colony) Publius Mestrius Pomponianus Capito together with his wife

Mestria Aquilina, the priestess of Minerva, provided the funds for the construction of the praetorium, the seat of the chief officials. This building, a large complex near the city forum, was where official banquets took place and hospitality was offered to important guests. The donors pridefully provide a detailed description of the construction and its furniture, thus giving us an idea of the refined dining practices of the elite: "the praetorium with two vaulted chambers and their furniture, which is listed below: five chamber beds, five mattresses, five cushions, ten benches, two chairs, a dining couch decorated with three mattresses, three small cushions, three long cushions, an iron hearth, twenty tables, twenty beds, twenty small cushions."[17] To judge from archaeological finds—especially from the luxurious so-called Villa of Dionysus (fig. 6), with the remains of domestic architecture as well as glass vessels used for dining but also as containers of perfume[18]— luxurious banquets were an important feature of social life in the Roman city. Moreover, the existence of extensive bath complexes and toilets testify to Dion's elevated urban culture.[19]

ENTERTAINMENT

Musical performances were an important element both of the private encounters of a sophisticated urban society and of the public festivals that it celebrated, the more so since the cult of the Muses had been very prominent in Dion and the entire region for centuries. The performers were specialized professionals: extensive training is required for the playing of the *hydraulis*—an early form of the pipe organ that operated with the pressure of water, a rare specimen of which was found in Dion in 1992 (fig. 7; first–second century AD)[20]—and the *nabla*, a string instrument represented in relief in the grave monument of a woman (cat. no. 67). As the husband, who commissioned the monument, explains, "he sculpted a *nabla* under the right arm of the wife, because she had always been devoted to the Muses, while she lived." Playing the *nabla* required training and skill, so it has rightly been assumed that this anonymous woman

Fig. 6.
Villa of Dionysus. Aerial view from the northwest.

Fig. 7. Dion. *Hydraulis* (water organ) after conservation.

Fig. 8. Roman theater. Aerial view from the northwest.

was a professional musician.[21] It has also been suggested that she performed in the local cult of the Muses,[22] but the Latin epigram does not support this interpretation. Her husband, author of the epigram, may himself have been a professional poet.

As we infer from the representation of theatrical masks (late second–early third century AD; cat. nos. 31–33), the existence of a theater (fig. 8),[23] and the celebration of a festival that included musical competitions, theatrical performances were an important aspect of cultural life. We may assume that an association of theater artists—the so-called association of *Dionysiakoi technitai*, or "Dionysiac artists"—had its seat in Dion.

Athletic competitions were an important activity in the gymnasium and part of the annual festivals. Not unlike hunting, participation in athletic training and competitions was an important leisure activity of young men, some of whom must have dreamed of great victories. Does Aurelius Olympionikos, whose name means "the winner of the Olympic games" (ca. 200 AD), owe his name to an Olympic victory or to the hope that he might win one?[24]

A funerary altar of the late second or early third century AD brings us from the heights of theatrical culture and music to the depths of the human fascination with violence. The altar is decorated with the representation of a standing man with spear and whip, a seated woman, a dog, two lions, and a lion and a bull. One of the most brutal contributions of the Romans to culture in the east was the introduction of gladiatorial combats and hunts of wild animals (*venationes*) that usually took place in connection with the festival in honor of the emperor. A merchant of wild animals from Smyrna, Konopas, was buried in Dion. What brought him to this city was his trade, probably with lions, which were used not only for hunts of wild animals but also for the execution of convicts.[25]

SOCIAL DIVERSITY AND SOCIAL MOBILITY

Unlike the inscriptions of the pre-Roman period, which primarily reflect elite activities—with the exception of grave inscriptions—in Roman Dion, private and public inscriptions give us insight into the life of members of the lower social strata. Admittedly, Roman political institutions promoted the rule of a wealthy oligarchy, but at the same time, they allowed for social mobility at a larger scale than had been possible in pre-Roman Macedonia. The Roman army was an important promoter of social mobility. Men from the eastern provinces could find employment as soldiers. When they did not possess Roman citizenship, they could volunteer for service in the auxiliary units for a standard period of twenty-five years. Men who possessed Roman citizenship, such as the citizens of the Roman colony of

Dion, were allowed to serve in the regular legions. Thus, army service provided employment for those who did not own land or had no other attractive prospects. Upon retirement the non-Roman veterans received citizenship, and depending on merit and fortune, soldiers could climb up the ranks and acquire wealth.

A significant number among the population of Dion in the early phases consisted of veterans of the Roman army, and in later periods, men who either came from Dion or settled there after their retirement from the army were soldiers. One of them was Caius Pomponius Aquila, son of Marcus, standard-bearer (*signifer*) in the third Scythian legion, whose grave monument was set up by his daughter Aquilina.[26] Another standard-bearer enjoyed a significant civil career upon his return to Dion, where he became an *aedilis* and mayor.[27]

We have already seen that slaves and freedmen are visible in the private and public inscriptions of Dion, especially in epitaphs. From the second century BC onward, the manumission of slaves became far more common. According to Roman law—and unlike Greek law—the manumitted slaves of Roman citizens acquired Roman citizenship, and thus were eligible for social advancement, if not for themselves then at least for their descendants. Some of the slaves, especially those who represented their masters in trade or super-vised large estates as stewards, could also acquire substantial wealth.

One family known from several inscriptions is an example of such a success story. In the early third century AD, Publius Anthestius manumitted two of his slaves, Iucunda and Amphio. They must have been a couple even as slaves, but a legitimate marriage became possible after their manumission. Iucunda had enough means to make dedications to Venus Hypolympidia ("Worshiped under Olympus") and Diana.[28] Together with her husband, she also provided the funds for the construction of two halls and an arch, which they dedicated to the Egyptian gods Isis and Serapis. Her husband, Publius Anthestius Amphio, had a spectacular career after his manumission, climbing the ladder of all the municipal offices and serving as *augur*, *aedilis*, and finally *duovir quinquinnalis*, that is, mayor in a year in which the official enumeration of the population (*census*) was carried out.[29] For her service to the community, Iucunda was honored with a statue by the wives of the citizens of the colony and the free population that lived in the territory (*colonarum et incolarum conjuges*).[30] Amphio and Iucunda together dedicated a statue of their daughter Maxima in the sanctuary of Isis.[31]

While other slaves and freedmen did not have such careers, they could still acquire the means to make public dedications or to pay for funerary monuments. Eracleo, the archivist in the public archive of Dion (*tabularius*), was a public slave (*publicus*). He is known for a dedication he made to Jupiter Optimus Maximus, the main divinity of Dion and the equivalent of Zeus.[32]

THE VISIBILITY OF WOMEN

Following a general trend that can already be observed in the third century BC throughout the Greek world, the position of women in social life was different in Roman Dion than in Classical Macedonia—I am not referring to queens and princesses but to ordinary women. To judge from dedications funded by women to gods and funerary monuments, women administered their property independently. When they were married, they jointly owned property with their husband, not only their dowry but also money earned with their work. Grave monuments that were erected by couples "from their shared pains" (*ek ton koinon kopon*) or "from the work of their own shoulders" (*ex idion omon*)[33] are visible evidence of their contribution to the finances of their household.

An indication of the new, larger freedom of women is also the fact that the free married women of Dion, as in some other cities of the Roman Empire,[34] belonged to a corporate body that had an assembly, which probably met during the organization of the festival of a goddess, for example, Demeter or Isis. This corporate body honored one of the most prominent women of Dion, Iucunda.[35]

Women of means were quite visible through dedications and donations, and some of them also had access to education. In Roman Dion, women exercised professions that went beyond the occupations we usually associate with ancient women, such as weaving and childcare. We have already encountered a professional player of the *nabla*. Another woman with an unusual occupation was Iulia Eutychiane, "the famous physician of men and midwife of women" in the late second century AD, commemorated by her husband Ulpius Zosas.[36] The archaeological finds from Dion include medical instruments (first century BC; cat. no. 52), and we can be sure that such an important city offered possibilities both for medical training and for state-of-the-art medical treatment. A doctor from Herakleia Sintike in Thrace settled in Dion (late first century AD) and "while he lived, saved many people from hard illnesses and grievous pains."[37] But without the grave epigram that Zosas set up for his wife, we would not be in a position to know that such medical instruments had been handled by a woman. If the Zosas who is named in a mosaic inscription in a private house ("for the fortunate Zosas")[38] is Eutychiane's husband, then we even know where Eutychiane lived. In any case, she certainly belonged to the well-off families of Dion.

CULTURAL COMPLEXITY

Roman Dion was a city where different traditions met and merged. We recognize this in the mixture of Greek and Latin—and a few Thracian—names, and in the parallel use of the Greek and Latin languages, but above all in the coexistence of different religious traditions and groups of worshipers. This mingling of traditions was one of the results of the migration of different population groups.

Dion is the city of Zeus. Although some of the worshipers of Zeus in the Imperial period still recognized the traditional Zeus

Olympios in this god, perception of the god had undoubtedly changed not only under the influence of the Roman Jupiter (Jupiter Optimus Maximus), whose cult played a central part in the rituals of the colony, but also under the influence of the religious trends of the Imperial period. A very important development, which modern research designates as "pagan monotheism," "henotheism," or "megatheism,"[39] is the elevation of one god above all others, the attribution to this god of significant properties—presence, efficacy, unlimited power, protection of justice—and the effort of worshipers to establish a personal relationship to this god through acts of devotion. Such elements indeed characterize the cult of the Egyptian gods, prominently present in Dion (cat. nos. 25, 27). Through initiation in the mysteries of Isis, devotees expected protection in this life and a blessed afterlife. The cult of Zeus must also have been influenced by these trends.

To judge from the personal names of the inhabitants, Dion and its territory had a mixed Greek and Italian population. But through trade and slave trade, Dion also received immigrants from other areas. Two women with the Semitic name Sambatis—which is related to sabbath, the seventh day—must have been immigrants from the Near East.[40] One of them addressed her dedication for the well-being of her daughter to *Parthenos*, the "Maiden," that is, the Syrian goddess Atargatis.

People have been dreaming since the beginning of humanity, but to mention in an inscription that one had been visited by a god in a dream is a relatively recent development, starting around the late third or second century BC. People who made dedications "in accordance with a dream" (*kat'onar*), or "in accordance with a divine command (*kat' epitagen*), wanted to show that they had succeeded where others had failed: they had attracted the attention of a deity, and they had directly communicated with the divine. There are two such dedications from the sanctuary of Isis in Dion.[41] They show the imprint of two feet—the larger represents the presence of the deity, the smaller that of the worshiper (late second–third century AD; cat. no. 26).

We wish that Roman Dion had been visited by an orator of the Second Sophistic such as Dion of Prusa, a traveler such as Pausanias, a Christian missionary such as Saint Paul, or even better a satirist such as Lucian. But no such travelers' impressions survive, and no author of a novel selected Dion as the stage of his plot. Fortunately, we have the silent testimonies of material culture—buildings, statues, artifacts, grave monuments—that have been unearthed in decades of systematic excavations. Moreover, the Greek and Latin inscriptions, public and private, preserve the thoughts and feelings, the experiences and stories of common people about whom the great authors usually remain silent.

1   The Roman names in Dion have been collected by Tataki 2006. On Roman Dion: Papazoglou 1988: 103–24.
2   E.g., Sarmounno and Sermikastes in *Supplementum Epigraphicum Graecum*, vol. 61: no. 497.
3   *Année Épigraphique* 1950: no. 20; 2003: no. 1582d.
4   *Corpus Inscriptionum Latinarum*, vol. 3: no. 593.
5   Pingiatoglou 2014. For Asclepius: *Supplementum Epigraphicum Graecum*, vol. 58: no. 565.
6   *Corpus Inscriptionum Latinarum*, vol. 3: no. 592.
7   *Supplementum Epigraphicum Graecum*, vol. 49: no. 700.
8   Horsley 1994.
9   *Supplementum Epigraphicum Graecum*, vol. 39: no. 580. Other foster children in Dion: Oikonomos 1915: 27–8 no. 47; Demaille 2015: 548 no. 1.
10 *Corpus Inscriptionum Latinarum*, vol. 3: no. 592.
11 *Supplementum Epigraphicum Graecum*, vol. 52: no. 596.
12 *Supplementum Epigraphicum Graecum*, vol. 52: no. 597.
13 Rigsby 1994: 192–93.
14 Oikonomos 1915: 14 no. 9; Demaille 2015: 551 no. 13.
15 *Supplementum Epigraphicum Graecum*, vol. 33: no. 516.
16 The baths in Dion: Pandermalis 1999a: 138–51.
17 Pandermalis 2002; *Année Épigraphique* 2000: no. 1295. Other examples of benefactions by magistrates include a temple of Liber (Dionysus) that was constructed at the expense of a mayor and his wife; *Année Épigraphique* 1950: no. 20. Dedications to Liber Pater were made by aediles; *Année Épigraphique* 1950: no. 21; 1954: no. 23; 2006: no. 1262.
18 Pandermalis 1999a: 152–203; Pandermalis 2003.
19 Pandermalis 1997b; Pandermalis 2000.
20 Pandermalis 1995.
21 Pandermalis 1994; *Année Épigraphique* 1998: no. 1200, and 2001: no. 1756.
22 Busch 2001.
23 Pandermalis 1999a: 74–83.
24 *Supplementum Epigraphicun Graecum*, vol. 39: no. 584.
25 Robert 1949: 126–28; *Supplementum Epigraphicun Graecum*, vol. 52: no. 600 bis; Demaille 2015: 555 no. 29.
26 Šašel Kos 1979: 82 no. 188. For another soldier of the same legion: *Corpus Inscriptionum Latinarum*, vol. 3: no. 592.
27 *Année Épigraphique* 1915: no. 112.
28 *Année Épigraphique* 1998: no. 1208; 2008: no. 1228. Discussion of the family of the Anthestii in Dion: Demaille 2008.
29 *Année Épigraphique* 1998: no. 1209.
30 *Année Épigraphique* 1998: no. 1210; *Supplementum Epigraphicum Graecum*, vol. 34: no. 631.
31 *Année Épigraphique* 1998: no. 1211; *Supplementum Epigraphicum Graecum*, vol. 34, no. 632.
32 *Année Épigraphique* 2003: no. 1582a. Another public slave: Oikonomos 1915: 19 no. 21; Damaille 2008: 551 no. 12.
33 *Supplementum Epigraphicum Graecum*, vol. 39: no. 581; vol. 52: no. 600.
34 Corporate bodies of women: Thonemann 2010.
35 See note 28.
36 Samama 2003: 183–84 no. 81.
37 *Supplementum Epigraphicum Graecum*, vol. 61: no. 494. Discussed by Papageorgiou 2011.
38 Papageorgiou 2011: 704.
39 Athanasiadi and Frede 1999; Chaniotis 2010; Versnel 2011: 280–307.
40 An epitaph: Stefanidou-Tiveriou 1998: 179. A dedication: Arvanitaki 2013; *Supplementum Epigraphicum Graecum*, vol. 60: no. 637.
41 *Supplementum Epigraphicum Graecum*, vol. 34: nos. 623, 625; Christodoulou 2011.

GREEK MYTHS AT DION: DIVINE FAMILY IN A HUMAN LANDSCAPE

RICHARD P. MARTIN
Stanford University

Dion—"the place of Zeus." Landscape dictates the name (fig. 1). Mount Olympus, towering more than 9,500 feet at the edge of its territory, was where Zeus presided over his divine family. What more appropriate name for this regional center of Macedonian religion than one honoring the highest divinity in the Greek pantheon, Zeus Hypsistos?

Zeus himself was "highest" from the beginning. One of the few Greek gods whose name can be traced by modern linguists back to Indo-European—the parent language of Greek, Latin, Sanskrit, Persian, and most of the tongues of Europe—*Zeus* is the "shining" or "gleaming" sky. The root of his significant name also gives us the Latin *dies*, "day" (not to mention the Old Irish word for *god* and a Germanic divine name that ultimately yields the English *Tuesday*). Already in the third millennium BC, the ancestors of the Greeks were praying to the Shining Father in a phrase that became *Zeu páter* (Zeus Father). The same two words, carried by Indo-European speakers when they migrated far outward from their original home in Southern Russia, produced the Sanskrit *Dyàus pitár* and the Latin *Iuppiter* (the origin of the god's appellation in ancient Italy: Jupiter). As ancestral sky-god, Zeus belongs as close as possible to the heavens. The snow-capped range dividing Thessaly from Macedonia perfectly suited him and his entourage.

Mapping his relations with the other divine beings who accompany him in myths can be a useful way of "reading" the landscape at Dion. While Zeus holds sway at the pinnacle of the pantheon, his extended family, descendants, siblings, consorts, and kin were also important objects of worship. The intertwined stories of these mythical personages might allow us to re-imagine the sort of thoughts and associations an ordinary ancient man or woman would experience on moving through Dion's sacred spaces. Such an effort aims at hearing the symphony of polytheism, or peering through a "forest of symbols."[1]

We must begin with the chief god himself. Cleanthes of Assos in Asia Minor, writing approximately two generations after the death of Alexander the Great, began his hymn of praise: "Most glorious of immortals, of many names, all-mighty always / Zeus, chief of Nature, governing all by Law . . . ."[2] Although as a pupil of Zeno, the renowned founder of Stoicism, he turns Zeus into a cosmic principle illustrating their shared philosophy, Cleanthes' depiction builds on long-accepted characteristics of the divinity. Zeus controls rain and snow, thunder and lightning, providing signs (to those who can interpret) of impending cosmic change from his mountain dwellings, whether Olympus or, in Athens, the heights of Mount Hymettos and Mount Parnes. He boasts, among nearly a thousand other titles, those of "Rainmaker" and "Thunderer." He incinerates those who demand to see him in his natural form—even his lover, the Theban woman Semele, carrying their child Dionysus when immolated by Zeus. Sewn into the thigh of Zeus, the premature baby-god completed his gestation. On reaching manhood, he became the wide-roving god of wine, ecstasy, and theater.[3] Like many Macedonian cities, Dion celebrated Dionysus. The excavated House of Dionysus with its splendid mosaic of the triumphant god shows his continuing presence in later centuries. Thanks to the foundation of dramatic contests at Dion by Archelaos in the late fifth century BC, audiences there may well have been the first to see the most penetrating dramatic portrayal of the power of Dionysus, the *Bacchae* of Euripides, written when the poet was working at the king's court around 407 BC.[4]

The cosmic Zeus is best known in early Greek literature from the *Theogony* of Hesiod, a long poem dating from about 700 BC but probably owing its main narrative of divine succession to much older Near Eastern myths. Ouranos, the original sky-god, had been castrated and driven out by his son Kronos, who, in turn, acquired the nasty habit of swallowing his own children. Zeus, spirited away at birth by his mother Rhea, returned to rout his father Kronos and defeat, with his thunder-weapons, the

Fig. 1. View of the site of Dion from the east. In the background is the Olympus range.

Titans of the previous generation. When all is safe, he spreads his new order and power through the world by a series of sexual encounters with goddesses and mortal women. One such dalliance, with Thuia, daughter of Deukalion (survivor of the great Flood), produced Makedon, who became the legendary ancestor of the Macedonians.[5]

The *Iliad* attributed to Homer gives us a more rounded and dramatic picture of the great god. From the start, the trajectory of its central protagonist, the hero Achilles of Thessaly, is inextricable from the actions of Zeus. The poet's opening invocation of the Muse brings the two together (*Il.* 1.1–5):[6]

> Sing, goddess, the anger of Peleus' son Achilles
> and its devastation, which put pains thousandfold upon
>   the Achaians,
> hurled in their multitudes to the house of Hades strong souls
> of heroes, but gave their bodies to be the delicate feasting
> of dogs, of all birds, and the will of Zeus was
>   accomplished.

Achilles is, in terms of mythic genealogy, a great-grandson of Zeus (by way of the god's son Aeacus, father of the hero's own father, Peleus). But that is not why Zeus feels compelled to extort recognition for the disenchanted warrior at Troy (also known as Ilion). It is, instead, Achilles' mother, the divine sea-nymph Thetis, who maneuvers the supreme god into granting her son honor, since Zeus owes her a favor for help in defeating the Titans. When Achilles complains that the Greek commander Agamemnon has unfairly taken away his beautiful war-prize, the woman Briseis, and that he has therefore decided to absent himself from battle until reparations are made, Thetis begs Zeus to make all the Greeks feel the loss of their finest fighter (*Il.* 1.493–510). The god reluctantly agrees to let the Trojans start winning, at the Greeks' expense. The *Iliad* meticulously tracks the consequences—the slaughter of Achilles' companions; the death of his closest companion Patroklos, sent to fight as his substitute; and the hero's ensuing rage, now directed against his external enemies, the Trojans (rather than his fellow Greeks).

Throughout the poem's twenty-four books, Zeus choreographs the action. His thunderbolt is the ultimate weapon, blazing across the sky and smoking the ground with sulfur to terrify the Greeks when they are too successful at pushing back the Trojans (*Il.* 8.130–36). Reading such a clear sign from Zeus, Nestor, the grizzled old warrior, warns the young Greek fighter Diomedes that this is no time for glory, since Zeus is against them: "no man can beat back the purpose of Zeus, not even one very strong, since Zeus is by far the greater" (*Il.* 8.143–44). Sometimes, Zeus accompanies his lightning with a shake of his talismanic magic shield, the *aigis* that stuns mortals. At other times, he balances the "portions of death" in a set of golden scales until the fate of one side or the other sinks, portending its destruction (*Il.* 8.69–75; 22.209). He communicates his will by signs, like the flight of an eagle, his emblematic bird (compare the avian

sculpture found in the Dion shrine, fig. 2, cat. no. 7), or the sudden appearance of a rainbow (identical with a goddess—Iris—who takes his commands to earth).[7] He can intervene, for instance, to put fear into Ajax (*Il.* 11.543). As the pace of the poem picks up, Zeus steps in more directly. He himself pushes Hector forward as if by his own great hand (*Il.* 15.694–95), and enables his favorite of the moment easily to heave a stone that ordinarily would be too heavy a burden for two men (*Il.* 12.449–50). To audiences of the poem—no doubt, to the many at Dion who must have heard it regularly or studied it—Zeus could thus be imagined as an all-aware, all-powerful, but dangerously unpredictable father-god. To stay on his good side, it would be advisable to be punctilious about prayer and sacrifice.

At the same time, Zeus, as depicted in Homer's epics, resembles the very audience members who eagerly listened to the poetry, or watched drama, such as those who filled the seats in Dion's theater (fig. 3). That is to say, the god himself can be imagined as a dispassionate spectator, peering down from his mountain fastness. The terrible war at Troy is for him an absorbing entertainment. He seats himself on the side of Mount Ida near the site of conflict to look out at the plain and the ships of the Greeks beached in the distance (*Il.* 8.47–52). Later, when he has finally allowed the other Olympian gods to take sides with their favorites on the killing field, Zeus enjoys hearing the consequent clash and is "amused in his deep heart for pleasure" (*Il.* 21.387–90).

As god of the broad, open sky, Zeus was also a promoter of justice: after all, he could literally oversee all the workings of humanity and his fellow divinities. In the poetic stylizations of the *Iliad*, he is invoked as the mighty power who upholds what is right by punishing the violators of oaths (*Il.* 3.302). Zeus maintains justice even for other gods, as when he promises to let his complaining brother Poseidon later destroy the defensive wall built (without proper honorific sacrifices) by the Greeks at Troy (*Il.* 7.443). His sense of justice makes him acknowledge the claims of reciprocity: if mortals have given him honor through the sacrifice of animals, he feels a sense of obligation, even affection. When Hector is losing the race for his life against the enraged Achilles, careening around the wall of Troy, Zeus mournfully ponders rescuing him, since Hector "burned in my honor many thigh pieces of oxen on the peaks of Ida with all her folds, or again on the uttermost part of the citadel" (*Il.* 22.170–72).

Zeus, in poetry as in the realities of daily living, was the proponent of civic and domestic order. As *Ephestios* he is "protector of the hearth;" as *Xenios* he protects strangers and guests; as *Ktesios* he guards family property; and as *Philios*, the bonds of friendship. As *Hikesios* he guarantees the rights of suppliants, and as *Horkios* he sees to it that those who break oaths are severely punished. Given this lattermost function, his key regional sanctuary at Dion was the logical spot at which to set up inscriptions recording political agreements, such as the letters of King Philip V and the treaty of King Perseus with the Boeotians, shown in the present exhibition (cat. no. 5).

There is, however, a darker side to Zeus's "order" when it comes to family relations. One form of his absolute control resides in the threat of domestic violence. At one point in the *Iliad*, recognizing that Hera has intervened in battle against his will, he threatens her with a lashing and reminds her of an earlier incident when he angrily suspended Hera from the heavens, a chain on her hands and anvils tied to her feet (*Il.* 15.18–22). In the midst of the Trojan conflict, Zeus terrifies the other gods with threats of similar whipping or worse. Whoever takes sides, he declares, will be expelled to Tartarus, "where the uttermost depth of the pit lies under earth, where there are gates of iron and a brazen doorstone, as far beneath the house of Hades as from earth the sky lies" (*Il.* 8.6–17). Mockingly, he challenges the gods to try to bind him with a golden cord and drag him from the sky—they will fail.

Yet Zeus can be a fond father, when he wishes. Twice in the *Iliad*, he comforts divine daughters when they slink back with minor injuries from clashes on the battlefield. Smiling, he gently rebukes Aphrodite: "not for you are the works of warfare. Rather, concern yourself only with the lovely secrets of marriage" (*Il.* 5.430). Artemis, trembling at his knees, is addressed like a little girl (*Il.* 21.509–10): "Who now of the Uranian gods, dear child, has done such things to you, rashly, as if you were caught doing something wicked?" It was Zeus's own wife, she blurts out, who boxed her ears. Against this treatment of immortal relations, one can juxtapose his fondness for mortal offspring. We might pity Zeus, because his own sense of pity—even for his own son—is of necessity limited by political considerations on Olympus. When the Greek hero Patroklos, companion of Achilles,

Fig. 2. Sanctuary of Zeus.
    Marble statue of an eagle at
    the time of discovery.

Fig. 3. Aerial view of the
    Hellenistic theater at Dion
    before reconstruction.

is about to slay Sarpedon, a son of Zeus who is allied with the Trojans, the chief god expresses his dilemma to Hera: should he "snatch him out of the sorrowful battle and set him down still alive in the rich country of Lykia, or beat him under at the hands of the son of Menoitios" (*Il.* 16:435–43)? Do as you wish, says Hera, but don't be surprised if other gods disapprove, for they too have mortal children. Mortals are meant, inevitably, to die. Zeus, preferring to keep the peace on Olympus, allows Sarpedon to be slaughtered, although in grief for his son he does piteously weep tears of blood onto the earth. In this horrifying image, Zeus's normal mastery of the weather comes to signify the cosmic disruption caused by his mourning.

This survey of some poetic representations of Zeus and kin is meant to highlight how the Greeks took seriously the concept of a "family" of gods, albeit a highly dysfunctional one. As we turn from the supreme god to the stories of other divinities at Dion, it is important to keep in mind Zeus's role as father, for this unites almost all the cults on the ground there. The Muses, for example, who were celebrated along with Zeus in the grand contests set up by King Archelaos, are his daughters by the Titaness "Memory" (*Mnemosyne*)—a sister of his own mother, Rhea (*Theogony* 133–35). As we learn in the *Theogony* of Hesiod, Zeus slept with her for nine nights in a row, thus producing nine offspring: "Clio (Glorifying) and Euterpe (Well Delighting) and Thalia (Blooming) and Melpomene (Singing) and Terpsichore (Delighting in Dance) and Erato (Lovely) and Polymnia (Many Hymning) and Ourania (Heavenly), and Calliope (Beautiful Voiced)."[8] Hesiod singles out the last-named as patroness of kings; it is Calliope who gives them the ability to manage assemblies and resolve legal disputes with their rhetorical gifts. The specific arts assigned to individual Muses—such as history to Clio, tragedy to Melpomene—were a much later antique invention.

In a beautiful description, Hesiod's poem imagines their procession from Pieria, the Muses' mountain birthplace (some thirty miles northwest of Dion), across the countryside to Mount Olympus, their father's dwelling. Constantly singing hymns in praise of their sire, Zeus's daughters "give pleasure to his great mind within Olympus, telling of what is and what will be and what was before, harmonizing in their sound. Their tireless voice flows sweet from their mouths; and the house of their father, loud-thundering Zeus, rejoices . . ." (*Theogony* 36–41). The Muses establish their own dwelling near their father's (fig. 4), "not far from snowy Olympus's highest peak. That is where their bright choral dances and their beautiful mansions are, and beside them the Graces and Desire have their houses, in joyous festivities" (*Theogony* 61–65). A visitor to the shrine of the Muses at Dion might imagine their presence while recalling Hesiod's verses about their therapeutic powers. Even someone suffering, "when a poet, servant of the Muses, sings of the glorious deeds of people of old and the blessed gods who possess Olympus . . . forgets his sorrows at once and does not remember his anguish at all; for quickly the gifts of the goddesses have turned it aside" (*Theogony* 98–103).

Indeed, the authority of Hesiod's own long poem comes, so he claims, from his face-to-face encounter with the Muses in the foothills of his local mountain, Helicon in Boeotia, while he pastured his sheep. Initiating him with the gift of a laurel branch and a boast of their divine abilities, which include telling "lies like the truth" on occasion, they breathe into Hesiod a "divine voice" so that he is inspired to narrate the origins of the gods (including the Muses' birth) in the creation story that forms his *Theogony*.

These delight-giving daughters of Zeus function as a choral group, a divine mirroring of the sort of song-and-dance activities in which young Greek women (less often men) were engaged, in hundreds of cities throughout antiquity. Most likely, Dion at its height saw such choral performances nearly every month connected to one or another god's ritual. Moreover, the Muses' attraction to sources of water can be seen in Hesiod's description of their bathing in mountain springs before they begin their choral processions. This topographical preference is reflected in the location of their shrine at Dion.[9] It is worth recalling that the major source of water at Dion, the river Baphyras, was also a god. A statue head of the personified river, dating from the second century AD, is in the exhibition (cat. no. 46). Theoretically, he too, like the three thousand rivers of the world according to Hesiod, arose from the union of the cosmic river Okeanos with the primeval goddess Tethys (*Theogony* 337–70). Unlike some Greek river deities (for instance, Acheloos, who fought with Heracles over the hero's eventual bride Deianeira), no myth survives specifically about Baphyras. From the two references to Baphyras in Greek literature, we learn, first, that a species of small squid (*tethides*) could be found near his waters; and second, that the legendary singer Orpheus met his death near the river, at the hands of women maddened by wine and angry at him for having lured away their husbands either with his enchanting music, or because he invented homosexuality.

An interesting tie-in binds the river to one of the Muses' favored cult-spots: the second-century-AD travel writer Pausanias reports that Baphyras, further upstream, was called *Helicon*. In his day, its waters ran underground for about two-thirds of its length before surfacing to become navigable near Dion. But this was not always the case, as Pausanias explains: "The people of Dion say that at first this river flowed on land throughout its course. But, they go on to say, the women who killed Orpheus wished to wash off in it the blood-stains, and thereat the river sank underground, so as not to lend its waters to cleanse manslaughter." The bones of Orpheus, after being washed by a flood from their original burial spot at Leibethra (on the coast just southeast of Dion), were reportedly re-interred near Dion itself.[10]

Water and the gifts of the Muses come together in a somewhat different configuration when we turn to another god whose presence at Dion is less detectable but probably important: Apollo. A child of Zeus by Leto, along with his twin sister Artemis, he established the famous divination site at Delphi, where a prophetess, the Pythia, enigmatically pronounced the will of Zeus. Along with his role as god of divination, Apollo was also famous for playing the kithara, a resounding, concert-sized stringed instrument. Internationally known musical contests celebrating the god—and imitating his own singing—were regularly held at Delphi, starting in the seventh century BC. No doubt King Archelaos had these in mind when organizing his own cultural contests at Dion.

locks of their hair to local rivers, as a symbol of sacrifice and transition. The ancient male visitor to Dion might thus have mused on his own life stages upon seeing Baphyras, and the shrines of the Muses and Apollo. At the same time, as the excavations of 1999 revealed, female visitors would have the chance to contemplate the role of Artemis in her relation to the river Baphryas, her shrine and statue having been found near the water.[12] The virgin huntress must have played the role of a river

Fig. 4. Mount Olympus. The Oropedio Mouson (Muse Plateau).

As *Mousagetes* (leader of the Muses), Apollo was depicted accompanying his nine half-sisters in their choral dance. We tend to think of such activity as entertainment, but for the Greeks learning harmony, proper bodily movement, song, and related skills were a crucial part of education, known as *mousikê* (art of the Muses—the root of the English *music*). As Plato noted in his long, late dialogue the *Laws*, education (*paideia*) owed its very origins to Apollo and the Muses.[11] Hesiod's poetry curiously connects this function of Apollo to rivers: along with all the streams in the world, Tethys gave birth to thousands of nymphs, the Okeanids, "a holy race of daughters who, together with lord Apollo and the rivers, raise boys so that they become men on the earth, for this is the lot they have from Zeus" (*Theogony* 346–48). On reaching manhood, young men would dedicate

goddess—Artemis Baphyria—as well as the divinity who oversaw the initiation of young girls into womanhood.[13]

Apollo was father of the healing god Asclepius, whose worship is prominently represented at Dion.[14] By most accounts, this semidivine grandson of Zeus, like Dionysus, had a difficult birth process. One version says Apollo killed the mortal woman Coronis, pregnant with Asclepius, for betraying his love, and then rescued their child from the funeral pyre. So miraculous a healer did Asclepius become that he resuscitated mortals who had died, for which transgression Zeus struck him dead with a bolt of lightning. Epidauros in the Peloponnese, close to a very old sanctuary of Apollo Maleatas, became the most famous site where the hero-healer exercised his ability even after his own demise. There, the sick would seek to encounter Asclepius or his helpers in a dream, while spending the night within the sacred precinct.[15] Testimony concerning the successful cures brought about by this "incubation" process were prominently displayed at Epidauros. No similar text has emerged yet from Dion, although an inscribed praise-poem to the god was among the early twentieth-century finds.[16] Worship of Asclepius spread in the fifth century BC to Athens, where the poet Sophocles, involved in the cult, composed a paean to the god. In Dion, as in other sites, the Asclepius shrine had easy access to water, actually being incorporated into a bath complex. Fittingly, statues of the extended family of Asclepius, including his daughters "Health" (*Hygieia*), "All-Cure" (*Panakeia*), "Healing" (*Iaso*), and "Curing" (*Akeso*), adorned the pool areas.[17]

We return, at last, to Zeus and his relationships in order to contextualize two of the longest-lasting and most highly developed varieties of worship at Dion—the related goddess cults of Demeter and of Isis (fig. 5).[18] The first was widespread throughout the Greek world and, from the evidence of archaeology, may go back to Mycenaean times, although Demeter's name, unlike those of other major divinities, is not attested in the Linear B tablets of the fourteenth to twelfth centuries BC.[19] The second arrived quite late from Egypt in the Classical period—most likely due to traders— and rapidly established itself, especially in such mercantile centers as Athens.[20] Always open to innovation, whether in technology, art, or religion, the Greeks appear to have merged the newer rites with their age-old inheritance, creating forms of veneration for the Egyptian mother-goddess that lasted until the fifth century AD.

Zeus played a double role in the story of Demeter and her daughter, who was snatched away to the Underworld and made his consort by its king Hades. Not only was the chief god the father of Persephone, it was Zeus who actually granted his brother Hades the permission to abduct her, while she picked flowers with her age-mates. As the *Homeric Hymn to Demeter* (ca. sixth century BC) tells the story, Demeter in protest at the arranged marriage stops the growth of grain, which she controls. Not only do humans face starvation: the gods, given the lack of foodstuffs, may not obtain sacrifices they desire. Zeus agrees to a compromise, forcing Hades to let Persephone revisit earth and reunite with her mother Demeter. But because the girl has been tricked into eating a pomegranate, she must return for part of each year to the murk and gloom of her husband's subterranean realm. Over the centuries, interpreters have attempted to read the myth, too reductively, as an allegory of the agricultural year. Of equal or greater interest are the ways in which the myth relates to the life cycles of female worshipers, and to the great Mysteries, still an unrevealed secret after two millennia.

Fig. 5.
Sanctuary of Isis.
Reconstruction of the
Temple of Isis and
the altar in front of it.

The mother-daughter bond was celebrated all over Greece in an annual festival exclusively for women, the Thesmophoria. Over the course of several days, participants would imitate a "primitive" lifestyle meant to mime how humans lived before the discovery of Demeter's specialty, cultivated grains. Separate days in the ritual complex recalled, through fasts and feasts, both Demeter's mourning for the lost Persephone and their joyous reunion. Furthermore, the celebration of familial reintegration was extended into a ritual model for the prosperity of the community: the festival of "carrying what was put down" (the meaning of *thesmo-phoria*) involved retrieving decayed remains of slaughtered pigs from underground pits to be used as crop fertilizer. In short, the ritual foregrounded renewed life on both the personal and civic levels.

About twelve miles west of Athens, an additional set of rituals seems to have been grafted onto Demeter's women-only worship starting in the Archaic period. At Eleusis men and women of any nationality or status could be "initiated" through a set of procedures that apparently involved seeing or handling secret objects during a nighttime rite. Initiates into the Mysteries thereby gained hopes for a happy afterlife, perhaps along the model of Persephone's annual "resurrection"—although one should avoid a Christianizing interpretation. The connection of Demeter herself with the world below may be thought natural, given her ability to "send up" the grain from the hidden depths. This, in turn, provides another bond with Zeus, who, like her, was worshiped in several places under the title "of the earth" (*Khthonios*).[21] At Dion, then, moving from the great sanctuary of Zeus to that of his sister on the same site could have seemed natural. For that matter, the mental distance to the Dion shrine of Zeus's grandson Asclepius could also have seemed short, since Demeter herself was known in other locales for healing, especially of eye ailments.[22]

From Demeter's sanctuary to that of Isis, on the other hand, might seem to require a major stretch of the religious imagination, although, spatially, at Dion the goddesses are near neighbors (fig. 6). As it turns out, even before the incursion of Alexander the Great had made Egyptian religion familiar to Macedonian soldiers and settlers, similarities between these two divinities had been observed. The well-traveled historian Herodotus, writing around 430 BC, reported that for the Egyptians Demeter was

"Isis" and Dionysus "Osiris."[23] Furthermore, he asserted that the Demeter festival of the Thesmophoria was actually Egyptian in origin, having been brought to Greece by the legendary daughters of Danaus.[24] References to the worship of Isis in Egyptian texts come as early as 2300 BC. A daughter of Earth and Sky, she first appears in mourning for her missing husband (also brother) Osiris, after the jealous Seth (another brother) throws him into the Nile in a box. After Seth further dismembers Osiris and scatters his limbs, Isis reassembles the body in a prototypical mummification and has intercourse, resulting in the child Horus. A statuette of Horus, also known by the Greek name Harpocrates, has been found in the Isis precinct at Dion (cat. no. 27). Iconography related to Isis commonly celebrates the goddess suckling her baby.

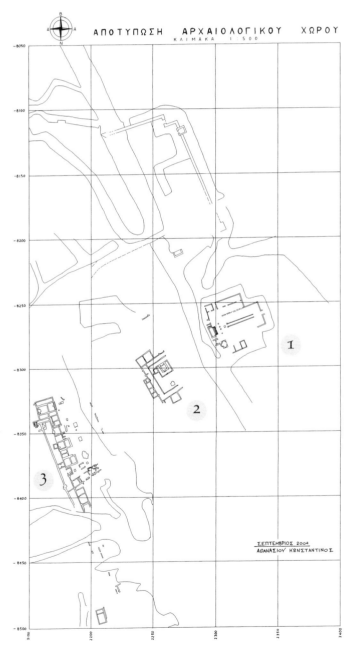

Fig. 6.
Plan of the sanctuaries outside the southern city gate:
(1) Sanctuary of Isis
(2) Sanctuary of Zeus Hypsistos
(3) Sanctuary of Demeter

Her multiple associations made Isis a goddess of fertility, including grain production and human procreation. As one who had resuscitated Osiris, she became a divinity of the afterlife; as his lover and wife, she was tied to erotic activity; and as a mother, she was widely worshiped by women. All these aspects may have been resonant in the minds of those who visited Isis in Dion. An inscription makes clear her links there to childbirth as Isis Lochia (of the Birth-Bed)—a title given to Artemis in the native Greek cult. In this regard, it is noteworthy that Egyptians made Isis mother of Artemis and Apollo.[25] The function of Isis to bring men and women together in marriage may explain why a statue of Aphrodite Hypolympidia was dedicated in her shrine (cat. no. 29).[26] Rather than replacing the worship of Demeter, it seems, Isis acted as an echo and amplifier of its major themes.

If Dion, finally, owes its name to associations of landscape, the placement of Isis within the site is also symbolic (fig. 7). She was "born in the regions that are ever moist," according to Plutarch (ca. 118 AD).[27] One of her greatest festivals, in Roman times, commemorated her sea voyage to find Osiris and marked the opening of sailing season. The North African writer Apuleius (ca. 124–170 AD) memorably set the denouement of his Latin novel *Metamorphoses*, when its hero converts to the goddess's cult, during a *navigium Isidis* held in Cenchreae, the port of Corinth. Isis may be alone among the deities of Dion in having no familiar relation with Zeus, yet her proximity to the icy clear streams that began their course in the rills of Olympus unites this goddess of the marsh and plain with the god who rules the sky.

Fig. 7. Aerial view of the Sanctuary of Isis (right) and the Sanctuary of Zeus Hypsistos (left).

1. A relevant ethnographic effort is Turner 1967. His title, *The Forest of Symbols*, comes from *Correspondances* by Charles Baudelaire.

2. Translation is mine, based on Meijer 2007: 210–12.

3. Fuller details and reading on these gods can be found in Dowden 2006; and Seaford 2006.

4. For the establishment of contests: Diodorus Siculus 17.16.

5. This detail is preserved in Hesiod's *Catalogue of Women* (fragment 7 Merkelbach-West).

6. All translations of the *Iliad* are from Lattimore 2011. Minor modifications in spelling have sometimes been made.

7. Aigis: *Il.* 17.593–96; eagle: *Il.* 24.315–21; rainbow: *Il.* 17.547, 24.190.

8. *Theogony* 76–79. Translations from Hesiod are from Most 2006.

9. See Pandermalis 2000: 28.

10. The tidbit about squid is from Archestratus, the fourth-century-BC Sicilian author of a gastronomic poem cited by Athenaeus (*Deipnosophistae* 7.326d); the Orpheus lore comes from Pausanias 9.30.8–11 (trans. Jones 1935).

11. Plato, *Laws* 654a6–7.

12. See Pandermalis 2000b: 272–79.

13. On Artemis and the initiation of young women: Sourvinou-Inwood 1988.

14. See Pandermalis 2000: 84–85, 140–42.

15. Details of myth and cult can be found in Edelstein, Edelstein 1945.

16. See Pandermalis 2000: 85. On the text, from the second century AD (a version of a poem attested in several other sanctuaries): Käppel 1992: 193–206.

17. See Pandermalis 2000: 140–47.

18. On these and other cults of goddesses at Dion: Pingiatoglou 2010a: 179–92.

19. A good summary of Demeter's myths and rituals is in Richardson 1974.

20. For the history of the cult elsewhere in Greece: Dunand 1973 (published before the relevant discoveries at Dion).

21. For Demeter *Khthonia*: Pausanias 2.35.4–8, 3.14.5; for Zeus as chthonic divinity: Pausanias 2.2.8.

22. On Demeter as healer: Rubensohn 1895.

23. Hdt. 2.123, 2.156.

24. Hdt. 2.171.

25. According to Herodotus (2.156), who claims Aeschylus borrowed this genealogy in his tragedy on the Danaids.

26. See Pandermalis 2000: 90. On the connections between Isis and Aphrodite: Heyob 1975: 49–50.

27. *De Iside et Osiride* 355f–356a.

ZEUS OLYMPIOS AND HIS CULT IN GREECE

FRITZ GRAF

Ohio State University

THE SANCTUARY OF ZEUS OLYMPIOS IN DION

The sanctuary of Zeus Olympios outside the city walls of Dion was the main sanctuary of the town of Dion (fig. 1). "Although not a large city, but adorned with public squares and a large number of statues," according to Livy,[1] the city thought it to be "the best visible spot" for the display of its own decrees.[2] At the same time, and with much larger consequences for the destiny of Dion, it was also the federal shrine and religious center of the Macedonians, comparable to other shrines such as Dodona for the Epirotans or Thermos for the Aetolians.[3] It is unclear whether it had this position before King Archelaos (r. 413–399 BC) instituted its Olympian games: ancient historians claimed that the shrine was very old, that its altar was founded by none other than Deukalion, and that it was the second-oldest altar of Zeus, after the altar of Zeus Lykaios in Arkadia and before the altar of Zeus in Dodona.[4] Whatever this earlier history might be, it is not yet recovered in the archaeological record: it was Archelaos's foundation that became crucial for the further development of the shrine into a royal Macedonian center. During Hellenistic times, the sanctuary housed a large number of royal documents including treaties and letters (cat. nos. 1–5), dedications, and images of the Macedonian kings; excavations have secured the bases of the images of the kings Kassandros and Perseus. On the eve of his Asian campaign, Alexander and his army assembled here to celebrate the games that Archelaos had instituted, as did other Macedonian kings. After his campaign, he planned to build a large temple in the sacred grove with its altar, but his successor Perdikkas shied away from the costs.[5] Thus, it was the altar, in Hellenistic times surrounded by porticoes, that remained the religious center and gained impressive dimensions: recent excavations have found a large number of the one hundred iron rings to which the sacrificial bulls for the literal hecatomb were tied on both sides of the altar—enough meat to feed the Macedonian nobles whom the kings invited to the festival (fig. 2).[6] Polybios's report of the devastation that the Aetolians brought to the city and the shrine in 219 BC sheds some light on its wealth: "He [Skopas] also burned down the colonnades around the sanctuary and destroyed all dedications that decorated it and served the visitors of the fairs; he also overturned all images of the kings."[7]

Fig. 2.
Sanctuary of Zeus Olympios. Reconstruction of the ceremony of the "hecatomb" at the great altar.

Fig. 1.
Sanctuary of Zeus Olympios. Aerial view from the west.
Right: Roman theater. Center: Sanctuary of Zeus Olympios (front), great altar to Zeus Olympios (back).

The Olympia that Archelaos founded not only included athletic contests, as did their namesakes and perhaps inspiration in Elis, they also included musical contests; accordingly, there is a theater and a stadion near the shrine. The contests always remained closely connected with the Macedonian kings: before his Asian campaign, Alexander celebrated nine days, "naming each day after one of the Muses."[8] Two centuries later, the Mousaïstai, the local association of performers, dedicated an image of the last Macedonian king, Perseus, to Dionysus and the Muses, confirming the ties between the kings and the musical contest.[9]

In the absence of an early history, one has to ask how this sanctuary—an extramural grove of a mountain god that lies in a plain, albeit in viewing distance of the name-giving mountain—acquired its characteristics of a royal and federal shrine. How does it fit with other shrines of Zeus, and what is the background of Zeus Olympios among the Greeks?

ZEUS OLYMPIOS IN HOMER

The starting point has to be Homer, as in so many other questions of Greek religion. From a common and often used Homeric formula, it is clear that the gods were thought to have "Olympian houses" (Ὀλύμπια δώματ᾽ ἔχοντες)—houses occupying the ambivalent space that is simultaneously the top of Greece's highest mountain, at whose foot the city of Dion was built, and somewhere high above it, in the sky. This justifies the Homeric singers to call them collectively the Olympians (Ὀλύμπιοι). But they do so in surprisingly few instances, only three times in the *Iliad*, and never in the *Odyssey*, and in each case in a well-defined context: once opposing Zeus and "the other Olympians" who fight him; another time constructing an opposition between human warriors and Olympians;[10] a third time, it is the Muses, "the daughters of Zeus," who are "Olympians" due to their habitat as well as their genealogy—they might well have inspired the cult of the Mousaïstai of Dion.[11] Much more often, and more frequently in the *Iliad* than the *Odyssey*, it is Zeus alone who is qualified as Olympian, both with and without his personal name. It is surprising how often in both poems *Olympios* alone designates Zeus, and only Zeus, regardless of the fact that the other main gods, as well as Zeus's siblings and children, could also claim this title if it simply designated the place where they have their abodes. Early in the *Iliad*, Achilles tells his mother

> μῆτερ, ἐπεί μ᾽ ἔτεκές γε μινυνθάδιόν περ ἐόντα,
> τιμήν πέρ μοι ὄφελλεν Ὀλύμπιος ἐγγυαλίξαι
> Ζεὺς ὑψιβρεμέτης, νῦν δ᾽ οὐδέ με τυτθὸν ἔτισεν. (*Il.* 1.353)
> Since you bore me to but a brief span of life, Mother,
> surely Olympian Zeus the Thunderer ought to grant me
> honor; but he grants me none at all.

Later, when during the banquet on Olympus Hephaistos calms his angry mother, Zeus is several times simply Ὀλύμπιος, "the Olympian," as in Hephaistos's final advice to his mother:

> ἀλλὰ σὺ τὸν ἐπέεσσι καθάπτεσθαι μαλακοῖσιν,
> αὐτίκ᾽ ἔπειθ᾽ ἵλαος Ὀλύμπιος ἔσσεται ἡμῖν. (*Il.* 1.582–83)
> Mother, speak gentle words to him, and the Olympian will once more show us grace.

Being Olympian and connected with the mountain, then, is crucial for Zeus, and for Zeus alone, whom the *Iliad* also depicts as enthroned on the highest peak of this mountain (*Il.* 1.499). After all, he is ὑψιβρεμέτης, the god of clouds and storms, who "thunders up high" and "collects the clouds," who in nature gathers round the high mountaintops. As such, he is not only the radically transformed heir of the Indo-European god of the clear sky that we find in his etymological connection with the Latin *dies*, but also influenced by the Near Eastern weather gods, whose iconography he also inherited in the many small bronzes of Archaic Greece that show him stepping wide and wielding lightning. And although "father Zeus" is linguistically connected closely with Dyaus Pita in the Indian Rigveda, with whom he shares the sky and fatherhood of important gods, the Indian god is different from the Greek one by not being an active king and ruler of the present world, as Indra is. This role aligns Zeus much more with the Hittite Storm God Teshub or with some of the Near Eastern Baalim: in Hittite images, Teshub too wields lightning (and an axe or club) and is sometimes carried on the shoulders of two mountains. It is against such a background that one must see Zeus Olympios in Homer's poems, a background that reflects an Indo-European heritage embedded in a complex Near Eastern *koine*: it is this complex and creative world that has formed Zeus the "king of the gods" and the "father of gods and humans," and has deeply influenced the way later Greeks perceived their Zeus in the many cult places that share this epithet.

ZEUS AND GREEK MOUNTAINS

If Olympus is a mountain—in our own geography, the highest mountain of Greece, which separates Macedonia from Thessaly; in the understanding of the ancient Greeks, six different mountains, including the one we call Olympus—mountain shrines of Zeus, not least the one on this very mountain, make us curious.[12] The Homeric emphasis on Zeus as the god of Olympus corresponds to the traces of a cult that were found on one of the central peaks of this mountain, Agios Antonios (elevation 2,817 m).[13] A layer of charcoal and ceramics shows that on this peak the god received sacrifices during Hellenistic and Roman times, and three inscriptions give the name of Zeus Olympios. Pre-Hellenistic strata are absent, which in the absence of more systematic research allows several options for an earlier history. On the one hand, it cannot be excluded that elsewhere on Mount Olympus an older cult gave ritual expression and worship to Zeus, god of Mount Olympus; mountain cult in Greece can be old.[14] But it might also be that the Homeric conception did not have its root in a real cult at an elevation to which neither shepherds nor hunters, not to mention worshipers with their sacrificial animals, would climb, and that the fame of the Homeric poem triggered such a cult several centuries later.

There are several other mountains in Greece where Zeus regularly received cult.[15] Several of these cults are as old as the eighth and early seventh centuries BC and are thus more or less contemporary with the *Iliad*—but they are all much easier to reach than the peaks of Mount Olympus. A small open-air shrine on Mount Hymettos in Attica (elevation 1,062 m) is representative of the minor mountaintop shrines that focused on Zeus as the god of rain; several of these shrines are attested in Attica. A platform near the summit of the mountain supported an enclosure with a simple altar; the ceramic finds around it date as early as the late eighth century BC. Later graffiti on shards identify the god as Zeus Semios, "Zeus of Signs," that is, of the weather signs connected with the mountain. Much later, Pausanias calls the Zeus worshiped on top of Mount Hymettos Zeus Ombrios, "Rain Zeus."[16] All of this corresponds to the role of the same mountain both in antiquity and in modern times as a regional indicator of rain because the clouds gather around its summit.[17]

Other mountaintop shrines on the Greek mainland have a similar connection with Zeus as the god who sends rain and signals the weather to come; this is expressed either in stories about Zeus who saved the humans from droughts or in epithets such as Ombrios or Hyetios, "Rain Zeus." A few other, less well-attested cults of a mountain Zeus are less clear as to their function, such as Zeus Pelinnaios on Chios.[18] That epithet, found in an early fourth-century-BC inscription and in much later lexica, connects the god with the highest mountain of the island, the impressive Mount Pelinnaion (elevation 1,260 m). The inscription that preserved the epithet attests to an isolated sanctuary whose priest could not be expected to live continuously on its premises, so that sometimes worshipers had to perform a sacrifice without a priest. Since the find spot of the inscription is near Chios Chora, far from the mountain range, we cannot know whether there really was a sanctuary on the mountaintop, or whether it was instead much closer to human settlements.

To a certain extent, the role as rain god almost forces Zeus to be relevant for more than just one place: the storm clouds that assembled around Mount Hymettos could not be expected to rain only over the small agrarian community at the foot of the mountain but were likely to water larger parts of Attica. Two mountaintop sanctuaries confirm this and expand the range of the cult.

Mount Oros, the highest peak of the island of Aigina (elevation 531 m), was the site of an open-air altar where, according to Isokrates and Pausanias, King Aiakos once sacrificed to Zeus in a drought that afflicted all Greeks, and obtained rain for all of them. "And when they were saved, they built a shrine common to all Greeks in Aigina where Aiakos had made his prayer;" thus Pausanias calls the god Panhellenios, "All-Greek Zeus."[19] Again, this mountaintop Zeus is a god of rain, and as at Mount Hymettos, the clouds around Mount Oros bring rain not just for the locals. Nor would they realistically bring rain for all of Greece; however, in this case, the title hides a much more important political claim about a local Zeus as the god of all the Greeks.

The shrine of Zeus Panhellenios, "Common to all Greeks," must reflect a historical claim of Aigina and goes well beyond help in a drought. The precise implications are hazy, however, in the absence of texts. But the substantial archaeological remains of the site and its pottery, which ranges from Geometric to Roman times, again point to a major cult that has more than just a local function; more-concrete meanings are, however, unknown.[20]

ZEUS LYKAIOS IN ARCADIA

An even higher degree of complexity, but also a considerably less vague meaning can be found for the best-known and most famous of these mountaintop shrines, the sanctuary of Zeus Lykaios on the summit of Mount Lykaion in Arcadia (elevation 1,382 m; fig. 3). "Some Arcadians," the traveler Pausanias tells us, "call the mountain Olympus, and others Sacred Peak. On it, they say, Zeus was reared"—a myth that underpins the supraregional claims of the mountaintop sanctuary of Zeus Lykaios.[21] A detailed report by Pausanias connects the priest of this Zeus with occasional rain rites at a sacred spring on the mountain and that concern all of Arcadia: "Should a drought persist for a long time, and the seeds in the earth and the trees wither, then the priest of Lycaean Zeus, after praying towards the water and making the usual sacrifices, lowers an oak branch to the surface of the spring, not letting it sink deep. When the water has been stirred up there rises a vapor, like mist; after a time the mist becomes cloud, gathers to itself other clouds, and makes rain fall on the

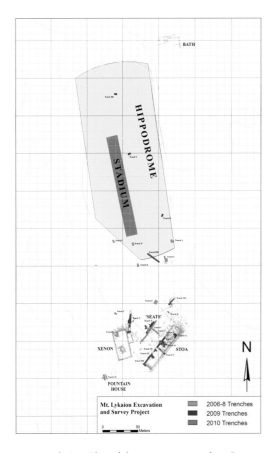

Fig. 3. Mount Lykaion. Plan of the sanctuary complex. Courtesy of Mt. Lykaion Excavation and Survey Project.

land of the Arcadians."[22] The spring is not far from the open-air sanctuary of the god whom the author also calls Olympios, whose cult is common to all Arcadians, and whose altar, according to a Hellenistic historian, went back to the origins of humanity: "Pelasgos, the author claims, built the first altar of Zeus Olympios in Arkadia for Zeus whom they call Lykaios."[23] Pelasgos is the founding hero of humanity and ancestor of the Pelasgians, who preceded the historical Greeks. Pausanias describes the core of the sanctuary as forbidden to mortals, who lose their shadows when they enter, and he is impressed by its strange altar but also by the secrecy that surrounds the rites performed there: "On the highest point of the mountain is a mound of earth, forming an altar of Zeus Lykaios, and from it most of the Peloponnesus can be seen. Before the altar on the east stand two pillars, on which there were of old gilded eagles. On this altar they sacrifice in secret to Zeus Lykaios. I was reluctant to pry into the details of the sacrifice; let them be as they are and were from the beginning."[24] As often, the secret sacrificial rite is not as secret as the scrupulous Pausanias would have liked. It is talked about since the time of Plato and was famous through its uncanny association: participation in the rite, which was tinged with the horror of human sacrifice, could result in the temporary transformation of young men into werewolves who roamed the wilderness before returning to human society. Archaeological research has shown that Pausanias's "mound of earth" was the site of an altar that, from Protogeometric times (tenth century BC) onward, was an accumulation of ash and sacrificial remains that formed a high conical ash-altar that hid its core, a flat block cut from the natural rock.[25]

The shrine was also the place of major athletic contests that, like the Olympic games in Elis, were held every four years, with an impressive stadium and hippodrome on a meadow below the sanctuary that demonstrate the importance of the disciplines of running and horse races. Two inscriptions from the late fourth century BC confirm these disciplines and attest not just to the Pan-Arcadian but to the Panhellenic character of these games, with participants from as far away as Sicily. Pausanias claims the foot race and the stadium for a sanctuary of Pan nearby; archaeology rather suggests that Pan and Zeus were worshiped side by side in the same complex shrine, as were Zeus and Pelops in Olympia. The myth of Zeus's birth on this mountain buttresses similar Panhellenic political claims and ambitions.

ZEUS OLYMPIOS AND OLYMPIA

The best-known cult of Zeus Olympios, the cult in Elis in the Western Peloponnesus, looks at first as if it were a very different matter.[26] Obviously it is no mountaintop cult, nor is securing rain relevant for the cult. The sanctuary lies in the flat land beneath a low hill, the Hill of Kronos, and two rivers, the Alpheios and its contributor the Kladeos. What drove the cult were the athletic games, the most prominent of all Greek sports events, which were held every four years; the four-year period of the Olympiads became the backbone of Greek chronology. According to the list of victors, which might go back to Ephoros of Kyme (ca. 400–330 BC), the first Olympic games were held in 776 BC, with the footrace as the only event. In the narrative tradition, however, which is reflected in the account of Pausanias (5.8.1–5), the games were founded by a competing group of heroes, from Pelops to Heracles and the Elean king Oxylos, reflecting competing claims on the games during the Archaic period.

Early cult in Olympia is somewhat elusive, although archaeological finds go back to very late Mycenaean times. Its core seems to be a prehistoric mound that was later understood to be the grave of the hero Pelops. As often in Greek sanctuaries, this heroic cult was combined with the cult of a major god, in this case Zeus, as Apollo and Hyakinthos were joined in Amyklai, or Apollo and Neoptolemos/Pyrrhos in Delphi. The sanctuary was radically reshaped and expanded after 700 BC to include a first stadion, with the horse races added not much later on the flat plain at the Alpheios. A first monumental peristyle temple, the Heraion, was constructed around 600 BC; eight hundred years later, Pausanias saw one of its original oakwood columns still in place.[27] The cult of Zeus Olympios originally was centered around an open-air altar as in Dion, but surrounded by olive trees; presumably already then the altar had the shape of the conical accumulation made from "the ash of the thighs of the victims sacrificed to Zeus" that Pausanias described (fig. 4).[28] In his time, the ash altar sat on a stone platform, with an overall height of twenty-two feet and the steps cut into the ash that led from the platform up to the top.[29] The ritual connected the sacrifice on this altar with the running contest in the stadion, whose axis was aimed at the very altar: "When the sacred parts were placed on the altar, there was no fire burning. The runners were at the distance of a stadion from the altar, and a priest

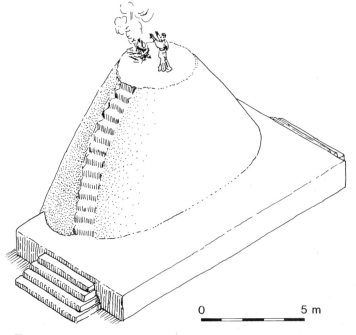

Fig. 4.
Sanctuary of Zeus at Olympia. Reconstruction of the altar.
After J. Whitley, *The Archaeology of Ancient Greece* (Cambridge, 2001), p. 135 fig. 7.1. Courtesy Howard Mason and James Whitley.

stood in front of them who gave the start signal with a torch. The victorious runner lit the fire on the altar, and so he went away as Olympic victor."[30] The winning runner thus was running up the steps cut into the ash cone with a torch, to light the sacrificial fire. Given the tradition that the very first games consisted only of the footrace, and the concomitant prominence of the stadion already during the very first expansion of the shrine, this footrace is old and central to the cult: from early on, the fastest young runner showed the excellence needed to make the sacrifice acceptable and pleasant for Zeus Olympios. Only later was Zeus thought to need a monumental residence: the Dorian temple, the largest in the Peloponnese, was finished in about 475 BC, with Phidias adding the famous gold-ivory statue of the enthroned god a few decades later (fig. 5). If we can trust the victory lists, the contest was supralocal as early as the eighth century BC and soon became Panhellenic: Pindar's *Olympian Odes*, written at the time when the temple of Zeus was being built, map prominent victors among Greek aristocrats from Rhodes to Sicily. In a similar way, the iconographic program of the temple moves the sanctuary out of local claims to supraregional and Panhellenic interests. The eastern pediment, with Zeus at its center, showed the preparation for the race between Pelops and Oinomaos that can be read as both foundational myth for the spectacular horse races and for the name of the Peloponnese. The western pediment, with a splendidly commanding Apollo at its center, narrated the fight between Centaurs and Lapiths, a story that combines Thessalian and Athenian traditions; shortly after the Persian Wars, this was an easily recognizable allusion to Greece's victory over barbarian aggression—the two pediments thus combine pan-Peloponnesian and Panhellenic claims. The famous twelve metopes that showed Heracles' twelve labors in turn represent the civilizing force of Zeus's most prominent son, which covers the geography of the entire known world and beyond, from the stable of the Elean king Augias to the Thracian king Diomedes, the queen of the Amazons somewhere far east, and Cerberus brought out of the Netherworld. The myth of Oinomaos and Pelops also plays on other associations: Pelops's father, Tantalos, is associated with Western Asia Minor, as is the name of his helpfully devious charioteer Myrtilos, which resonates with the Hittite divine and royal name Muršilis. The chariot was the weapon of choice of the Hittite aristocracy, adopted by the kings of Mycenae and given as a gift to Pelops by Poseidon, his lover, Lord of Horses, and major Mycenaean divinity. Whatever the value of these associations and the layers of historical depth they hide rather than reveal, the aristocratic and royal echoes of Pelops and horse races seem to be important for Archaic Olympia.

On closer look, the cult in Olympia shares some key features with the cult in the mountaintop shrines with which I started this survey. It shares the ash altar with the cult in the Lykaion sanctuary, which appears to be somewhat older, and with the cult on Mount Olympus even if only in later legend. If the early date of the stadion is a reliable indicator, running was a key physical activity both on the Arcadian mountain and on the plain in Elis. A connection with military prowess in early Greek ideology, and in the practice of young men in warfare, imposes itself: in Cretan documents from Hellenistic times, to be a runner characterized the social and ritual position of adolescent males—the ability to run fast and over long periods of time contributed to military success in the rugged territory of both Crete and the Peloponnese. The association of the stadion with Pan on Mount Lykaion, on which Pausanias insisted, makes sense: Pan, the goat-god, is a supremely nimble and fast runner in the mountains of Arcadia. It needs emphasis, on the other hand, that in both places the contests moved toward the inclusion of a greater number

Fig. 5. Perspective reconstruction of the sanctuary of Zeus (Altis), Olympia, by Friedrich Adler, 1827. The temple of Zeus, the great ash altar, and the Pelopion, view from the southwest.

of the aristocratic elites, whose sport, the chariot race, was as easily performed on the plain of the river Alpheios as it was somewhat awkwardly and with strain on the Arcadian mountaintop.

However, Olympia is unique in combining Zeus with Hera, the male and warlike disciplines of footraces and chariot races with the exclusively female footraces at the equally penteteric Heraia, where unmarried girls contested in three age classes under the eyes of the priestess of Hera. The same festival saw the dedication of a peplos to Hera, woven by a selected group of sixteen mature women: the arch-female art of weaving complemented the unusual girls' athletic contest for a much fuller mirror of gendered human society than that offered by any of the male-only mountaintop cults. The cult in the plain between Kronos Hill and the Alpheios developed from a much richer background into an event that already in the Late Archaic Age was able to represent all of Greece under the somewhat paradoxical protection of a Zeus whose epithet derived from the highest Greek mountain, far north at the border between Thessaly and Macedonia.

ZEUS OLYMPIOS AND ATHENS

The aristocratic and Panhellenic associations of Zeus Olympios, father of gods and men but also the main divinity of rulers, had already become manifest and obvious for the ancient observers in another shrine, the huge temple of Zeus Olympios in Athens, which after the mid-sixth century BC the tyrant Peisitratos started to build outside the city of Athens, near the river Ilissos[31]— according to tradition not on a new sacred spot, but at a place where Deukalion, the flood hero, had built a temple to mark the fissure into which the flood waters had drained.[32] When Peisitratos's son Hippias was overthrown in 510 BC, the ambitious building remained unfinished for centuries. Athenians associated it with the undemocratic hubris of monarchs: Aristotle mentions it in a list of buildings that attest how tyrants (starting with the Egyptian pharaohs) employed the poor for grandiose works "so that they are unable to revolt because they have no time."[33] As if to prove Aristotle's point, the unfinished building attracted exclusively foreign kings, who had no compunction about advertising their royal ambitions. The first was the grandiose and as conqueror highly successful Antiochos IV (who called himself Epiphanes, "Visibly Helpful Divinity"), who in 174 BC commissioned a Roman architect to finish "the only temple in the world that was begun in a way fitting to the god's greatness," as claimed by Livy, who also praises the "royal generosity" of the king who filled the world with his buildings.[34] Powerful friends ("friendly kings") of Augustus planned to finish the temple in his honor, as Suetonius tells; but somehow the plan did not materialize—perhaps because Augustus, equally ambitions but less ostentatious, objected to it.[35] More than a century later, Hadrian, the most generous benefactor of Greece and especially Athens, succeeded in finishing it, dedicated it in 131/132 AD, and made it the seat of the Panhellenion, the assembly of all the Greeks. As his biographer tells us: "After his return from Africa to Rome, he immediately traveled on to

Greece, and he inaugurated the buildings that he had begun there: thus, he dedicated the temple and altar of Zeus Olympios to himself; and in the same way, when traveling on through Asia, he dedicated several temples to himself."[36] Numerous inscriptions show that among his many titles was the name of Zeus Olympios and even Zeus Olympios Soter, "Olympian Zeus the Savior." The biographer leaves it open whether this title was a consequence of the inauguration of the Athenian temple or an incentive; an inscription, however, dates the temple "in the third year of Zeus Olympios and the Panhellenion," which suggests that the title and the temple were intimately connected. In any case, the firm association of Zeus Olympios with royal power and with Panhellenism that we previously observed in Olympia is obvious; it is also relevant to understand Dion.

BACK TO DION

As it turns out, Zeus, who resides on a tall mountain—be it the true Olympus or a lesser mountain—derives from this position a role that moves him above and beyond the boundaries of a single polity. In purely physical terms, the view from the mountaintop is wider than the view from below, and the weather that he sends does not confine itself to narrow local boundaries. As the Homeric formula of "father of gods and men" expresses, he plays a more universal role that, in the epic poem, sets him above the fighting Greeks and Trojans (it is, one recalls, Hera's intervention that prevents Zeus from protecting Hector) and that, at the least, makes him the protector of an ethnic or tribal group such as the Arcadians or the Macedonians. To worship him in an extramural shrine, outside the confines of a town, expresses this transcendence.

At the same time, Zeus was seen as the king among gods and men; whatever form Greek polities were taking, he never fully gave up his royal associations. Hadrian, the Zeus Olympios who presided over the Panhellenion, returned full circle to what Homer and the mountain cults of Archaic Greece had previously spelled out—and what the Macedonian kings in the sanctuary of Zeus Olympios at Dion claimed as their own political program. It is these two traits, that he is a king and that his influence transcends a single city, that are inherent in the worship of Zeus Olympios as it was shaped by Homer's poems.

This is relevant, although in a very ambivalent way, for the early history of Zeus Olympios in Dion. The relationship of the sanctuary with the cult atop Mount Olympus has often been debated.[37] It is obvious that the location on one of the highest peaks in Greece allowed only a few people during the summer to perform a sacrifice, and it is very unlikely that the shrine had its own priest: the cult could thus have been dependent on the cult in Dion. A dedication of Roman Imperial date to Zeus Olympios, found in the peak cult place, is dated in the office year of a priest. His title, however, is lost, and the assumption that it was the priest of the shrine in Dion is only one possibility: we do not know whether his office was ever used for dating purposes. At any rate, the cult in Dion might well be older than the sacrifice on the mountain, and it might have included the mountain only after King Archaelaos had elevated it to a pan-Macedonian status; we recall that on Chios there must have been a sanctuary of the mountain god Zeus Pelinnaios far from the mountain peak. And that the mountain cult was older than the cult in Dion, and even older than Homer—peak sanctuaries are well-known from Minoan Crete and from Bronze and Iron Age cultures in the Alps:[38] there are more questions than answers. The same is true for the question whether Archelaos's innovation was influenced by the Panhellenic cult in Olympia. One would like to assume it. However, the Olympia founded by the king did not just contain athletic contests such as the Elean games but also musical ones, and if one looks for models, the cult of the Muses in Thespiai could also be relevant, and Archelaos might have competed with two major Greek cults.[39] The combination of athletic and musical contests looks not so much back to models of the classical age but forward to the new festivals founded in Hellenistic and Imperial times, with their much richer programs.[40]

In a radically historical reading, the claims of some of these sanctuaries of Zeus Olympios to date back to the foundational age after the Flood need an explanation. The sanctuaries of Dion and of Athens are connected in their mythology with Deukalion, the altar "of Zeus Olympios, who was named Zeus Lykaios," on the Arkadian Mount Lykaion, which was founded by Pelasgos and was the first ever altar of Zeus. But this makes sense, not as memories of very old age but as underscoring important later claims. These cults legitimated either royal power or, in Peisistratos's case, a tyranny, and at the same time supralocal "tribal" associations, of the Arcadians or the Macedonians. In both cases, these institutions were construed as being connected to a sanctuary that went back to the beginnings of our actual world order. This is the same mechanism that, in Hesiod's *Catalogues,* derived the eponymous heroes of the major Greek tribes from Deukalion, his son (Hellen), grandsons (Doros, Aiolos), and great-grandson (Makedon). The large-scale tribal order was perceived as almost primordial and thus exempt from political change, and the monarchic institutions sheltered under the same claim.[41]

A recently published inscription from Thessaly has confirmed some of these interpretations. In a third-century-BC decree from Aigai, a priest of Zeus Olympios expresses the gratitude of all Thessalians to their relatives, "Aiolians, Coans, and Magnesians," for having participated in the "rite and sacrifice for Zeus Olympios and the heros Thettalos." It turns out that this otherwise shadowy Thessalian festival of Olympia was invented as a means of asserting translocal tribal claims on either side of the Aegean: although royal associations were impossible in a time when the Thessalians were firmly under Macedonian kings but loath to own up to it, Zeus Olympios again offered himself as the god to protect claims to a unity that transcended a geographical area and gave some nominal independence to the otherwise all too dependent Thessalians.[42]

---

1. Livy 44.7.3: *urbem . . . sicut non magnam, ita exornatam publicis locis et multitudine statuarum.*

2. See *SEG* 48.784, line 4: εἰς τὸ ἱερὸν τοῦ Διὸς τοῦ Ὀλυμπίου ἐν τῶι ἐπιφανεστάτωι τόπω[ι].

3. Hatzopoulos 2013.

4. *Templum veterrimae Macedonum religionis* (a temple worshiped by the Macedonians since very old times) (Justin. 24.2.8); the list of altars in *P.Oxy.* 4306, frg. I col. i, 19–29; see Voutiras 2006, 335.

5. Diodor. 17.16.3 (festival), 18.4.5 (temple).

6. Pandermalis 1998: 291–92.

7. Polyb. 4.62.2: ἐνέπρησε τὰς στοὰς τὰς περὶ τὸ τέμενος καὶ τὰ λοιπὰ διέφθειρε τῶν ἀναθημάτων, ὅσα πρὸς κόσμον ἢ χρείαν ὑπῆρχε τοῖς εἰς τὰς πανηγύρεις συμπορευομένοις· ἀνέτρεψε δὲ καὶ τὰς εἰκόνας τῶν βασιλέων ἁπάσας.

8. Diodor. 17.16.3.

9. Pandermalis 1999b: 415–17.

10. *Iliad* 1.399 (the story of the planned attack "of the other Olympians" on Zeus), 20.47 (where the Olympians join the battle of the humans, in a pregnant juxtaposition: μεθ᾿ ὅμιλον Ὀλύμπιοι ἤλυθον ἀνδρῶν.

11. *Il.* 2.491.

12. On the six Olympoi: the Scholion on Apollonios of Rhodes, *Argonautica* 1.598.

13. Voutiras 2006: 340–43.

14. See below for the Lykaion cult.

15. For a list: Langdon 1976: 100–112.

16. Paus. 1.32.2.

17. It is the one spot in Attica where this writer was surprised and thoroughly drenched by a rainstorm a few years ago.

18. See Graf 1984: 37–40.

19. Isokrates, *Evagoras* 14; Pausanias 2.29.8.

20. On the excavation: Langdon 1976: 81 n. 12.

21. Paus. 8.28.2 (Loeb translation).

22. Paus. 8.38.4 (Loeb translation).

23. *P. Oxy.* 3406 frg. I, col. i, 19–25; see Voutiras 2006: 335.

24. Paus. 8.38.7.

25. Romano and Voyatzis 2010.

26. For a good overview: Mallwitz 1972; Mallwitz 1988.

27. Paus. 5.16.1.

28. For details: Mallwitz 1972: 82–85.

29. Paus. 5.13.8–10.

30. Philostratos, *Gymnastikos* 5 (my translation).

31. For an overview: Dowden 2006: 77.

32. Paus. 1.18.7–8..

33. Aristotle, *Politika* 5, 1313 b 20 (my translation).

34. Livy 41.20.8.

35. Suetonius, *Augustus* 60.

36. *Historia Augusta, Hadrian* 13.6 (my translation).

37. Most recently by Voutiras 2006: 340–42.

38. Minoan peak sanctuaries: Peatfield 1990; Nowicki 2001. Alps: Steiner 2010.

39. Thespiai: Hurst and Schachter 1996, esp. D. Knoepfler, "La réorganisation du concours des Mouseia à l'époque hellénistique: Esquisse d'une solution nouvelle," 141–67.

40. Wörrle 1988 is exemplary.

41. See Hesiod, frg. 7 and 9 Merkelbach-West.

42. Parker 2011.

MOUNT OLYMPUS AND ITS NATURAL WEALTH

KATERINA BOLI, MARIA KATSAKIORI

The Goulandris Natural History Museum, Kifissia

Covering an area of 500 square km, almost circular in shape, and with many peaks, Mount Olympus is known the world over (fig. 1). Its nature is outstanding by virtue of the extraordinary variety of plants and animals, with rare and endemic species, its rich avifauna, and its intriguing geological history.

On account of its natural richness, Mount Olympus has been dubbed the "Parthenon" of Greek nature. Olympus National Park was established by a royal decree in 1938, following a law of 1937 that had set the basis for the designation of national parks and introduced the legal framework for nature conservation in Greece.

In 1976 Mount Olympus was included within the European Network of Biogenetic Reserves by the European Council. In 1981 UNESCO placed it on the list of World Biosphere Reserves, and in 2006 it was designated as a protected area within the European Natura 2000 Network.

THE FORMATION OF MOUNT OLYMPUS

Mount Olympus has a unique geology and represents a tectonic "window." Its history differs from that of other mountains in Greece, although its beginning is the same and is recorded on the bottom of the Tethys, the shallow sea that covered the whole of Greece 250 million years ago. Sediments from shells of marine organisms that accumulated on the bottom of the Tethys, explosions, tectonic plate movements, and other complex processes led to the creation of "submarine" mountains that gradually emerged to form the current terrain of Greece, including the Pelagonic mountain range, stretching from Macedonia to the northern part of Evia island.

On the rocks of this tectonic zone, a "window" later opened, allowing the rocks of Mount Olympus—dolomite and limestone—to emerge. The crystalline schist substratum, through which Mount Olympus rose, now surrounds the massif, bearing witness to how it was created. During the Ice Age, Mount Olympus acquired plateaus and depressions. Streams of melting ice swept away huge quantities of crushed rocks, which spread from the mountain's foothills down to the sea. Eventually Mount Olympus came into its current form, no more than 10,000 years ago. Geological processes formed an intense relief, with steep slopes and impressive chasms, sharp sheer rock peaks but also dozens of smooth ones. Canyons define its boundaries while ravines carve deeply into the massif.

Mount Olympus borders on the plain of Katerini to the north and the Thermaikos Gulf to the east, while the Ziliana stream marks its border with Mount Kato Olympus to the south. In the west, the pass of Petra separates Mount Olympus from Mount Titaros, while an extensive plateau separates it from the Kamvounia mountain range.

Kato Olympus is completely different. It is smooth, lower, and covered in thick vegetation. Like Mount Olympus, however, it also reaches the sea to the south through the valley of Tempe, although its western slopes fade into the plain of Elassona.

Carved by natural forces, compact—with fifty-five peaks rising from 2,000 to 2,918.8 m—the circular massif of Mount Olympus manifests the mountain's fascinating geological history. A history without which Greek nature would seem impoverished and Greek civilization less important.

Fig. 1. View of Mount Olympus.

ROCKS

Mount Olympus is mainly dolomitic limestone and dolomite, although at the lower and medium altitudes these are mixed with other types of rock (gneiss to the west and flysch to the northeast). Above 2,000 m, limestone becomes most prevalent, dominating the natural landscape. Alluvial deposits are typical of the eastern foothills, evidence of the Ice Age on Olympus. They were formed by large quantities of crushed rock carried away by melting glaciers. These deposits cover an area of approximately 30 km, from the environs of Palaia Vrontou to Skotina and from the edges of the mountain to the sea.

The predominance of limestone rock has a decisive influence on the morphology of the massif, the climate, and hydrological conditions. The striking formations that characterize the relief of Mount Olympus are due to heavy erosion of the limestone by rainwater. Moreover, the limestone makes the climate drier, as it increases heat and absorbs rainwater and snow melt. Likewise, its porosity affects hydrological conditions. Thus at high altitudes on Mount Olympus, where limestone predominates, there are no springs.

Fig. 2. The Orlias waterfall.

Fig. 3. The Megala Kazania.

Mount Olympus holds more water within this intermediate mountainous zone, because of its morphology and because impermeable rocks penetrate masses of porous dolomitic stone that favor the accumulation of water. Two karstic aquifers are formed in the mountain massif. The first emerges at high altitudes and decompresses at 1,150–1,200 m by forming springs, such as those of Orlias (fig. 2), Palavos at Prionia, Pyxari, Nera, Palia Prionia, Apostolidi, Kolokythies, Kostis, Itamos, Kleftovrysi, and Mastorouli, among others. There are also other springs that dry out from late August to early September. At 800–850 m, a second karstic aquifer of less importance produces the springs of Agio Spilaio, Kokonis, Giannaka, Mana, Skandaliara, and Agia Kori, mainly at the edges of streams and torrents.

GEOMORPHOLOGY

The intense erosion of the limestone by rainwater and snow melt gave Mount Olympus its striking formations: peaks made of thin, broken slabs of dolomite, sinkholes, and precipitous cavities at high altitudes (e.g., Mikra and Megala Kazania [Small and Large Cauldron, fig. 3], Mikri and Megali Gourna [Lesser and Great Doline], Doline of Stefani, Doline of Stavroetia), depressions (e.g., Agios Antonios, Kalogeros, Metamorfosi, Fragkou Aloni, Kakavraka, Chontza, Griva), alpine meadows and plateaus (Bara, Muses), gullies (Prophitis Ilias, Livadaki), and steep slopes and deep gorges, especially on the eastern and northern slopes. On those slopes, the rugged relief, with deeper ravines and a well-formed hydrographic network, results in greater erosion and possible faster rates of uplift. The western and eastern slopes of the mountain are gentler, with lower gradients.

The two ravines of Mount Olympus, Mavrolongos-Enipeas (14 km long), and Mavrantzas-Sparmos (13 km long), cut the massif almost in two. The valleys of the stream of Ziliana at the edge of Kato Olympus, the Xerolakki stream in the northwest, and the streams of Papas and Orlias in the northeast are equally impressive.

Fig. 4. The Mytikas summit from the Skolio peak.

Fig. 5. The Enipeas Gorge.

Fifty-five peaks on Mount Olympus rise to between 2,000 and nearly 3,000 m. Despite the fact that the massif is mainly characterized by rocky and precipitous peaks, there are dozens of others that are smooth, quite a few of which are over 2,000 m.

The Mytikas summit (2,918.8 m, fig. 4) and the peaks Stefani (2,912.3 m) and Skolio (2,911 m) rise dramatically and steeply at the topmost point, almost in the center of the massif, forming an arc. In the west, their cliffs define the Megala Kazania, an impressive, funnel-shaped, precipitous cavity that is 700 m deep and 1,000 m wide. On the eastern cliffs of these three peaks, successive folds are formed, the so-called *zonaria* (belts) and *loukia* (gutters), narrow, steep rock fissures.

Agios Antonios (2,815 m) to the south and Profitis Ilias (2,788 m) and Toumpa (2,801 m) to the north are among the few smooth peaks at high altitudes. Between Stefani and Profitis Ilias, at an altitude of 2,695 m, lies the Muses Plateau.

THE ENIPEAS GORGE

The most striking "fissure" on Mount Olympus, and the best-known pass leading from the foothills to its highest peaks, is the Enipeas Gorge (fig. 5). Roughly 10 km long, it dramatically opens in the very heart of the massif, offering unrivalled views of the Mytikas and Stefani peaks. Through it runs the small Enipeas River, named after the ancient god Enipeus. Due to his love rivalry with Poseidon over the beautiful Tyro, daughter of the king of Elis, Zeus cursed him, decreeing that Enipeus should never reach the sea. Thus the river rises in Prionia at an altitude of 1,060 m, only to halt just before the sea, near Skala of Litochoro. Finding shelter in the dense vegetation, and attesting to the purity of the water, are hedgehogs, weasels, foxes, ferrets, salamanders, yellow-bellied toads, and water snakes. The charm of its myth, the rich vegetation along its banks, the cascades and ponds with crystal-clear water (fig. 6), the ruins of the water mills at the entry of its ravine, and the monastery of Agios Dionysios in the thriving environment compose a site of great natural beauty and cultural heritage.

Mount Olympus is an oddity in terms of its geomorphology and wide range of microclimates. Evergreen broadleaf species therefore grow above their regular altitude limit, whereas the Bosnian pine, a cryophile species, grows here as low as 400 m, an extremely rare phenomenon. Several forest species coexist and compose unique scenes, such as those near the monastery of Agios Dionysios, where pines, firs, beeches, yews, hornbeams, elders, and common hazels form thick stands.

At lower altitudes, the plane tree predominates, while the willow appears sparsely or in small stands in rocky sites by the riverbank. Growing on the rocks are chasmophytes and ferns, such as the rustyback, the wall rue, the nettle-leaved bellflower (a Balkan endemic), and the clove-scented bellflower. Typical species of the ravine also include the mullein-leaved insula, the Julian savory, and the insectivore hairy-flowered butterwort. The thick vegetation provides shelter and food to hedgehogs, weasels, foxes and martens, fire salamanders and yellow-bellied toads, European grass snakes and leopard snakes, dragonflies, butterflies, and more. Many birds of Olympus feed and nest here, while the steep slopes of the gorge are among the most important habitats of the mountain for rare raptors, such as the short-toed snake eagle and the common kestrel.

Fig. 6. The Enipeas waterfall.

CLIMATE

Olympus is well-known for its microclimates. The great variations in climate from one place to another are due to the rocks, the great variety in the physical relief, the fragmentation and diverse orientation of the slopes and their relation to the sea, and the great and sudden difference in altitude from the foothills to the peaks.

In the foothills of Mount Olympus, the climate is Mediterranean, with mild, wet winters and hot, dry summers. The northeastern coastal regions receive more rain than the southwestern inland areas, encouraging lusher vegetation. The greater the altitude, the more these phenomena are exacerbated. Winters suddenly become harsher, rainfall and snowfall heavier, summers cooler and drier. For approximately every 200-m increase in altitude, the temperature is estimated to fall by one degree centigrade.

In Mount Olympus's alpine zone, it is generally windy on a daily basis. Wind speeds can reach up to 120 km per hour. In some places, blizzards amass huge snowdrifts, up to 10 m deep. In other places, including abysses and deep ravines, snow never melts and remains a permanent feature.

The harsh climate is like that of Northern Europe. Snow covers the mountain for almost nine months of the year, from September to May. Winters are severe and protracted. Summer is short, and downpours—often accompanied by hail and strong winds—are common, as is snow, even in the summer months.

VEGETATION FROM THE FOOTHILLS TO THE HIGHEST PEAKS

From the Mediterranean zone in the foothills to the eerie, alpine landscape of the peaks, Mount Olympus constantly reveals different aspects. Visible and invisible changes are evident: variations in bedrock composition, soil attributes, and geomorphology, along with changes in the altitude, climate, and exposure of the various slopes, all mark differences in the vegetation, establishing a multitude of animal habitats and comprising different facets from one altitudinal zone to the next and from one side of the mountain to the other.

THE MEDITERRANEAN ZONE (300–500 M)

The Mediterranean vegetation type covers the eastern slopes of Mount Olympus up to 500 m. Evergreen broadleaf species, such as holm oak, kermes oak, strawberry tree, Greek strawberry tree, green olive tree, juniper, and tree heather coexist with deciduous ones, such as ash, maple, Judas tree, terebinth, smokebush, and nettle tree. Evergreen broadleaves expand beyond 500 m and cover a large area of the eastern slope up to 1,000 m. On the more humid northeastern and northern slopes, a mixed forest of deciduous and evergreen oaks prevails, dominated by downy and Hungarian oaks with a significant presence of tall holm oaks. On the western, southwestern, and southern slopes, where forests came under pressure from overgrazing and where the climate is continental, kermes oak dominates the landscape up to an altitude of 1,200 m. At the top boundaries of the Mediterranean vegetation

zone, black pine and Bulgarian fir appear, with the latter reaching as low as 300 m.

THE BLACK PINE ZONE (500–1,400 M)

On Mount Olympus, two species of pines predominate: the black and the Bosnian pine. Pine forests occupy 45 percent of the total area of the mountain. By contrast, oak and beech, which are predominant on most other Greek mountains at similar altitudes, are by no means as widespread on Olympus. Beech woods represent roughly 5 percent of the overall vegetation, while oak covers just 4 percent.

On the eastern slope, black pines gradually replace evergreen broadleaves and predominate up to 1,600–1,700 m, together with stands of Bulgarian fir. In valleys with high humidity, beech appears in thick stands. The presence of oak is restricted to individual trees among the conifers, while few stands are seen locally.

On the northern slope, black pines replace oaks and predominate from 700–800 m up to the forest limits, at 1,800 m. By the torrents Xerolakki and Papas, black pines occasionally form dense stands with fir, which descends down to 600 m, at the boundaries of the oak forest. The upper parts of the Xerolakki basin host small beech stands, mixed with fir.

Similarly, on the western and southern slopes, the kermes oak zone is also replaced by black pine, which prevails from 1,200 m to 1,500–1,600 m, occasionally even up to 1,800 m. Black pine stands here are less robust than those on the eastern slope. From 1,100 m and upward, Bosnian pine gradually takes over to become the dominant species at 1,400 m and above.

✳ Black pine (*Pinus nigra*): Native to Europe and widespread throughout Greece. According to European Union classification, its forests are considered a priority habitat, i.e., of particular importance, because of their distribution and the rich biodiversity they support.

THE BOSNIAN PINE ZONE (1,400– 2,500 M)

At 1,400 m, the landscape of the mountain changes. Black pine and deciduous broadleaf forests are gradually replaced by Bosnian pine (fig. 7).

On the eastern slope of Mount Olympus, Bosnian pines appear sporadically at an altitude of 1,000–1,100 m. They progressively succeed black pine forests and dominate to form entire forests at altitudes between 1,400 and 2,000 m. Bosnian pines grow up to 2,600 m as bushes, to withstand extreme winds and cold. On the northern slope, Bosnian pines dominate from 1,700 m upward.

On the western and southern slopes, by contrast, the vegetation at corresponding altitudes is completely different. From 1,600 m and culminating at the alpine meadows, the mountain is covered by shrubs and herbaceous vegetation, with European box being the most abundant species.

Fig. 7. *Pinus heldreichii.*

* Bosnian pine (*Pinus heldreichii*, syn. *P. leucodermis*): A hardy conifer, very resistant to low temperatures and endemic to the Balkan peninsula and Southern Italy. It creates single-species forests only on Mount Olympus and a few other Greek mountains with limestone substrates.
* Common or European box (*Buxus sempervirens*): A small but particularly hardy shrub that grows up to an altitude of 2,100 m. It is one of most characteristic species of Mount Olympus.

ALPINE VEGETATION (2,500 M AND ABOVE)

At altitudes of 2,500 m and above, the vegetation consists of creeping scrub, alpine meadows, and saxicolous plants, rooted in screes and crevices in the rocks. Dwarf Bosnian pines and junipers form a narrow belt, separating the pine forests and the alpine meadows that host herbaceous vegetation. Alpine screes, which are abundant at the extremes of Mount Olympus, and rock crevices host endemic and rare species that managed to adapt to the harsh environmental conditions of the high altitudes.

PLANTS

The flora of Mount Olympus number more than 1,700 species to date. Orchids (*Orchis papilonacea*, fig. 8), anemones, crocus, and endemic species such as *Aubrieta thessala* and *Centaurea litochorea*, as well as an abundance of species typical of the Mediterranean zone, such as the pink rock-rose and thyme, are representative of the huge wealth of plant life in the foothills of the mountain.

* Helen's bee orchid (*Ophrys helenae*): There are over fifty species of orchid on Mount Olympus. Endemic to Greece, Helen's bee orchid was named after the mother of the botanist who first described it. It is easily distinguishable due to its cherry-red, velvety lip.
* "Thessalian" aubrieta (*Aubrieta thessala*): A species also endemic to Mount Olympus, it grows in limestone substrates and is found at a wide variety of altitudes, from 300 m in ravines up to 2,300 m (fig. 9).
* Knapweed of Litochoro (*Centaurea litochorea*): One of the endemic knapweeds of Olympus and extremely rare, it has been observed in just a few places on the eastern and southern slopes of the mountain. It owes its name to the small town of Litochoro, in the vicinity of which it was first recorded in 1973.
* Autumn crocus (*Crocus cancellatus*): Greece hosts one of the highest counts of crocus species. The species *cancellatus* is one of the most common and among the first to bloom in the autumn (fig. 10).
* Thyme (*Thymbra capitata*): More than forty species of thyme grow in Greece, some of them on Mount Olympus.

The black pine forests host shrubs including the broadleaf spindle-tree, European box, hairy cotoneaster, smokebush, terebinth, wild rose, scorpion senna, hairy broom, Austrian broom, the suffruticose Balkan endemic "malouda" (*Staehelina uniflosculosa*), grasses such as the wood melick and bluegrass, ferns such as the hard

shield fern and hart's tongue, and wild flowers such as the peach-leaved bellflower, the bastard palm, the hedge woundwort, and the impressive scarlet lily. Among the endemic species, one can find Heldreich's onion, Kalopissi's orchid, the helleborine of Olympus, Sakellariadis's broom, Heldreich's janka, the few-flowered campion, and the pseudo-greek violet.

* Scarlet lily (*Lilium chalcedonium*): Endemic to the mountains of the Balkans, this lily, with its impressive red flowers, is one of the most beautiful plants on Mount Olympus (fig. 11).

* Heldreich's janka (*Jankaea heldreichii*): Endemic to the mountain and one of its most interesting plants, it is a relic of earlier geological eras, one of five members of the Gesneriaceae family that grow in temperate climates. On Mount Olympus, *Jankaea heldreichii* has taken refuge in the shady ravines, surviving the great climatic changes that led to the extinction of all other related species. It was recorded for the first time in 1851 by the German botanist and naturalist Theodor Heinrich Hermann von Heldreich (1822–1902), and described by the Swiss botanist Pierre Edmond Boissier (1810–1885), who named it janka in honour of Victor von Janka (1837–1890), curator of the Botanical Department of the Budapest National Museum and well-known for his work on the flora of the Balkans (fig. 12).

* Helleborine of Olympus (*Epipactis olympica*): Endemic to Mount Olympus, it grows in beech forests at altitudes from 800 to 1,100 m.

* The pseudo-Greek violet (*Viola pseudograeca*): First described as a separate species in 1985 and endemic to Mount Olympus, it grows on rocky slopes and in forest clearings between 900 and 2,800 m (fig. 13).

In the Bosnian pine zone, there are few woody species, including dwarf juniper, common box, and wild rose. Many endemic species also grow there, including *Asperula muscosa*, *Hieracium graecum* subsp. *szilyanum*, and *Viola delphinantha*.

* Dwarf juniper (*Juniperus communis* subsp. *nana*): Well adapted to conditions at high altitudes, it lends a hue of dark green to the bright yellow slopes of the mountain in the summer months.

* Moss-like woodruff (*Asperula muscosa*): A steno-endemic species of Mount Olympus found in dry, rocky places, in black pine and Bosnian pine forests, and more rarely in beech woods.

* Greek hawkweed (*Hieracium graecum* subsp. *szilyanum*): Endemic to Olympus, it grows on limestone rock at high altitudes, between 2,100 and 2,500 m. The subspecies' name was given in honor of a Hungarian state official.

* Long-spur violet (*Viola delphinantha*): With its purple-violet flowers that grow on numerous erect stems, it is one of the few violets to have a woody rootstock. Its spread is confined to a few mountains in Greece and Southern Bulgaria. On Mount Olympus, it usually occurs at altitudes between 1,500 and 2,500 m.

The range of plant life in the alpine zone of Mount Olympus is vast. More than a hundred species have been recorded at altitudes of over 2,800 m, very few of which are common. Species endemic to the Balkans and others that grow on Mount Olympus and nowhere else in the world, those on the IUCN Red List of Threatened Species (of the International Union for Conservation of Nature and Natural Resources), and those that are not widespread in the southeastern Mediterranean all contribute to making Mount Olympus famous for its flora.

* Violet of Olympus (*Viola striis-notata*): Violets, popularly known in Greek as *menexes* (from the Turkish *menekşe*) or *io* (Gr. ἴον), number more than five hundred species. The violet of Olympus is endemic to the area, as the name suggests, and is found at altitudes of over 2,400 m. It takes a creeping form, growing just a few centimeters above the earth, and from July to September its violet-blue flowers can be seen peeking out from the rocks.

* Theophrastus's mouse-ear chickweed (*Cerastium theophrasti*): A perennial plant endemic to Mount Olympus and common at altitudes over 2,600 m (fig. 14). It was described in 1977 by Professors Arne Strid and Hermann Merxmüller and named after the ancient philosopher Theophrastus, who has been called the "father of botany."

* Yarrow of Olympus (*Achillea ambrosiaca*): Endemic to Mount Olympus and abundant in the alpine scree from 2,200 to 2,800 m.

11.   12.   13.   14.

FUNGI

A total of 326 species of fungi have been identified on Mount Olympus, 67 of which are rare.

* Pepperpot earthstar (*Myriostomacoliforme*): Rare in Europe and Greece, it has been recorded near Litochoro under holm oaks.
* Apricot jelly fungus (*Guepinia hellveloides*): Equally rare in Greece, it has been identified in the coniferous forests of the National Park (fig. 15).
* Russula-like waxy cap (*Hygrophorus russula*): Greece marks the southernmost boundary of its spread in Europe. Although russula-like waxy cap is thought to have become extinct in Northern Europe, it is found in abundance in Olympus National Park, in a symbiotic relationship with the holm oak (fig. 16).
* Train wrecker mushroom (*Neolentinus lepideus*): Considered rare on Mount Olympus, it has been recorded only once. Equally rare species, not just on Olympus but also in Greece as a whole, include the orange mat coprinus (*Coprinellus radians*), which grows in the leaf litter of beech forests, and resinous polypore (*Ischnoderma resinosum*), which prefers rotting tree trunks and beech tree stumps. *Zeus olympius* was described as a new genus and species in 1987 (fig. 17). It was spotted on the path from Prionia to Spilios Agapitos Refuge, on low branches of Bosnian pines. In 2013 it was found once more on Mount Olympus and on the Bulgarian side of Mount Rodopi. A weak parasite, it is included on the global Red List of Threatened Species as critically endangered.
* *Nectria ganymede*: Another new species discovered on the carpophores of *Zeus olympius*, this is an endangered species since a fire can destroy the single location where it has been found.

MAMMALS

The National Park and the broader area host around thirty-five mammal species, most of which are residents. Some of the mammals that used to dwell on the mountain massif in earlier times, such as the lynx and red deer, are now extinct. Wildlife is represented today by the Balkan chamois, roe deer, wild boar, fox, wild cat, beech marten, badger, hare, squirrel, and weasel, and small mammals such as bats and mice (wood mouse, yellow-necked mouse). In the area of Petra, Kato Olympus, and the Muses Plateau, the brown bear has recently been recorded. The presence of wolves is linked to livestock.

* Chamois: One of the most illustrious residents of Mount Olympus, the Balkan chamois is now among the rarest mammals in Greece (fig. 18). It belongs to the Alpine genus and the Balkan subspecies (*Rupicapra rupicapra balcanica*). The breed possibly derives from a gazelle species that lived in Central and Eastern Asia three million years ago. It has a robust aspect with upright, backward-curling horns and a brown, mask-like stripe on its face. Sloping hillsides, cliffs, and alpine meadows make up the chamois's ideal habitats. In late summer and in autumn, it roams at altitudes of 1,880 m and above, while in winter it descends lower to steep wooded slopes. The Muses Plateau and the peaks of Stefani, Skolio, and Toumpa are typical summer habitats. In the past, it was fairly widespread on the Greek mountains, but more recently the population has decreased in contrast to Europe. There are an estimated 500–600 individuals, spread over the mountain of Central Rodopi, Mount Pindos, Central Greece, Mount Olympus, and the mountain ranges of Tzena-Pinovo and Nemertsika. At present, 150 chamois live in the area of Mount Olympus.

15.

16.

17.

18.

BIRDS

Mount Olympus has been designated as an Important Bird and Biodiversity Area (IBA). More than 148 bird species have been recorded so far, including rare and common species, some with restricted habitats and others that live in areas and altitudes ranging from the foothills to the alpine meadows. Some species nest in steep places, others on rocks and wooded slopes, in deep gorges, and near streams, and others next to the human settlements perched onto the mountain's slopes.

A wide variety of birds are found in the lower zone of Mount Olympus, which is covered with rich areas of maquis shrubs and kermes oak, meadows, creeks, and farms. Birds encountered here include European goldfinches (fig. 19), common nightingales, cirl buntings, European greenfinches, black-eared wheatears (fig. 20), subalpine and Sardinian warblers, common whitethroats, rock partridges (fig. 21), Eastern olivaceous warblers, European turtle-doves, European bee-eaters (fig. 22), hoopoes, red-backed shrikes, European nightjars, and woodchat shrikes. Black storks (fig. 23)

Birds of prey such as the northern goshawk, golden eagle (fig. 24), and peregrine falcon, as well as the booted eagle, species such as the red crossbill, Eurasian bullfinch, willow tit, Tengmalm's owl, cuckoo, European serin, Eurasian treecreeper, whinchat, mistle thrush, goldcrest, woodlark, common swift, and woodpecker species (gray headed, black, and white backed) feed and breed in the Bosnian pine forests.

In the extreme conditions of high altitudes, in the alpine meadows and on mountain peaks, only a few species manage to survive. Birds such as the golden eagle, wall creeper, alpine chough, horned lark (fig. 25), wheatear, European stonechat, African stonechat, and common rock thrush (fig. 26) are among them.

In recent years, the bearded vulture, cinereous vulture, Egyptian vulture, and red-billed chough have become extinct, and probably the hazel grouse as well. The populations of golden eagles, rock pigeons, and rock partridges also appear to be dramatically reduced.

can be seen looking for food near the water while peregrine falcons occasionally hunt their prey and alpine accentors seek winter refuge.

Woodpeckers, tree creepers, tits, warblers, goldcrests, icterine warblers, finches, robins, Eurasian nuthatches, rock partridges, eagle owls, European honey buzzards, common buzzards, red-footed falcons, Eurasian hobbies, and short-toed eagles feed and breed in the forests of black pine, beech, and fir as well as in the forest clearings. The rare semicollared flycatcher dwells in the dense deciduous forests, while the spectacular Eurasian golden oriole prefers sites near the water. Mount Olympus provides habitat for eight of the ten woodpecker species in Greece.

AMPHIBIANS AND REPTILES

Amphibians living in creeks and seasonal ponds, such as the fire salamander (fig. 27), common newt, Macedonian newt, yellow-bellied toad, and Balkan stream frog as well as reptiles, the European green lizard (fig. 28), Greek slow worm, four-lined snake, Hermann's tortoise (fig. 29), European cat snake (fig. 30), and nose-horned viper indicate the importance of Mount Olympus.

The majority of the nine amphibian and twenty-one reptile species recorded are protected at the European level, including the European pond turtle, four-lined snake, and Hermann's tortoise. Common species observed at low altitudes are the Balkan frog, European glass lizard, Kotschy's gecko, Dahl's whip snake, Caspian whip snake, and Montpellier snake, as well as endemic or rare species such as the marginated tortoise, Erhard's wall lizard, and the leopard snake. The European pond turtle has been recorded only in the archaeological site of Dion.

27.

28.

29.

30.

The ecosystems of intermediate altitudes host reptiles and amphibians, such as the Greek stream frog in deciduous and mixed forests, the agile frog in deciduous forests, the common toad in conifers, the slow worm in meadows and deciduous forests, the European copper skink in meadows and forest openings, the dice snake and the European cat snake, the smooth and the Macedonian newt, which live in the seasonal ponds, the Hermann's tortoise, and the four-lined snake.

There are few species of amphibians and reptiles in the Bosnian pine zone. These include the yellow-bellied and green toad, the European green lizard, the smooth snake, and the grass snake.

Around two hundred species of invertebrates have been recorded on Olympus to date. They share their habitat with butterflies, dragonflies, grasshoppers, and beetles and other coleoptera. Some species are important at the European level, including the grasshopper *Poecilimon thessalicus*, endemic to Greece; the butterfly *Lycaena ottomanus*, which loves humid valleys among the evergreen forests and is endemic to the Balkan peninsula; the exceptionally rare beetle *Buprestis splendens*, which lives in the trunks of old pines; the stag beetle; and *Cerambyx cerdo*, or great Capricorn beetle, whose ecosystem of choice is found among the black pine.

31.

32.

33.

In clearings and meadows, easily spotted butterflies are named for figures from Greek mythology: Io (*Inachis io*), after the priestess of Hera from Argos, with whom Zeus fell in love (fig. 31); Ifikleidis, after the nephew of Heracles; Podaleirius, after the son of Asclepius (*Iphiclides podalirius*, fig. 32); Lycaon, after the king of Arcadia (*Hyponephele lycaon*), who tried to deceive Zeus and was punished by being transformed into a wolf (fig. 33); but also Machaon (*Papilio machaon*), after Asclepius's son.

MAPPING THE MOUNTAIN: THE HEIGHT OF OLYMPUS

2nd century BC:
The mathematician and geographer Xenagoras made the first attempt at determining the height of Mount Olympus, from the Temple of Pythius Apollo on the western slopes of the mountain. Attested by Plutarch, it is the first measurement placing the height of the mountain at 6,096 feet (2,609 m according to modern calculations). Even though Mytikas is not visible from Pythio, and apparently it was a lower peak that Xenagoras measured—perhaps Kakavrakas (2,618 m) or Flampouro (2,473 m)—the geographic value of the measurement is great. Nearly twenty centuries had to pass before accurate measurements were achieved.

1831:
A British army officer, while mapping the Thermaikos Gulf, also surveyed the peaks of Mount Olympus. He reported almost entirely accurate coordinates, measuring the highest peak at 2,973 m.

1862:
The German geographer Heinrich Barth was the first to officially record the Mytikas peak as the highest on Mount Olympus.

1921:
The Swiss engineer-surveyor Marcel Kurz, the first man to set foot on Stefani peak, carried out the first comprehensive mapping of Olympus, commissioned by the Greek government. Contemporary press published the height of Mytikas as 2,917 m.

1997:
Professors K. Katsambalos, A. Bandelas, and P. Savvaïdes, from the Polytechnic School of the Aristotle University of Thessaloniki, published the results of measuring with GPS in *Olympus*, the journal of the Greek Guiding Association [SEO]. Mytikas was recorded at 2,918.8 m.

CATALOGUE

THE SANCTUARY OF ZEUS OLYMPIOS

THE SANCTUARY OF ZEUS HYPSISTOS

THE SANCTUARY OF DEMETER

THE SANCTUARY OF ISIS

THE VILLA OF DIONYSUS

THE GREAT BATHS

FINDS FROM THE CITY AND
THE NECROPOLIS

Detail of cat. no. 30.

1

LETTER OF KING ANTIGONOS GONATAS TO AGASIKLES

277–239 BC
Marble
H. 34 cm; W. 22.5 cm; D. 6.5 cm
From Dion. Sanctuary of Zeus Olympios. Built in the foundation of a later Stoa building.
Archaeological Museum of Dion, ΜΔ 7422

The sixteen-line inscription on this fragment of an inscribed stele contains the text of a letter from Antigonos Gonatas, King of Macedonia, to Agasikles, the royal local supervisor in Dion, demanding that it be displayed in the sanctuary there. The subject of the letter is the settlement of a dispute between one Noumenios and his children over occupancy and ownership of a large area of ground. The king rules that no transaction can be carried out by Noumenios's children without their father's consent.

The inscription is also of topographical interest, as there is a reference in the text to Noumenios having settled his children "between Asikos and the Pyrrolian Lake." Both the plain of Pieria, near the modern salt lake of Kitros, and the area of Chalcidice, near the modern lake of Koroneia, have been suggested as the possible locations of this estate. As the case may be, the publication of the letter in the sanctuary of Zeus Olympios shows the important position occupied by Dion in the state religion of Macedonia.

This flat-topped stele is made of coarse-grained marble, off-white with veining from oxidation. It was reused as construction material in the foundations of a portico built when the sanctuary of Zeus Olympios was reconstructed, after it had been destroyed in 219 BC by an Aetolian army.

Selected bibliography
Pandermalis 1995: 169; Hatzopoulos 2000: 65–70;
Pandermalis 2000: 53.

2

LETTER OF KING PHILIP V TO THE MAGISTRATES OF DION CONCERNING THE ASYLIA OF CYZICUS

ca. 180 BC

Marble

H. 29 cm; W. 28 cm; D. 8.5 cm

From Dion. Sanctuary of Zeus Olympios. Found in a pit at the southwest corner of the sanctuary.

Archaeological Museum of Dion, MΔ 7424

The inscription on this fragment of a stele contains the text of a letter from King Philip V to the local magistrate Eurylochos, the *peliganes* (the body of distinguished citizens that corresponded to the local council), and all the other citizens of Dion. According to the inscription's content, the bearers of the letter were envoys from Cyzicus who were seeking recognition of their city's sacrosanct status. The term *asylia* refers to the Hellenistic practice of declaring religious places as precincts of asylum, territorially inviolable by civil authority. The letter attests the development of diplomatic relations between Philip V and this city in Asia Minor in the early second century BC, while the lengthy reference to the recipients reveals the administrative organization and social structure of the city of Dion. Another fragmentary inscription found in Dion bears witness to the development of a specific administrative process that culminated in the passage of a corresponding resolution by the local authorities.

The stele is made of gray marble with veining. It is missing its bottom part, and the acroteria on the gabled pediment are broken.

Selected bibliography

Pandermalis 1997b: 234ff.; Pandermalis 2000: 55; Pandermalis 2009: 261ff. fig. 2.

3

4

FRAGMENTARY INSCRIPTION RECORDING AN ALLIANCE BETWEEN KING PHILIP V AND THE CITIZENS OF LYSIMACHEIA

202–197 BC
Marble
H. 43 cm; W. 30.5 cm; D. 14.5 cm
From Dion. Sanctuary of Zeus Olympios. Found built in
the south wall of the church of Agia Paraskevi.
Archaeological Museum of Dion, MΔ 63α, 63β

Inscribed on this stele is part of a treaty of alliance between King Philip V of Macedonia and the citizens of Lysimacheia in Thrace. The stele is preserved in fragmentary condition, with the two fragments joined. On one fragment, reference is made to a condition of the treaty that no alliances were to be made with third parties hostile to the signatories. Preserved on the other fragment is a lengthy oath, sworn by the Lysimachian envoys, and followed by the oath sworn by Philip V. The stele is made of very coarse-grained blue-gray marble.

Founded in 309 BC by Lysimachus, one of Alexander the Great's generals, the Thracian city of Lysimacheia experienced a number of overlords, including Macedonian kings. The inscription from Dion substantiates information provided by the historian Polybius about the stationing of a Macedonian garrison in the city, intended to protect it from the Thracian tribes that finally destroyed Lysimacheia in the war between Philip V and the Romans (197 BC).

Selected bibliography
Oikonomos 1915: 2–7; Pandermalis 1981: 285ff.;
Pandermalis 2000: 56.

LETTER OF KING PHILIP V CONCERNING A BOUNDARY SETTLEMENT

206–205 BC
Marble
H. 57 cm; W. 61 cm; D. 14.5 cm
From Dion. Sanctuary of Zeus Olympios.
Found in the temenos.
Archaeological Museum of Dion, MΔ 391 (MΔ 6669)

This fragment of a stele—originally the right-hand edge—preserves part of a letter from King Philip V to the inhabitants of Pherrai and Demetrias. In the letter, the Macedonian king defines the boundary line between the two Thessalian cities with reference to specific locations. The text contains an order that the inscription should be publicly displayed in the sanctuary of Zeus Olympios and the exact date: the sixteenth year of the reign of Philip V, on the twelfth day of the intercalary month (*embolimos*), which corresponds to early September 206 BC.

The stele is made of very coarse-grained blue-gray marble. The top, bottom, and left-hand side of the stele are missing.

The Macedonian kings had extended their suzerainty to this area from as early as the late fourth century BC, and it was common practice for them to rule on issues related to Thessalian cities. Demetrias in particular, named after its founder Demetrius I, known as Poliorcetes, was the base of the Macedonian kings and their starting point for invasions of Thessaly and Southern Greece. Displaying the letter in the sanctuary of Zeus Olympios not only served the archival requirements of the Macedonian state, it also helped to inform the multitudinous visitors to the sanctuary, both Macedonians and Thessalians.

Selected bibliography
Pandermalis 1977: 340ff.; Pandermalis 2000: 57.

5

TREATY BETWEEN KING PERSEUS AND THE BOEOTIANS

172 BC
Marble
H. 34.5 cm; W. 77 cm; D. 18 cm
From Dion. Sanctuary of Zeus Olympios. Found east of the altar to Zeus Olympios.
Archaeological Museum of Dion, ΜΔ 7439

This fragment is the upper part of an inscribed stele. On the upright below the pediment, a two-line inscription has been finely carved:

ΣΥΜΜΑΧΙΑ ΒΑΣΙΛΕΩΣ / ΠΕΡΣΕΩΣ ΚΑΙ ΒΟΙΩΤΩΝ
Alliance between King Perseus and the Boeotians

The pediment is adorned with antefixes with relief decoration, a band, and molding. The stele is made of white marble with a reddish surface, and it has a clamp on the bottom for fixing this part to the main body of the stele. The bottom left part is missing.

The inscription is the heading of the treaty of alliance that the Macedonian king Perseus (179–168 BC) entered into in 172 BC with the Boeotian Confederacy, with the aim of acquiring support in Southern Greece and strengthening his power against the Romans. We know about this alliance from a reference to it in the *Ab Urbe Condita* by the Roman historian Livy (42.12.6), who recorded that the text of the treaty had been engraved on three stone steles. One was set up in Thebes, the seat of the Boeotian Confederacy; another in Delphi, a Panhellenic sanctuary; and the third in a "famous" place, the name of which was not preserved in the ancient text. The discovery of the Dion inscription completed the historical evidence, while at the same time underlining the exceptional importance of the venerated sanctuary of Zeus Olympios to the functioning of the Macedonian state.

Selected bibliography
Pandermalis 1997b: 233ff.; Pandermalis 2000: 54; Pandermalis 2009: 262f.

6

CULT STATUE OF ZEUS HYPSISTOS

2nd century AD

Marble

H. 85.5 cm; W. 46 cm; D. 63.5 cm

From Dion. Sanctuary of Zeus Hypsistos. Found in the naos of the temple.

Archaeological Museum of Dion, MΔ 7815

The cult statue of Zeus Hypsistos was found fallen next to its masonry base. This exceptionally fine sculpture is made from a single piece of coarse-grained white marble with large crystals. The head, left forearm, and fingers on the right hand are missing. The god is depicted seated on a throne with a gabled back. His right hand rests on his thigh and holds a thunderbolt, half of which remains. The raised left arm held a scepter, of which only fragments are preserved. He wears a himation, which is folded over the left shoulder and covers the lower part of his body, and sandals with a triple strap.

This iconographic type of enthroned Zeus extends back to the chryselephantine statue by Phidias at Olympia, known only from the description given by Pausanias in his *Description of Greece* (5.11) and from depictions on ancient coins. While this statue— created in the Imperial period following Hellenistic models—is not directly comparable to the original, it forms part of a series of works that adopt the main characteristics of the type with minor differences. The appearance of this type of statue, together with its Latin votive inscription referring to Jupiter Optimus Maximus, show that in this particular temple Zeus was worshiped by Greeks and Romans alike and was identified with the central figure in the Capitoline triad of divinities.

Selected bibliography

Pandermalis 2003: 419; Pandermalis 2009: 269 fig. 15.

7

8

STATUE OF AN EAGLE

2nd century AD
Marble
H. 63.5 cm; W. 34.5 cm; D. 15 cm
From Dion. Sanctuary of Zeus Hypsistos. Found in the naos.
Archaeological Museum of Dion, MΔ 7816

Carved in the round, this eagle was found in the naos (the innermost chamber) of the temple of Zeus Hypsistos, near the cult statue of the god. The deity's sacred bird is depicted in a frontal pose, perched on a curved base, and holds a thunderbolt in its hooked claws. Its finely sculpted head is turned, gazing at the statue of his lord, Zeus. The plumage on the inside of the bird's open wings and on its body is depicted in decorative fashion. The sculpture, made of grayish marble, is intact, although there is some slight damage to the right wing and the head has been reattached.

Bearer of the thunderbolt, message carrier (ἄγγελος), and symbol of the epiphany of the god, the eagle was the most common votive offering in the temples of Zeus Hypsistos. As an iconographic subject, it adorned altars and votive stelae along with other characteristic symbols of the cult of Zeus, such as the bull and the oak wreath. The eagle perched on a thunderbolt, a symbolic reference to the tutelary deity of the royal house of the Temenids, is also found in the iconography of coins of the Macedonian state.

Selected bibliography
Pandermalis 2003: 418; Pandermalis 2009: 269 fig. 14;
Pingiatoglou 2011: 600 no. 374.

STATUE OF AN EAGLE WITH INSCRIPTION

Imperial period
Marble
H. 46 cm; W. 28 cm; D. 24 cm
From Dion. Sanctuary of Zeus Hypsistos. Found in the naos.
Archaeological Museum of Dion, MΔ 8715α, 8715β

A four-sided base supports this small statue of an eagle, which stands on the head of an ox. The details on the sculpture are depicted imprecisely, and the back view is rendered in a cursory fashion. The eagle, missing its head and part of the throat, is made of white marble. The grayish marble base is intact but shows some minor damage. On the front of the base, a five-line votive inscription is engraved in fine lettering:

ΑΓΑΘΗ ΤΥΧΗ / ΔΙΙ ΥΨΙΣΤΩ ΑΡΟΥΡΑ / ΠΛΟΥΤΙΑΔΟΥ
ΠΑΙΔΙΣΚΗ / ΑΓΟΡΑΝΟΜΗΣΑΣΑ ΝΩΝΑΙΣ / ΚΑΠΡΑΤΕΙΝΑΙΣ
ΑΝΕΘΗΚΕΝ / ΚΑΙ ΕΠΙΜΕΛΕΙΑΣ ΦΡΟΥΚΤΟΥ
To the Good Fortune. Aroura, slave of Ploutiades, participant in the Nonae Capratinae, dedicated [this] to Zeus Hypsistos through the good offices of Phrouktos.

The devotee Aroura, evidently a young slave girl (παιδίσκη), dedicated a thank offering to the sanctuary of Zeus Hypsistos after the festivities (Nonae Capratinae) during which she was responsible for the provisions (αγορανόμος). The setting up of the offering was facilitated by the good offices of one Phrouktos, as is noted in smaller letters slightly farther down, in a later addition. The inscription attests the celebration of the Nonae Capratinae, a Roman festival, in Dion. Held on July 5 or 7 by the slave women of Rome in honor of Juno Caprotina, this festival saw the reversal of social roles, jokes made at men's expense, and the use of symbols associated with fertility.

The dedication of a statue to the sanctuary of Zeus Hypsistos for a festival in honor of Hera (Lat. Juno) was the first indication that the two divinities shared a cult. The later discovery of a cult statue of Hera in the city walls confirmed this hypothesis.

Selected bibliography
On the Roman festival, see Bremmer 1987; on Hera-Juno, see Pandermalis 2006: 570.

9

STATUE OF AN EAGLE STANDING ON AN IONIC COLUMN WITH DEDICATORY INSCRIPTION TO ZEUS HYPSISTOS

Imperial period

Marble

H. 80 cm; W. 30 cm; D. 30 cm

From Dion. Sanctuary of Zeus Hypsistos.

Archaeological Museum of Dion, ΜΔ 8906α, 8906β, 8906γ

Standing atop this unfluted column with an Ionic capital is the statuette of an eagle with outspread wings, carved in the round. The column is green marble, and the capital and eagle are white marble. The head of the eagle is missing. On the body of the column, which tapers slightly toward the top, a three-line votive inscription has been carved:

ΔΙΙ ΥΨΙΣΤΩ / Λ ΤΡΕΒΙΟΣ / ΛΕΩΝ / ΕΥΞΑΜΕΝΟΣ

Ex-voto from L. Trebius Leon to Zeus Hypsistos

The offering made by Trebius Leon must have been placed on a stylobate, along with other similar votive offerings, at the eastern end of the Sacred Way that led to the temple of Zeus Hypsistos.

The column, whether as a stand-alone monument or as the base for an eagle, was a common form of offering in sanctuaries of Zeus Hypsistos. The eagle in this example seems to be landing on the capital, a depiction related to its role as the messenger that transmitted the will of the mightiest god to mortals. As ancient sources attest, from as far back as Homeric times, an eagle flying from the right at the moment of sacrifice or prayer was a sign that Zeus would react positively to a devotee's petition.

Selected bibliography

Pandermalis 2003: 417; Pandermalis 2009: 267 fig. 11; Tzanavari 2012: 589ff.

10

CATALOGUE OF NAMES

251–52 AD

Marble

H. 58 cm; W. 30 cm; D. 3 cm

From Dion. Sanctuary of Zeus Hypsistos. Found in the naos of the temple.

Archaeological Museum of Dion, ΜΔ 8907

Inscribed on this marble slab are the names of those who had been chosen by lot to take responsibility for organizing the monthly feasts (δοχαί) attended by the devotees of Zeus Hypsistos. The slab, made of off-white marble with gray veining and now missing a fragment at its lower left, was built into the front of the pedestal on which the deity's cult statue stood. In addition to the list of names, the inscription gives details of the penalties and fines inflicted on those who neglected their duties.

The existence of religious societies devoted to the cult of local divinities was a common phenomenon in the Imperial period. Their regulations made provision for organizing sacrifices and rites, accompanied by shared meals, as part of the sanctuaries' festivities or at regular intervals. Most interesting about the inscription is the reference to the months of the Macedonian calendar. The first to be mentioned is Xandikos, which took its name from the Xandika, the purification rituals practiced by the army. The ancient Macedonian calendar was lunisolar, consisting of twelve synodic lunar months, and required extra, intercalated months to stay synchronized with the seasons. The names of the months were: Xandikos, Artemisios, Daisios, Panemos, Loios, Gorpiaios, Hyperberetaios Dios (Zeus), Apellaios, Audunaios, Peritios, and Dystros. The Macedonian year began on the first of Dios (October 1), which coincided with the beginning of the celebrations in honor of Zeus Olympios.

The inscription gives an exact date of 251–52 AD: "[in] the imperial year ΓΠΣ" (283). After the Roman conquest of Macedonia, a calendar system was introduced that retained the names of the months, but calculated the years from the "year of Augustus" or the "imperial year" (σεβαστόν ἔτος). That calendar began on September 2 in 31 BC, the day of Octavian's victory at Actium.

Selected bibliography

Pandermalis 2003; Pandermalis 2009: 269; Nigdelis 2010: 333.

11

HEAD FROM A STATUE OF DEMETER

Late 4th century BC
Marble
H. 24 cm; D. 19 cm
From Dion. Sanctuary of Demeter, South Hellenistic temple.
Found in a layer of destruction at the stylobate level.
Archaeological Museum of Dion, MΔ 200

Only the head and neck of this female figure have survived. The hair is chipped and there are some incrustations on the stone. The oval, fleshy face has small eyes and heavy lids, a half-open mouth with a strongly marked dividing groove between the lips, and a narrow, triangular forehead. There is a deep crease around the neck and another around the base of the neck. The strands of thick hair are defined by irregular grooves. Parted in the middle, her hair is combed to either side around the ears, while behind the ears locks fall down to the shoulders. There are holes in the earlobes for attaching earrings, and small holes in the hair for fixing a diadem. A himation, a garment associated with the Demeter of Knidos–type of statue, covers the back of the head. The late fourth-century date is substantiated by the shape and modeling of the face, the rendering of the hair, and the details of the eyes and mouth. This dating is further supported by comparisons with figures on funerary steles from the end of the fourth century.

Selected bibliography

Pandermalis, 1989a: 15; Pandermalis 1997a: 18; Pandermalis 2000: 63; Zimmer 2002: 560 no. 422; Pingiatoglou 2010b: 202 fig. 4; Pingiatoglou 2015: 54. For similar rendering of the small eyes and heavy eyelids, and the small mouth with the marked division between the lips and the hair, see Clairmont 1993: 2.909, 3.425a; Despinis 1997: no. 25 figs. 46–49. For the type with the himation "over the head," cf. Kabus-Preisshofen 1989: 91, 304 no. 98, pls. 21, 3.4. On a statue of a standing Demeter with a himation thrown over her head, see Beschi 1988: nos. 57, 70, 71, 81, 83, 84, 98; and for a seated Demeter, nos. 138, 143, 148.

12

HEADLESS STATUE OF A WOMAN WEARING A PEPLOS (*PEPLOPHOROS*)

350–300 BC
Marble
H. 92 cm; W. 35; D. 23 cm
From Dion. Sanctuary of Demeter, North Hellenistic temple. Found in the pronaos.
Archaeological Museum of Dion, MΔ 198

This figure of a woman stands on an oval plinth that has been shaped to match the stance of the legs, with the weight on the right and the slightly bent left leg in front and to the side. The figure wears an Attic peplos with a long overfall, tied high under the breast. Heavy, vertical drapery folds conceal the right leg, while the whole length of the left shows through clearly. The head, neck, and arms—all missing—were made separately. The head, neck, and breastbone were attached by inserting a metal tenon into a large, ellipsoid cavity (max. diam. 15.8 cm; d. 13.6 cm) carved out of the top of the torso. The sternum survives from the base of the neck. The separate arms were attached with iron tenons (one of which survives, on the right arm) in rectangular sockets under the shoulders. The back is less skillfully worked. The front end of the left foot is damaged, and there are gray incrustations on the surface of the marble.

Found during the 1973 excavation season, the statue is dated to the second half of the fourth century BC on the basis of comparisons with votive reliefs. The dress and stance are related to a statuette from the sanctuary at Derveni in the Archaeological Museum of Thessaloniki, and it has been compared to the statue type of Artemis known from copies and Attic votive reliefs of the second half of the fourth century BC. It has been proposed that this statue type was modeled on a cult statue of Artemis from the period, perhaps the Artemis Brauronia by Praxiteles. However, the Dion statue lacks the band worn diagonally across the chest like a leather strap that would indisputably link it to an image of Artemis.

Selected bibliography

Pandermalis 2000: 71; Pingiatoglou 2015: 55. On the insertion of rods in joins in ancient Greek sculpture, see Claridge 1990: 143. On comparable votive reliefs, see Baumer 1997: G 19/3, K 18 pl. 47, K 23 pl. 49. On the comparable statue type of Artemis, including the Artemis Brauronia, see Despinis, Stefanidou-Tiveriou, and Voutiras 1997: 49 no. 32 figs. 69–74, Despinis 1997.

13

RING STONE DECORATED WITH INCISED LION AND TREE

Late 15th–early 14th century BC (Late Helladic II–early Late Helladic IIIa)
Carnelian
L. 2.3 cm; W. 1.8 cm
From Dion. Sanctuary of Demeter, Megalon B. South Late Archaic–Early Classical temple.
Archaeological Museum of Dion, MΔ 608

The seal on this stone depicts a stylized lion facing left in front of a tree. The animal is shown in a resting pose, sitting back on its hind legs. Its thick mane falls straight down, while its tail is slightly raised. The trunk of the tree directly behind the lion's back is divided symmetrically into three branches. A fourth branch rises up behind its tail.

The lion is a popular subject in Minoan and above all Mycenaean seal carving. It is depicted both on its own, often in emblematic isolation and in narrative scenes, and indeed sometimes in a highly dramatic fashion.

This Mycenaean, amygdaloidal stone seal is made of cornelian and was found during the 1981 excavation season at the temple of Demeter. It is dated by comparison to similar seals from the end of the Late Helladic II–early Late Helladic IIIa (late fifteenth–early fourteenth century BC).

Selected bibliography
Pingiatoglou 2015: 117. On types of lion, see Thomas 1981: 227ff. On Mycenaean stone seals in temples of the historic period, see Sakellarakis 1976: 305.

14–18

FIVE OIL LAMPS

Terracotta lamps with open bowls make up the sanctuary's largest group of lamps. They belong to Howland's type 21B and 24A, characterized by a curved profile and black glazing, with a separate and unglazed disc-shaped base. They have squat and square nozzles with curved tops and oval holes. The clay and the quality of the glaze suggest that they were Attic imports.

Selected bibliography
Pingiatoglou 2005: 19; Pingiatoglou 2015: 111. On the types, see Howland 1958: 46.

14. OIL LAMP

5th century BC
Terracotta: reddish yellow clay (5YR.7/6)
H. 1.2 cm; L. 10.7 cm; Diam. 7.2 cm
From Dion. Sanctuary of Demeter. Found west of the South Late Archaic–Classical temple.
Archaeological Museum of Dion, MΔ 491

This intact, black-glazed lamp has an open bowl and an unglazed base made separately. The glazing has mostly flaked off. The handle has been restored from three fragments. There are signs of burning on the short nozzle with rounded top.

Selected bibliography
Pandermalis 2000: 66; Pingiatoglou 2005: 27 K7 pl. 4.

15. OIL LAMP

5th century BC
Terracotta: reddish yellow clay (5YR.7/6)
H. 1.5 cm; Diam. 7.7 cm
From Dion. Sanctuary of Demeter. Found west of the South Late Archaic–Classical temple.
Archaeological Museum of Dion, MΔ 496

The handle is missing on this black-glazed lamp with an open bowl. The unglazed base was made separately. The lamp's condition is not exceptional as the glaze inside is badly flaked.

Selected bibliography
Pingiatoglou 2005: 28 K11 pl. 6.

16 · OIL LAMP

450–400 BC or later

Terracotta: reddish yellow clay (5YR.7/6)

H. 2.4 cm; L. 11.5 cm; Diam. 7.5 cm

From Dion. Sanctuary of Demeter. Found west of the South Late Archaic–Classical temple.

Archaeological Museum of Dion, MΔ 498

This intact, black-glazed lamp, with an open bowl and an unglazed base made separately, is in good condition. In some areas the glaze is flaked. The lamp has a large, horizontal strap handle and a small, triangular nozzle, which shows traces of burning. There are two stepped grooves around the filler hole

Selected bibliography

Pandermalis 2000: 66; Pingiatoglou 2005: 34 K28 pl.12, Iβ; Pingiatoglou 2015: 111 fig. 206 pl. Xα.

17 · OIL LAMP

5th century BC

Terracotta: reddish yellow clay (5YR.7/6)

H. 2 cm; Diam. 8 cm

From Dion. Sanctuary of Demeter. Found west of the South Late Archaic–Classical temple.

Archaeological Museum of Dion, MΔ 508α

The glaze has flaked off in places of this intact, black-glazed lamp with an open bowl. The unglazed base was made separately.

Selected bibliography

Pandermalis 2000: 66; Pingiatoglou 2005: 28 K12 pl. 6, Iα; Pingiatoglou 2015: 111 fig. 207 pl. Xβ.

18 · OIL LAMP

425–375 BC

Terracotta: reddish yellow clay (5YR.7/6)

H. 3 cm; Diam. 8.5 cm

From Dion. Sanctuary of Demeter. Found west of the South Late Archaic–Classical temple.

Archaeological Museum of Dion, MΔ 1089

This two-wicked lamp with brown-black glaze is intact and quite well preserved. There is a wide band and a deep groove around the filler hole. Long, square nozzles, flattened at the base and with oval ventilation holes, are placed diametrically opposite one another. The separate base is unglazed.

Selected bibliography

Pingiatoglou 2005: 35 K29 pl. 13, IIα–β; Pingiatoglou 2015: 111 fig. 208 pl. Xγ. On the form of this vessel, Howland's type 24A, see Scheibler 1976: RSL 3, 26.

19

OIL LAMP WITH HEAD OF AN AFRICAN

1st century AD
Copper alloy
H. 7. cm; L. 20 cm; W. 6 cm
From Dion. Sanctuary of Demeter. Found north of the north
Roman temple.
Archaeological Museum of Dion, MΔ 552

Found in 1975 in the most northerly temple of the sanctuary of Demeter, this lamp was made using two molds. The top mold was in the form of an African head, while the lower part of the lamp and the surface on which it stands were made using the bottom mold, as there is no separate base.

Part of the bottom of the lamp and part of the end of the nozzle have been added. The face is narrow with large, heavy-lidded eyes; large, stylized, strongly separated eyebrows; and a pug nose. The triangular, protruding forehead is etched with two small, parallel, semicircular lines that suggest a frown or scowl. The long nozzle, which protrudes like a tongue from the jutting upper jaw, has a curved end and a circular ventilation hole. At the top of the head, there is a second, larger hole with a tall lip that was used as a filler hole. The hair is arranged in four rows of short, oblong curls, each with slanting, parallel incisions. The hairstyle, albeit stylized, recalls the curly locks that were customary in the Hellenistic period in Cyrenaica and Egypt. Behind the filler hole, at the top of the head, there is an upright, ring-shaped handle with horn-like projections in front.

Cast lamps with a horizontal join between two molds, usually depicting a human or animal head or a face, likely originated in the Hellenistic lamps that were produced using a mold that had an elaborately decorated top or a decorated lid over the filler hole. A number of cast African-head lamps from the Hellenistic and especially the Imperial period have been found in both the eastern and western provinces of the Roman Empire. The exotic nature of the African form had long enchanted artists in antiquity, dating back to the archaic era. Its use to decorate lamps probably emerged from the tasks associated with black slaves. As regards the structure of the head and the face, the shape of the nozzle that projects out of the mouth, and the placing of the filler hole at the top of the head, the lamp from the sanctuary of Demeter is in the tradition of the clay mold for a cast lamp (now lost) bearing the signature ΔΑΜΑΡΙΩΝΟΣ (Damarionos) from Delos. However, the hairstyle and the forehead area on the Dion example are stylized. Moreover, the horn-like protrusions in front of the handle have their closest parallel only in the half-moon-shaped protrusions on Italic lamps of the first and second centuries AD. These observations point to a later date than that of the Damarionos lamp, in the first two centuries of Roman rule and up to the end of the first century AD.

Selected bibliography

Deonna 1908: 136 fig. 33; Bruneau 1965: 145 nos. 4751, 4759; Bailey 1980: 217 nos. Q 1036–Q 1055; Boucher 1980: 50 nos. 271–75; de Spagnolis and de Carolis 1983: 81, 83; Pingiatoglou 2005: 85, 88; Pingiatoglou 2010b: 213 fig. 11; Pingiatoglou 2015: 114 fig. 212 pl. Χδ. Cf. the bronze statuettes of Africans holding lamps: Snowden 1970: 187, and figs. 66, 111, 112. On the typology of cast lamps, see Marcadé 1984: 447 n. 9. On the dating of the Dion lamp, see Pingiatoglou 2005: 85, 88.

21   20   23   22

20—23

20. FEMALE FIGURINE OF A KORE HOLDING A BIRD AND POMEGRANATE

5th century BC

Terracotta: very pale brown clay (10YR.8/4)

H. 14.4 cm; W. 4.3 cm

From Dion. Sanctuary of Demeter. South Late Archaic–Classical temple.

Archaeological Museum of Dion, MΔ 452α

A compact figurine, this kore holds a bird in her right hand and a pomegranate in her left. Wearing a peplos with a long overfall and a polos headdress, she stands on a low, rectangular base. The face is damaged. The back of the figurine is flat.

Selected bibliography

Pingiatoglou 1990: 207ff., 214 fig. 7; Pingiatoglou 2015: 70 E5 figs. 124–26, pl. VIIIα.

21. FEMALE FIGURINE OF A KORE HOLDING A FRUIT

5th century BC

Terracotta: reddish yellow clay (7.5YR.7/6)

H. 10.5 cm; W. 4.7 cm

From Dion. Sanctuary of Demeter. South Late Archaic–Classical temple.

Archaeological Museum of Dion, MΔ 452β

This figure wears a high polos headdress and holds a fruit at chest level in the right hand, while lifting her himation with the left. The lower part of the kore is missing from about mid-thigh level.

Selected bibliography

Pingiatoglou 1990: 207ff., 214 fig. 7δ. Pingiatoglou 2015: 71 E11 figs. 129, 130. Cf. a statuette from Olynthos: Robinson 1933: no. 157 pl. 19; Higgins 1967: 81 pls. 3e,f.

22. FEMALE FIGURINE OF A KORE HOLDING A FRUIT

5th century BC

Terracotta: reddish yellow clay (7.5YR.7/6)

H. 9.3 cm; W. 3.5 cm

From Dion. Sanctuary of Demeter. South Late Archaic–Classical temple.

Archaeological Museum of Dion, MΔ 452δ

Reconstructed from two fragments, the head of this compact figurine is missing and the surface damaged. The right arm is held under the breast; below it the left hand holds a fruit. The back is smooth.

Selected bibliography

Pingiatoglou 1990: 207ff., 214 fig. 7β; Pingiatoglou 2015: 70 E7 figs. 127, 128.

23. FEMALE FIGURINE OF A KORE HOLDING A FRUIT

5th century BC

Terracotta: pinkish clay (7.5YR.8/4)

H. 9.3 cm; W. 3.2 cm

From Dion. Sanctuary of Demeter. South Late Archaic–Classical temple.

Archaeological Museum of Dion, MΔ 452ε

Wearing a peplos with a long *apoptygma*, or overfall, this compact statuette holds her right hand just below the breast and the left, somewhat lower, bears a fruit. The figurine stands on a low, rectangular base. The back is smooth.

Selected bibliography

Pingiatoglou 1990: 207ff., 214 fig. 7γ; Pingiatoglou 2015: 70 E6.

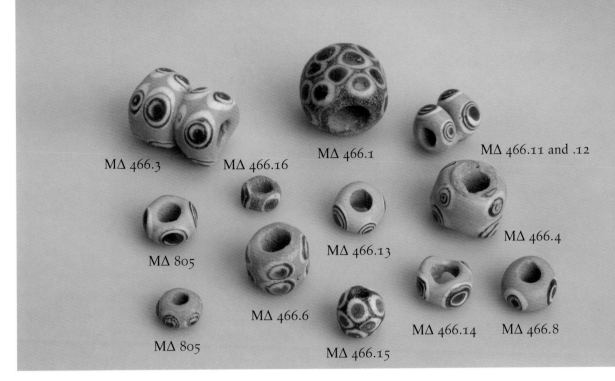

MΔ 466.3   MΔ 466.16   MΔ 466.1   MΔ 466.11 and .12

MΔ 805   MΔ 466.13   MΔ 466.4

MΔ 805   MΔ 466.6   MΔ 466.15   MΔ 466.14   MΔ 466.8

24 a–c

EYE BEADS

5th century BC
Glass
Diam. 1.3–2.8 cm
From Dion. Sanctuary of Demeter. North Late Archaic–
Classical temple.
Archaeological Museum of Dion, MΔ 466

These so-called eye beads are from a necklace. Most of them have a yellow ground, but one is green and two others are gray. All have blue and white eyes.

Selected bibliography
Pingiatoglou 2015: 120 figs. 220, 222.

24a. BEAD

5th century BC
Glass
H. 1.5 cm
From Dion. Sanctuary of Demeter. North Late Archaic–
Classical temple.
Archaeological Museum of Dion, MΔ 717

Fragment with blue eyes on white dots against a yellow ground.

24b. BEAD

5th century BC
Glass
Diam. 1 cm
From Dion. Sanctuary of Demeter. North Late Archaic–
Classical temple.
Archaeological Museum of Dion, MΔ 805

Blue and white eyes on a yellow ground.

24c. BEAD

5th century BC
Glass
Diam. 2 cm
From Dion. Sanctuary of Demeter. North Late Archaic–
Classical temple.
Archaeological Museum of Dion, MΔ 2834

Blue and white eyes on a yellow ground.

25

RELIEF STELE DEPICTING ISIS AS DEMETER WITH DEDICATORY INSCRIPTION

Second half of 3rd–early 2nd century BC

Marble

H. 31 cm; W. 34 cm; D. 8 cm

From Dion. Sanctuary of Isis. Found in the courtyard, northeast of the main temple to Isis Lochia.

Archaeological Museum of Dion, MΔ 410

Isis is depicted here in bust form as the goddess of fertility and abundance. Her drapery is tied with the "knot of Isis" on the right shoulder, and she holds a sheaf of corn and a scepter, with the solar disc acting as a finial. Over her left shoulder is a barely distinguishable object, perhaps a shield, and she wears a broad-brimmed hat to which a crescent moon or some other symbol of Isis was attached. The top right corner of the grayish marble stele has been reattached.

The iconographic elements here recall Herodotus's identification of Isis with Demeter (*Hist.* 2.59.1): "Isis is [known] in the Greek language [as] Demeter." In the upper left corner of the relief, a votive inscription reads:

Σαράπιδι Ἴσιδι / Ἀνούβιδι / Καλλίμαχος / καὶ Κλήτα / χαριστήριον /τῆς πλανητέ- / ας

The inscription refers to a couple named Kallimachos and Kleta who dedicated the relief to the divine trinity of Sarapis, Isis, and Anubis as "a thank offering to the wandering goddess." The dedication may be associated with the profits made from a business deal after a sea voyage, making the relief an important source for the study of the cult of the Egyptian deities in relation to seafaring and trade.

Selected bibliography

Pandermalis 2000: 89; Pingiatoglou 2010a: 189 fig. 4; Christodoulou 2011: 11–16; Pingiatoglou 2011: 498 no. 312.

26

SLAB WITH THE IMPRINT OF TWO FEET AND DEDICATORY INSCRIPTION

Late 2nd–3rd century AD
Marble
H. 50 cm; W. 39 cm; D. 3.8 cm
From Dion. Sanctuary of Isis, on the steps leading to the pronaos of the temple of Isis Lochia.
Archaeological Museum of Dion, MΔ 419

Three fragments of this relief slab have been reassembled to show two differently sized imprints of feet ("footsteps"). The variation in size between the two footprints has been interpreted as the symbolic reference to a couple, man and wife, who had a common purpose in fulfilling a vow or prayer. On the back of the slab, a half-finished, first attempt at carving a footprint has been preserved. The slab is white marble with a reddish tint on the surface. At the bottom of the slab's face is a carved votive inscription:

Ἰγνατία Ἐρεννία / Ἑρμανούβει / κατ᾽ ἐπιταγήν᾽
Ignatia Erennia [commissioned this] at the behest of Hermanubis.

The inscription reveals that Hermanubis had commanded the patron Ignatia Erennia to make the offering. Hermanubis was a syncretistic deity who combined the characteristics of Anubis, the divine guardian of the dead in Egypt, with those of Hermes the conductor of souls (psychopomp). He was one of the trinity of Egyptian deities who were worshiped across the Greco-Roman world.

Select bibliography
Pandermalis 2000: 99; Christodoulou 2011: 18–20.

27

STATUETTE OF HARPOCRATES WITH CORNUCOPIA

100–125 AD
Marble
H. 63 cm; W. 19.5 cm; D. 28 cm
From Dion. Sanctuary of Isis. Found in the courtyard, northeast of the main temple to Isis Lochia.
Archaeological Museum of Dion, MΔ 400

Identified as Harpocrates, son of Isis, this statuette of the naked boy-god is depicted standing, with a long, thick mane of hair down to his shoulders. On his head he wears a fillet, decorated above the forehead with the solar disc. His left leg is extended and partially conceals the right, which is attached to a low, cylindrical support. The index finger on his right hand originally rested on his lips, and he held a complete cornucopia in his left. The five white marble fragments of the statuette have been reassembled. A large part of the cornucopia is missing, as are some tiny fragments of the figure's extremities, the genitalia, and the emblem on the fillet in the hair. There are some reddish spots on the stone that may be the result of oxidation.

Harpocrates is the child form of Horus, the Egyptian sun god, who was born of the union of Isis and Osiris. In the Greco-Roman world, he was identified with Eros and was an inseparable member of the trinity of Greek deities. He was worshiped as a protector of children and tutelary deity of prosperity, as indicated by the cornucopia. The god's characteristic gesture of finger to mouth, indicative of his childish nature, has been interpreted from as far back as antiquity as symbolic, imposing silence on the initiates of Isis, as attested by Plutarch in *De Iside et Osiride*.

Selected bibliography
Pandermalis 1982: 734; Pandermalis 2000: 98; Pingiatoglou 2011: 499 no. 313.

28

STATUETTE OF ARTEMIS EILEITHYIA

3rd–1st century BC
Marble
H. 59 cm; W. 19 cm; D. 12 cm
From Dion. Sanctuary of Isis. Found in the courtyard,
east of the altar.
Archaeological Museum of Dion, MΔ 5450

The goddess is depicted here standing in a strictly frontal pose.
She wears a chiton and himation passed diagonally under the left
armpit and holds two torches, which are attached to the body.
The figure is rendered with Archaic stylistic characteristics, seen
in the stance, the form of dress, and the handling of the drapery
folds. From the point of view of artists in the Hellenistic period,
this anachronistic depiction emphasized the goddess's venerability
and the long-standing nature of her cult. A dedicatory inscription
found with this sculpture attests to the identity of the torch-
bearing goddess as Artemis Eileithyia, the protectress of women in
childbirth and newborns. The head and right arm of this white
marble statuette are missing. Dowel holes (or sockets) appear on
the neck and torch.

The statuette was found in the sanctuary of Isis Lochia but
dates to some earlier phase of the operation of the temple, when
Artemis was worshiped there. Worshiped by the Greeks as Lochia
and Kourotrophos, Artemis was the daughter of Leto and
assisted her mother in giving birth to her twin brother Apollo.
In the Hellenistic period, the connection between the content
of the cults of these two goddesses was the foundation for the
Egyptian cult in Dion.

Selected bibliography
Pandermalis 1982: 734; Giuman 1999b: 430–31. Pandermalis 2000: 97;
On Artemis Eileithyia, see Pingiatoglou 1981: 98ff.; Pingiatoglou
2015: 164; Christodoulou (forthcoming).

29

STATUE OF APHRODITE HYPOLYMPIDIA AND BASE WITH DEDICATORY INSCRIPTION

Statue: 150–100 BC; base: 2nd century AD
Marble
H. 113 cm; W. 48 cm; D. 36 cm
From Dion. Sanctuary of Isis. Head and base found in the
temple dedicated to Aphrodite Hypolympidia. Body found in
a canal near the sanctuary of Isis.
Archaeological Museum of Dion, MΔ 4, MΔ 383

This cult statue of Aphrodite Hypolympidia depicts the goddess
standing next to a tree trunk with her head slightly inclined
downward. Her stance is relaxed, with the right leg bent and the
left bearing the weight of the body. The left arm is bent and
rests on the jutting hip. She wears a diaphanous chiton, caught
up under the breast, and the himation wrapped around her wrist
falls loosely around the body and over the right leg. Her hair is
piled high on the head and bound up in an elaborate topknot.
The right arm of this white marble statue is missing. The head
has been reattached and has a repair that goes back to a break
in antiquity.

Known in the past as the Tiepolo Aphrodite or Artemis/Hecate,
this statuary type was widespread in the Hellenistic period. The
model for a series of copies and versions, mainly from Attica and
Rhodes, the original is believed to have been an over-life-size
statue from the Athens Agora, dated to between 170 and 150 BC and
probably identified with Aphrodite Hegemone. The Dion statue's
base was made after the statue itself, with the intention of placing
the statue in the goddess's shrine during the reconstruction of
the sanctuary of Isis in the second century AD.

The inscription mentions that the statue was commissioned
by the freedwoman Anthestia Iucunda in honor of Aphrodite
Hypolympidia and the Roman colonists who had settled in Dion:

Anthestia P(ublii) l(iberta) Iucunda Veneri Hypolympidia
et colonis

The interest of the inscription lies in the appellation of the goddess,
which attests to the fact that Aphrodite was worshiped at Dion
as the local goddess of the foothills of Olympus.

Selected bibliography
Pandermalis 1982: 733–35; Pandermalis 1984b: 275–76;
Pandermalis 2000: 104–9; Pingiatoglou 2010a: 189 fig. 5. On the
original, see Stewart 2012: 288–98.

30

MOSAIC OF THE EPIPHANY OF DIONYSUS

Late 2nd–early 3rd century AD
Stone tesserae
H. 150 cm; W. 220 cm
From Dion. Villa of Dionysus. Found in the Symposium Hall.
Archaeological Museum of Dion, MΔ 8993

This is the central panel of a mosaic pavement from the triclinium, or banqueting hall, in the Villa of Dionysus. The god stands in a chariot, holding a drinking horn (rhyton) and a staff adorned with ivy leaves (thyrsus). He is supported by the elderly Papposilenos, wearing an animal-skin tunic under a purple himation. The chariot is being pulled by a pair of sea-panthers, their reins held by two ichthyocentaurs who carry on their shoulders a krater (left) and a wine jar with a lid (right), both symbols of the cult of Dionysus. The polychromy of the depiction, the strong contrasts, and the attempt to give a sense of depth create the impression of a painted work. The Dion mosaic probably copies a large painted composition from the Hellenistic period.

This rare subject is connected with an ancient myth mentioned by a number of authors, the first of whom was Homer (*Iliad* 6.130–44). When Dionysus arrived in Thrace with his troupe (*thiasos*) of revelers, Lycurgus, King of the Edoni, hunted down and imprisoned the maenads and the satyrs. Dionysus himself, still a small child, was afraid and dove into the sea, whence he fled into the arms of the Nereid Thetis. The scene shown on the mosaic depicts the moment of the god's triumphal return—his epiphany—as he emerges from the waters.

Selected bibliography
Pandermalis 1987: 181–86; Pandermalis 1996: 212; Pandermalis 2000: 174–83. Cf. Kakrides 1986a: 292–93; Kondoleon 1994: 332 n. 84.

31–33

THREE PANELS FROM THE MOSAIC OF THE EPIPHANY OF DIONYSUS

These three panels are part of a group of six that framed the central scene of the Epiphany of Dionysus (see cat. no. 30). They are decorated with theatrical masks of Dionysian characters taken from the tradition of the pantomime: Dionysus, Lycurgus, a female figure (perhaps Ariadne), and three satyrs. The mosaic, which is most probably a copy of a Hellenistic painting, derives its subject from dramas such as Aeschylus's *Lykourgeia* tetralogy, which told of Lycurgus, King of the Edoni, and his rejection of the Bacchic cult.

Selected bibliography

Pandermalis 1987: 182–85; Pandermalis 2000: 175–83. Cf. Kakrides 1986a: 2, 315; Kakrides 1986b: 292–93; Lesky 2008: 381.

31. MOSAIC PANEL WITH THEATRICAL MASK OF SILENUS

Late 2nd–early 3rd century AD
Stone tesserae
H. 73 cm; W. 73 cm
From Dion. Villa of Dionysus. Found in the Symposium Hall.
Archaeological Museum of Dion, ΜΔ 8994

In this panel the head of an elderly figure with round eyes, fleshy nose, and thick lips is depicted with a closed mouth, suggesting that it is a mask used for pantomimes, a theatrical genre particularly popular during the Roman period. The primary textual source for theatrical masks, especially those of satyrs, is the *Onomasticon* of Julius Pollux of Naucratis, dated to the second century AD (see 4.142).

In this masterly portrait, one can recognize the wise Silenus, Dionysus's most elderly follower and the head of his *thiasos* (troupe), who is also presented as the nurse and tutor of a young Dionysus in the Orphic hymns, Sophocles' *Dionysiacus*, and Euripides' *Cyclops*.

Selected bibliography

Kakrides 1986a: 315; Pandermalis 1987: 183; Pandermalis 2000: 175.

32. MOSAIC PANEL WITH THEATRICAL MASK OF A SATYR

Late 2nd–early 3rd century AD
Stone tesserae
H. 73 cm; W. 73 cm
From Dion. Villa of Dionysus. Found in the Symposium Hall.
Archaeological Museum of Dion, MΔ 8995

In this panel is depicted the theatrical mask of a mature satyr. He has the characteristic pointed ears, open mouth, snub nose, and bulging eyes. A band decorates his head, while a drum is shown to his right.

Selected bibliography
Pandermalis 1987: 182.

33. MOSAIC PANEL WITH THEATRICAL MASK OF KING LYCURGUS

Late 2nd–early 3rd century AD
Stone tesserae
H. 73 cm; W. 73 cm
From Dion. Villa of Dionysus. Found in the Symposium Hall.
Archaeological Museum of Dion, MΔ 8996

This theatrical mask of a mature, bearded man with barbaric features is identifiable as Lycurgus, King of the Edoni, who chased Dionysus and his entourage out of Thrace. According to the ancient myth recounted by Apollodoros (*Library* 3.5.1), Lycurgus provoked the fury of the gods due to his impious behavior toward Dionysus. In that account, Zeus blinded Lycurgus, causing Dionysus to put him in an ecstatic frenzy, leading Lycurgus to think that his son was a grapevine and dismember him, following which the king mutilated himself. Lycurgus's end followed a prophecy from the Delphic oracle that the land of the Edoni would remain infertile until the king was put to death. To propitiate Dionysus, the Edoni were obliged to abandon a bound Lycurgus on Mount Pangaion, where he was torn to pieces by the horses or panthers of Dionysus.

According to Lucian (*Salt.* 52), in the Roman period Lycurgus's punishment was included in the list of subjects with which pantomime actors should be familiar. The king's closed mouth in this panel confirms that the mask was to be understood as used for pantomimes.

Selected bibliography
Kakrides 1986b: 292–93; Pandermalis 1987: 182; Farnoux 1992: no. 310; Pandermalis 2000: 183; Lesky 2008: 381.

FOUR STATUES OF PHILOSOPHERS

The excavation of the central part of the so-called Villa of Dionysus in ancient Dion was undertaken in June 1987. In the great triclinium (banqueting hall), where the mosaic was preserved intact albeit cracked, there were four headless statues of philosophers lined up along the north wall. It was evident that they had been placed there hastily and as a temporary measure, since they were standing directly on the mosaic and one of them blocked an adjacent doorway. Three of the four heads from the statues soon came to light when the atrium that communicated with the main entrance into the banqueting hall was excavated. The heads were subsequently reattached to the bodies without difficulty. It seems certain that the sculptures had experienced two disasters. When the first occurred, the sculptures were in the atrium, and with the collapse of the wall behind them, the heads fell off. The headless statues were subsequently pulled from the ruins and placed in the banqueting hall, where they were located when the second disaster struck—a great fire that completely destroyed the building. These statues must be connected with the splendid room west of the atrium, which was probably a library to judge by the built-in desks along the walls. All four philosophers are seated on thrones with their feet resting on footstools. All wear the sleeved tunica under the himation, and all hold the left arm bent in front of the body with a scroll in the hand. On two of the statues, the right elbow is bent: the hand, now missing, would have rested on the chin to convey a thoughtful pose. On the other two statues, the forearm (a separate insertion) was instead outstretched (*porrecta manu*). The four philosophers wear ornate, open-toed sandals. All the statues stand on integral bases of varying heights.

The differences among the four sculptures are just as important as the similarities: cat. no. 34 (inv. 5882) has a mane of hair and a full beard. The same was true of the headless cat. no. 36 (inv. 5880), to judge from the traces of beard preserved on the neck. By contrast cat. nos. 35 (inv. 5881) and 37 (inv. 5879) have very short hair in the *à penna* style. Moreover, cat. no. 35 is beardless while cat. no. 37 has a short beard, and in neither of those two is there any carving on the eyeballs to suggest an iris. More importantly, both of these two heads are significantly smaller than that of cat. no. 34; traces of curled locks on the back of the head of cat. no. 35 and that of cat. no. 37 suggest they have been resculpted over time.

Important differences can also be seen in the thrones: on cat. nos. 34 and 36, the throne has the usual depth, and the philosophers are comfortably seated. On cat. nos. 35 and 37, the thrones are narrower, and the philosophers are perched on them rather than seated in a relaxed fashion. Similar variations apply to the footstools: those of cat. nos. 34 and 36 are higher, while those of cat. nos. 35 and 37 are flat boards. Finally, the scrolls of cat. nos. 35 and 37 are rendered as the customary closed cylinders, whereas that of cat. no. 36 is depicted as unrolling and that of cat. no. 34 is completely open, suggesting that the latter had just been reading a text.

It is undeniable that the group depicted a clear hierarchy among the philosophers: cat. no. 34 was the most important, as the more elaborate furniture and the open papyrus indicate; cat. no. 36 was next in line and probably had a similar hairstyle, while the other two—with the less comfortable thrones—came after him.

The typology of the statues and above all the appearance of cat. no. 34 are reminiscent of the Epicurean philosophers. The School of Epicurus exhibited a similar hierarchy in its members, in which a distinct emphasis is placed on the precedence of the school's founder, who is depicted seated on an elaborate throne, followed in turn by Metrodorus of Lampsacus, who has a chair, and Hermarchus, for whom a simple cube is deemed sufficient.

There must have been a similar significance to the originally outstretched hands of cat. nos. 35 and 37, who were perhaps intended to be seen as posing a question, while the hands of cat. nos. 34 and 36 would have rested on their chins to indicate that they were deep in thought.

It appears that this group of philosophers was made by a New Attic–style workshop in the second century AD, inspired by models from the late fourth century BC, and was reused by the owner of the Villa of Dionysus in the early third century AD, with the heads of cat. nos. 35 and 37 recarved to depict his own portrait and that of his beardless son. Placing those two statues next to the villa's library and the banqueting hall with the Greek philosophers in cat. nos. 34 and 36 emphasized the prestige of these wealthy landowners and displayed their patronage of the arts and appreciation of Greek learning, which was experiencing a revival as the Second Sophistic spread throughout Greece and Asia Minor.

Selected bibliography

Pandermalis 1987: 181ff.; Pandermalis 2000: 166–73; Adam-Veleni 2012: 83.

34. STATUE OF A PHILOSOPHER

2nd century AD
Marble
H 86 cm; W. 35 cm; D. 54 cm
From Dion. Villa of Dionysus. Symposium Hall.
Archaeological Museum of Dion, MΔ 5882

In antiquity this statue was given precedence over the other philosophers in the group. Extremely fine drapery folds across most of the himation contrast with the bold carving on the bottom part that partially covers the left knee. The tunica has short sleeves. There is a hollow for the pupil in each eye and some carving of the outline of the iris. The throne has decorative lion's feet, as does the footstool. The papyrus is unmistakably open and folded back, as if the philosopher's reading had been interrupted.

35. STATUE OF A PHILOSOPHER

2nd century AD
Marble
H. 85 cm; W. 40 cm; D. 43 cm
From Dion. Villa of Dionysus. Symposium Hall.
Archaeological Museum of Dion, MΔ 5881

This statue took second place in the group's antique hierarchy. The drapery folds on the himation are full but simplified, suggesting a thicker fabric than the one dressing the philosopher in cat. no. 34. The sleeves on the tunica extend to the elbow. There is a hollow indicating the pupil in the eye but no carving of the outline of the iris. The figure is beardless and his hair is cut short; small curls on the back of the head remain from its original use. The socket for the right arm is hemispherical.

36. HEADLESS STATUE OF A PHILOSOPHER

2nd century AD
Marble
H. 74 cm; W. 40 cm; D. 43 cm
From Dion. Villa of Dionysus. Symposium Hall.
Archaeological Museum of Dion, MΔ 5880

Taking third place in the hierarchy of philosophers, this statue is headless although traces of a beard survive. The figure wears a short-sleeved tunica. The himation is folded in a fashion similar to that of the philosopher in cat. no. 34. Rather than rolled, the papyrus scroll is stretched over two cylinders, indicating that it is being read. The sandaled right foot is lifted in a lively manner.

37. STATUE OF A PHILOSOPHER

2nd century AD
Marble
H. 87 cm; W. 39.5; D. 42.5 cm
From Dion. Villa of Dionysus. Symposium Hall.
Archaeological Museum of Dion, MΔ 5879

The sleeves on the tunica extend to the elbows. The figure has short hair and a beard to match. The deep wrinkle on the forehead strikingly differentiates this figure from the philosopher in cat. no. 35. There is a hollow for each pupil, but no carving of the outline of the iris. The head shows strong signs of burning. The socket for the outstretched right arm is shaped like a square dowel hole.

38

STATUETTE OF HERACLES

2nd century AD
Marble
H. 50 cm; W. 25 cm; D. 18.5 cm
From Dion. Villa of Dionysus. The statuette's fragments were
found scattered throughout the villa.
Archaeological Museum of Dion, MΔ 8928

This headless statuette of the hero Heracles depicts him in
repose. Naked, he leans his right hand on a club and holds a bow
and arrow in his left, with the lion's skin over his outstretched
left arm. A deer stands by Heracles' side with its head turned
toward the hero. The sculpture is an exceptionally high-quality
copy of a model from the Imperial period. The fine-grained white
marble has been reassembled from a number of fragments. The
head, the lower parts of the legs, and part of the bow are missing.

Known as the Boston Hercules, this type goes back to a bronze
original of the fifth century BC, possibly attributable to the
sculptor Myron (460–450 BC). The addition of the deer in the
Dion copy is perhaps related to the myth of Telephus, son of
Heracles and Auge, daughter of Aleus, King of Tegea. As the
product of a sacrilegious act, Telephus was abandoned on
Mount Parthenion to die but managed to survive by suckling a doe.

Selected bibliography
Pandermalis 1989a: 144; Pandermalis 2000: 196ff.

39

40

HEAD OF AGRIPPINA THE ELDER
First half of the 1st century AD
Marble
H. 24 cm; W. 16 cm; D. 9.2 cm
From Dion. Villa of Dionysus. South chamber. From the
destruction layer above the chamber's floor.
Archaeological Museum of Dion, MΔ 2714

This woman's head is depicted with large, almond-shaped eyes,
a low forehead, a large nose, and closed lips. Her hair, parted in
the middle, is arranged in parallel strands that end in tight curls.
The facial characteristics and the hairstyle identify it as a portrait
of Agrippina the Elder (14 BC–33 AD), granddaughter of Augustus
and mother of the emperor Caligula. The portrait is of fine-
grained marble, white with a brownish patina, possibly due to
oxidation. Only the front of the head, missing a section at the
upper left, survives.

The iconographic type is well-known from the coinage of the
reigns of Caligula and Claudius, although it was created as far
back as the first decades of the first century AD. The carving of the
Dion head suggests that it is closer to early types than to later
portraits, which were made after Agrippina's death and intended
to vaunt the descent of the Julio-Claudian dynasty from Augustus.
The discovery of an early portrait of Agrippina in Dion could be
related to her brief presence in the east in the years 17–19 AD,
when she traveled around the eastern provinces of the empire with
her husband, the popular prince and brilliant general Germanicus.

Selected bibliography
Pandermalis 2000: 160–61; Pingiatoglou 2011: 573 no. 361.

HEAD OF A STATUE OF NIKE STANDING ON THE GLOBE
Late 2nd century AD
Marble
H. 33 cm; W. 24.7 cm; D. 21.5 cm
From Dion. Villa of Dionysus. South Chamber.
Archaeological Museum of Dion, MΔ 5858

A quiet smile plays across the face of this life-size marble head of a
woman. The youthful figure and the inlaid eyeballs add additional
touches of vitality. The hair, parted in the middle and twisted in two
braids, frames the face and ends in a bun at the back, from which
a long tail of hair originally hung down. The head is of fine-grained
white marble in good condition. There is damage to the back and
the sternum.

The head was found with other fragments of the body and the base
scattered among the atria of the south wing and in a nearby stream
of water. The base is reminiscent of the Berlin Nike type, in which a
flying Nike is depicted at the moment she lands with her feet on
a hemispherical base. This type has been compared with the monumental works of Phidias, especially the cult statue of the enthroned
Zeus holding a Nike at the sanctuary of Olympia. However, scholars
have more recently deemed it a classicizing creation of the mid-first-
century BC, inspired by an original of the late fourth century.

The location of the statue in the southern atria of the residential
complex suggests that it formed part of the decorative program of
the internal courtyards, as in the luxury Roman villas of Campania.

Selected bibliography
Pandermalis 2000: 162–65. Cf. Blümel 1931: 42–45; Schrader 1941:
21ff.; Vermeule and von Bothmer 1959: 332; Goulaki 1981: 218ff.;
de Caro 1987: 107–10; Davison 2009: 329ff.

41

42

KEY
1st–3rd century AD
Iron
L. 18.4 cm; W. 6 cm
From Dion. Villa of Dionysus.
Archaeological Museum of Dion, MΔ 1312

COMPASS
3rd century AD
Copper alloy
L. 17 cm
From Dion. Villa of Dionysus.
Archaeological Museum of Dion, MΔ 1266

This large iron key of the Laconian type consists of a long, flat rod that has been bent to form two discrete parts, the shank and the bit of the key. The shank ends in a partially preserved ring that was used to hang up the key. The bit, at a right angle to the shank, has two toothed projections (tines), corresponding to the same number of tumbler pins in the internal mechanism of the lock. When the key was fitted into the keyhole, the tines operated the tumbler pins and released the safety lever, opening and closing the wooden door. There is some oxidation on the iron, and the suspension ring is missing.

Selected bibliography
Pandermalis 2000: 233.

The compass is a geometrical instrument for drawing circles and measuring distances. It consists of two flat arms ending in sharp tips, hinged together at the top. The ancient sources refer to the compass using the word *diabetes* (from the verb *diabainō*, meaning to walk or stand with legs apart) or *tornos* (from the verb *teirō*, to bore a hole), terms that describe, respectively, the shape of the instrument and the way it works. When open, the arms of the compass take the form of the Greek capital letter Λ, which resembles the legs of a person standing with feet apart. Circles are inscribed by turning the instrument around a fixed point, to which one arm remains attached, while the other moves around it. This example is intact with a dark green patina.

Putting the mathematical theories of the ancient Greeks into practice, the compass embodied the basic principles of geometry and was one of the most useful tools for architects, sculptors, woodcarvers, and carpenters throughout antiquity. In mythology the inventor of this instrument is said to be the young Talos, who was thrown from the walls of the Acropolis by his mother's brother, the famous master craftsman Daedalus, who envied his powers of invention. However, Pliny the Elder credits the engineer Theodorus of Samos with inventing the compass (*Nat.* 7.57).

Selected bibliography
Cf. Orlandos 1958: 137–38.

43

HERMAIC STELE WITH A PORTRAIT OF HERENNIANUS

Late 2nd–early 3rd century AD

Marble

H. 110 cm; W. 30 cm; D. 22 cm

From Dion. Stele found in the Northeastern Hall of the Great Baths. Head found in the workshop of the Villa of Dionysus.

Archaeological Museum of Dion, MΔ 5438

A portrait herm with the bust of a mature male, the iconographic type—with the himation over the left shoulder—points to the typical depiction of a philosopher. This has been determined to be an original work of the Severan period based on stylistic features, such as the engraved pupils in the eyes, the contrast between the closely cropped hair in sketchy relief, and the much deeper undercutting of the curling locks of the beard. The fine-grained white marble has been reassembled from seven fragments. The bottom of the herm is missing.

On the flat face of the stele, above the relief depiction of the genitalia, a four-line inscription records the man's name as Herennianus. The versified text is a play on words about the existence of two identical herms, a state of affairs that was confirmed when fragments from another stele with part of the same inscription were discovered. The placement of two busts in honor of the same man attests to his prominent position in the local community.

Selected bibliography

Pandermalis 2000: 157–59.

44

STATUE OF PODALEIRIUS

Late 2nd century AD
Marble
H. 85 cm; W. 34 cm
From Dion. Northeastern Hall of the Great Baths.
Archaeological Museum of Dion, MΔ 372

Smaller than life-size, this naked youth stands in a quasifrontal, relaxed pose, with the head turned to the right. He leans on a support, probably a staff, which is covered by his himation. The young man is accompanied by a dog with its front paws slightly raised. The inscription on the integral base of the statue gives the name of the youth as Podaleirius (ΠΟΔΑΛΕΙΡΙΟC). The fine-grained white Pentelic marble has been restored. The right arm below the shoulder is missing, as are part of the head and part of the dog's trunk. There is some damage to the face and the base. Podaleirius, son of Asclepius, is mentioned by Homer as a hero in the Trojan War and a doctor specializing in the diagnosis of illnesses (*Il.* 2.729–33). The statue is part of a group depicting Asclepius, his wife Epione, and their children. The group, which was set up in a place of worship in the Great Baths complex in Dion, was made in an Attic workshop at the end of the second century AD, but it was modeled on a work of the fourth century BC.

Selected bibliography
Pandermalis 1988b: 214; Pandermalis 2000: 144–45;
Droste 2001: 279ff.

45

STATUE OF AEGLE

Late 2nd century AD
Marble
H. 108 cm; W. 35 cm
From Dion. Northeastern Hall of the Great Baths. The head
was reused in the facade of the south fortification wall.
Archaeological Museum of Dion, MΔ 373

This figure of a young woman, smaller than life size, stands in a full
frontal pose, with the parts of the body arranged symmetrically
along the vertical axis of the sculpture. She wears a sleeveless
chiton, a himation folded over the left shoulder, and sandals. The
hair is arranged in curling locks wound around the forehead and
secured in a bun at the back of the head. The inscription on the
integral base gives the young woman's name as Aegle (ΑΙΓΛΗ).
The hands and parts of the plinth are missing, and there is some
damage to the face, the himation, and the left arm.

Aegle, one of Asclepius's daughters, represented good physical
condition—the glow of health. The statue was part of the same group
to which the Podaleirius belonged (see cat. no. 44). The body of
the statue was found in the east chamber of the northern wing of the
Great Baths, along with fragments from other statues in the group,
while her head was found built into the external face of the Late
Roman walls.

Selected bibliography
Pandermalis 1988b: 214ff.; Pandermalis 2000: 146ff. See also Despinis
1997; Despinis, Stefanidou-Tiveriou, and Voutiras 1997: 120 no. 91,
figs. 246–49; Despinis 1997; Droste 2001: 280.

46

HEAD FROM A STATUE OF THE
PERSONIFIED RIVER BAPHYRAS

2nd century AD
Marble
H. 30 cm; W. 22 cm; D. 21 cm
From Dion. Southeast sector of the city.
Archaeological Museum of Dion, MΔ 1053 (MΔ 5469)

Made of very fine-grained white marble, this head of a young male has long hair and curling locks. There is some damage to the face, and there are signs of a turreted crown on the top of the head, although the diadem is missing. On the basis of its iconography, the figure has been identified as a personification of the Baphyras River, a navigable waterway that connected Dion with the Aegean and flowed through the eastern part of the ancient city.

Pausanias (9.30.8) mentions an ancient tale that associates the Dion River with Orpheus, the legendary musician and mystery-cult initiate. According to tradition, when the women of Pieria killed Orpheus on the slopes of Mount Olympus, they wanted to wash their bloodstained hands in the waters of the Helikon. Reacting against the impious deed, the river disappeared into the earth and, after flowing 22 stadia (roughly 4 km) underground, resurfaced outside Dion's city walls. From that time forward, the reach of the river between Dion and the sea has been called Baphyras (from the verb *baphō*, to stain).

Selected bibliography
Bakalakis 1982: 28–32.

47

TABLE AND TRAPEZOPHOROS (TABLE SUPPORT)

2nd century AD
Marble
H. 132 cm; L. 120 cm; W. 92 cm
From Dion. House of Leda. Found along the southern wall
of the large room.
Archaeological Museum of Dion, MΔ 7822

The rectangular table-top of this pedestal table (i.e., with one central leg) has a raised rim and a small, curved protrusion in the center of the upper side that is decorated with eagle heads. The table leg is decorated with a hybrid form consisting of a lion's head with a thick mane, a bowed body, and a paw with sharp claws. The carving of this hybrid form on a table leg reflects the more general context in which anthropomorphic and zoomorphic elements were used to decorate furniture and other household goods in the Imperial period. The white marble with some gray veins was assembled from a number of fragments. Sockets/dowel holes are set one above the other in the lower part of the support.

Pedestal tables were luxury items of furniture, often made of marble and more rarely of bronze or brass. Set against a wall in the triclinia of Roman villas, they were status symbols that displayed the householder's wealth. The height of the Dion pedestal table shows that it was not a side table on which to put dishes while serving a meal, but rather it acted as a sideboard (*mensa vasaria*) for storing and displaying precious vessels and decorative objects in the Hellenistic and Roman periods.

Selected bibliography

Pandermalis 1994: 131; Pandermalis 2000: 220. Cf. Richter 1966: 81–84, 112–13, 116; Stefanidou-Tiveriou 1993: 58ff., 145–46.

48

TRAPEZOPHOROS (TABLE SUPPORT)

2nd century AD
Marble
H. 88.5 cm; L. 37.5 cm; W. 26.5 cm
From Dion. House of Leda.
Archaeological Museum of Dion, ΜΔ 7819

A group sculpture of Leda and the Swan in a standing embrace decorates this table leg. The composition unfolds in front of an integral pier, which originally supported the tabletop. Zeus, disguised as a swan, has one wing around Leda, who attempts to push him away, grasping the bird's neck in her hand. She is depicted naked, with her drapery falling in front of her body; the swan's tail feathers can be glimpsed between her thighs. Part of the top of this white marble table leg is missing, and there is some slight damage to the base.

Made in a second-century-AD Neo-Attic workshop, this sculpture took an original work of the late Hellenistic period as its model. The iconography of the scene derives its subject matter from the myth of the liaison between Zeus and Leda, wife of Tyndareus, King of Sparta, which resulted in the births of the Dioscuri twins, Castor and Pollux, and the beautiful Helen.

Selected bibliography
Pandermalis 1994: 131; Pandermalis 2000: 225. Cf. Stefanidou-Tiveriou 1993: 131–36.

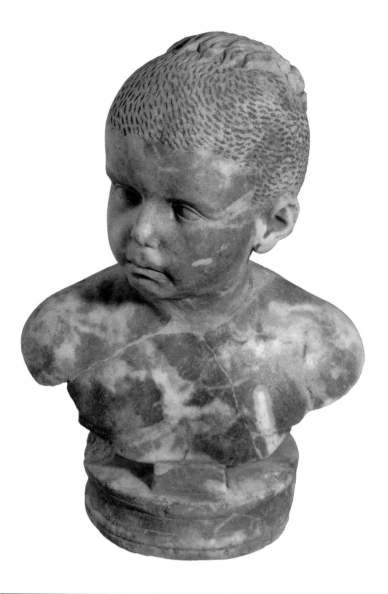

49

BUST OF A CHILD

Late 1st–early 2nd century AD. Reused mid-3rd century AD
Marble
H. 35 cm; W. 23 cm; D. 13.5 cm
From Dion. House of Leda.
Archaeological Museum of Dion, MΔ 8929

The head of this boy's bust is very fine in contrast to the less detailed treatment of the upper part of the body. Below the breast, the trunk has been cut away and replaced by a rectangular support. Between the bust and the round base is a small tabula, which makes the sculpture look as if it is turning freely in space. The fine-grained white marble, with brown and reddish patina, has been reassembled.

The type of this bust dates the sculpture to the early Imperial period, although the carving of the hair attests a later intervention. Only a tuft of curly hair on the crown of the head remains of the original hairstyle. The Dion bust is one of only a few examples with this sort of tuft, known in ancient Greek as *skollys* and usually depicted on busts of the Roman period as a long lock of hair worn on the side of the head.

In ancient Greece this special hairstyle for boys was a mark of piety, honoring the protective deity (*kourotrophos*) to whom the child's locks were ceremonially dedicated at the onset of puberty. The fact that the child's hair on the Dion bust was reworked at a later time into a *skollys* indicates that the sculpture was reused, probably in connection with the circle of the devotees of the cult of Isis. The facial features were not changed, despite the remodeling, possibly due to a dedication to the goddess after the child's death. Indeed, Isis, who was venerated also for her maternal tenderness, was believed to protect both living and dead children.

Selected bibliography
Pandermalis 2000: 221; Christodoulou (forthcoming).

50

MOSAIC WITH BIRDS ON EITHER SIDE OF A KANTHAROS

2nd century AD
Marble and glass tesserae
H. 57 cm; W. 64 cm; D. 3 cm
From Dion. House of Zosa.
Archaeological Museum of Dion, MΔ 7873α

The composition of this panel from a mosaic pavement reveals an attempt to render light and shade, as well as a decorative tendency in the use of polychrome glass tesserae. Two birds are depicted perched on the rim of a large kantharos. The stone and glass tesserae, which have been conserved, are in good condition.

The image reflects an iconographic subject that was particularly widespread in antiquity. The source of inspiration for a long series of copies and versions of the motif is thought to be a famous work by the mosaicist Sosus, who was based in Pergamum in the second century BC. According to Pliny the Elder (*Nat.* 36.60), the archetype depicted doves drinking from a basin full of water, which gave back their reflection. The best-known copy of Sosus's masterpiece is the mosaic found in Hadrian's Villa at Tivoli.

Selected bibliography
Pandermalis 1993: 197; **Pandermalis** 2000: 217–19.

51

OIL LAMP DECORATED WITH A PANTHER PROTOME

1st–2nd century AD
Copper alloy
H. 37 cm; W. 33 cm; D. 33 cm
From Dion. Water Organ Sector.
Archaeological Museum of Dion, MΔ 8908

Made up of cast and hammered parts, this intact two-wicked lamp has a conical base and a strongly curved handle that ends in the head of a panther. The animal head pushes through a wreath of stylized leaves. The handle is decorated with confronted palmettes in relief, while the details on the leaves of the wreath are incised. The nozzles have circular holes for the wick, and there is a leaf-shaped filler hole in the center of the disc. The form of the nozzles and the type of handle recall a series of pear-shaped, single-wicked lamps of the early Imperial period that have similar handles decorated with theatrical masks and animal heads. The metal shows a dark green patina.

Its monumental character, its fine craftsmanship, and above all the plastic rendering of the animal's facial characteristics make this lamp an outstanding example of the metalwork and aesthetic of the Roman period. In addition to lighting the interior spaces in Roman homes, monumental lamps served to impress and to create a theatrical atmosphere in the banqueting halls of luxury villas. In the Dion example, the feline head is skillfully combined with the power of light. When the lamp was lit, the beast would have seemed dazzled by the flame, recalling by association the myth of Dionysus's birth in fire (Dionysus Pyrigenes) and the practices of the Bacchic cult.

Selected bibliography
Conticello de Spagnolis and de Carolis 1988: nos. 100, 102; Bailey 1996: no. 3671; Pandermalis 1999b: 419; Bielfeldt 2014: 181–83.

52

SPECULUM

1st century BC
Copper alloy
W. 22 cm
From Dion. Water Organ Sector.
Archaeological Museum of Dion, MΔ 7476

The gynecological medical instrument referred to in the ancient Greek sources as a *dioptra* (Lat. *speculum magnum matricis*) consists of an upright in the form of a screw; a moveable cylindrical element with two levers to which are fitted two similarly moveable handles; and a *priapiscus*, a valve mechanism composed of three valves. This example is cast copper alloy, in good condition, with a greenish patina. One handle is missing.

The Roman speculum was used in a way similar to the employment of modern medical instruments for a colposcopy: when the valves were opened by turning the screw, the vagina was dilated, facilitating medical examination and treatment. Gynecological vaginal and uterine specula were in widespread use in Hellenistic and Roman times, a period in which immense advances were made in obstetrics and gynecology. The earliest reference to this instrument is found in a lost treatise by the greatest gynecologist of antiquity, Soranus of Ephesus (98–138 AD), which has survived in a sixth-century Latin paraphrases by Muscio (*Gynaecia* 2.34). The invention of the speculum may have been associated with the celebrated medical school of Herophilos in Alexandria, where Soranus himself had studied.

Selected bibliography
Pandermalis 1993: 197–98; Pandermalis 2000: 232. Cf. Milne 1907: 150–52; Bouzakis et al. 2008.

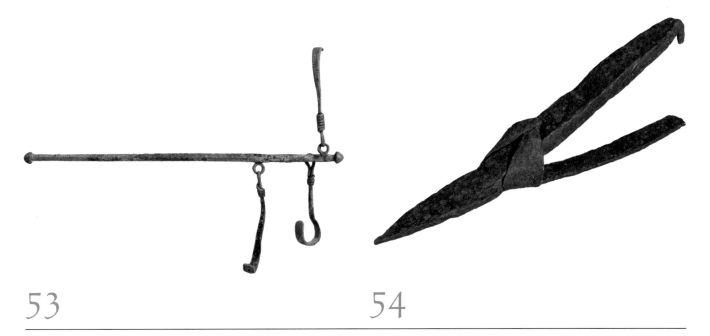

53

54

STEELYARD BALANCE

1st century BC
Copper alloy
L. 23 cm
From Dion. Found at the Roman Baths located in the area of
the sanctuaries.
Archaeological Museum of Dion, MΔ 1258

The Roman type of this small balance (*statera*) consisted of a horizontal beam of rectangular cross-section and three suspension hooks corresponding to three different points of suspension of the balance, or pivots. The calibrated scale for measuring weight that is engraved on three sides of the rod in this example is marked 0–IV, V, III–XI, XI–XXXVI (0–4, 5, 3–11, 11–36), and the midpoint is marked with an *S* for *semis*. The balance is in good condition with a green patina. The moveable weight and the pan of the balance, which hung by chains from the end of the rod near the hooks, have not survived from the original device.

The steelyard is a straight-beam balance with arms of unequal length. The mechanism requires an object to be placed in the pan and a point of balance selected according to the size of the load. The moveable weight is then dragged along the beam until the scales balance. Equilibrium is achieved when the movable weight counterbalances the mass of the object to be weighed. The point of calibration corresponding to the counterweight gives the weight of the load. The hook nearest to the pan was used in weighing larger loads, while smaller sizes were weighed using the other two hooks. The concept of the single-pan balance is usually thought to be a Roman invention. However, recent research has indicated that its use was known to the Greeks from as far back as the fifth century BC, long before the mathematical formulation of the law of the lever by Archimedes.

Selected bibliography
Pandermalis 1990: 12–13; Pandermalis 1999a: 233. Cf. Robens et al. 2014: 169, 536 ff.

PLOWSHARE

3rd century AD
Iron
L. 39 cm; W. 5.5 cm; D. 11 cm
From Dion. Found in the Roman building south of the
Hellenistic theater.
Archaeological Museum of Dion, MΔ 1417

The ancient plow was made up of an iron plowshare (*hynis*), a wooden sole (*elyma*), a handlebar (*echetle*), a curved beam (*gye*), and a long draw beam (*histoboe*) by means of which the yoked animals were attached to the implement. Only the iron plowshare survives from the Dion plow. It has an integral shaft that was attached to the top of the wooden sole by the sharp projection at one end. The second shaft, which was fixed to one end of the plowshare with an integral ring, consisted of a sort of lever that allowed the height of the drawbar to be increased or decreased in accordance with the height of the draft animals and, depending on the plowing requirements, to permit changes in the angle at which the plowshare entered the earth. This intact example shows some oxidation.

The Dion plowshare has some new features not usually found on Greek plows. Similar agricultural implements have been found in more northerly parts of the Balkans and at Petres, in the Florina region.

Selected bibliography
Bakalakis 1969: 344; Pandermalis 2000: 233; Vasileiadou 2011: 165–69, 249–50.

55

SIDE-SPOUTED JUG OR FEEDER
Early Iron Age (1000–700 BC)
Terracotta
H. 13 cm; Diam. base 4.2 cm; Diam. rim 5 cm
From Olympus. Tumulus cemetery of Hagios Basileios.
Tumulus B, pithos burial.
Archaeological Museum of Dion, MΔ 4705

This small, wheel-thrown pot is made of brown ochre clay and decorated with black-brown slip that is faded in places. It is an intact insulated jug or feeder with a depressed globular, quasi-biconical body, from which a pierced tubular spout projects. The handle is vertical and set to one side of the spout; the neck is cylindrical and has a funnel-shaped mouth. The base is annular.

The surface of the vessel is largely covered with geometric decoration, including broad bands of black-brown paint. Adjoining the upper part of the horizontal band that runs around the body of the jug are three groups of semicircles, each framed by a small triangle. A larger triangle fills the space between the handle and the spout. The series of semicircles is characteristic of the Early Geometric period and attests to relations between the foothills of Olympus and Thessaly/Euboia.

Selected bibliography
On the tumulus cemeteries of Olympus, see Pandermalis 1989b: 46–47; Poulaki-Pandermali 1997: 371–74; Havela 2012: 314.

56

KANTHAROS
Early Iron Age (1000–700 BC)
Terracotta
H. 9.5 cm; Diam. base 5.2 cm; Diam. rim 11 cm
From Olympus. Tumulus cemetery of Hagios Basileios.
Tumulus A, grave 12.
Archaeological Museum of Dion, MΔ 4756

Vessels of this type first appeared in Macedonia during the Bronze Age, and the shape became characteristic of local pottery. Made of wheel-thrown grayish clay with black glaze on the outside of the handles and the interior of the vessel, this kantharos is intact, with some flaking of the glaze on the inside.

The large bowl has a vestigial discoid base and strap handles that extend at a slight angle above the rim of the bowl. It is decorated with a broad, black band on the belly and two narrower bands on the shoulders and under the rim, with a zigzag line between.

In shape and decoration, the painted kantharoi found in tumulus cemeteries in the foothills of Mount Olympus have a number of similarities to corresponding vases from Thessaly, demonstrating that the geographical areas on either side of Olympus had developed a network of cultural and economic exchange.

Selected bibliography
Andronikos 1969: 182–85; Poulaki-Pandermali 2013: 75. On the tumulus cemeteries of Olympus, see Pandermalis 1989b: 46–47; Poulaki-Pandermali 1997: 371–74; Havela 2012: 314.

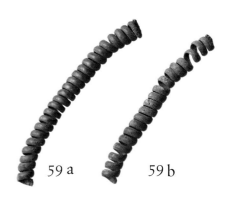

58

57

59 a

59 b

57–59

57. SPECTACLE-SHAPED BROOCH WITH FABRIC REMAINS

Early Iron Age (1000–700 BC)
Copper alloy, iron, and textile
L. 15 cm; Diam. coils 6 cm, 6.5 cm
From Olympus. Tumulus cemetery of Mesonisi. Tumulus 2, grave D.
Archaeological Museum of Dion, MΔ 8905

Completely preserved, this fibula is made from a single piece of bronze wire twisted into two coils with a figure-eight-shaped link between them. At the back of one coil, one end of the wire has been made into a hook to secure the pin. Attached to the other coil is the iron pin that secured the fibula to a garment at shoulder level. Due to the iron's oxidation, part of the fabric from the clothing of the deceased has been preserved onto the fibula.

So-called spectacle fibulae first emerged in Central Europe and spread to the Balkans in the ninth-eighth centuries BC. In Greece they first appeared in the Iron Age, where they are generally found in pairs as grave goods or offerings at shrines. The distribution of innovative dress accessories, such as spectacle fibulae and brooches, indicates cultural changes related to dramatic population movements such as the Dorian invasion.

Selected bibliography
Pandermalis 2000: 34–35. Cf. Alexander 1965; Andronikos 1969: 227–230; Bouzek 1997: 115–16.

58. SPIRAL BRACELET

Early Iron Age (1000–700 BC)
Copper alloy
L. 6 cm; Diam. 5.7 cm; Thickness 0.4 cm
From Olympus. Tumulus cemetery of Mesonisi.
Tumulus 2, grave D.
Archaeological Museum of Dion, MΔ 4924

Bangles, or armlets, with multiple spirals are jewelry items typical of the Early Iron Age. This bracelet from Dion was found around the left arm of a woman's skeleton in the tumulus cemetery on the slopes of Olympus, west of ancient Dion. It is made from a single strip of metal, flat on one side and curved on the other, twisted to form nine coils. The copper-alloy shows a light green patina.

Large, heavy armlets are unknown in prehistoric Greece, but in Central Europe they had a long tradition going back to the Early Bronze Age. Their appearance in Macedonia possibly marks the arrival of Early Dorian settlers in the Olympus region.

Selected bibliography
Cf. Andronikos 1969: 241ff.; Bouzek 1974: 122ff.; Rhomiopoulou and Kilian-Dirlmeier 1989: 122ff.

59. TWO SPIRAL PINS

Early Iron Age (1000–700 BC)
Copper alloy
a. α: L. 9.4 cm; Diam. 1 cm; Thickness 0.2 cm
b. β: L. 8.2 cm; Diam. 0.95 cm; Thickness 0.2 cm
From Olympus. Tumulus cemetery of Mesonisi. Tumulus 7, grave B.
Archaeological Museum of Dion, MΔ 4912α, 4912β

These two spiral coils were found on the cranium of a woman's skeleton in the tumulus cemetery west of ancient Dion. The metal shows a green patina. In the past, these coils were identified as the "tubes" mentioned in Homer and thought to be hair ornaments. More recent finds, which have preserved threads of fabric on the inside of the coils, have shown that they were attached to a head covering or hung from leather or fabric headbands worn on the forehead.

In Central Europe such coiled tubes were in use since the Early Bronze Age. In Greece they became widespread in the Iron Age and they are often found in women's tombs in the tumulus cemeteries, especially in Central Macedonia.

Selected bibliography
Cf. Andronikos 1969: 225–27; Rhomiopoulou and Kilian-Dirlmeier 1989: 101–7.

60

GRAVE STELE WITH FEMALE FIGURE

450–440 BC
Marble
H. 39 cm; W. 48.5 cm; D. 9 cm
Karitsa. Reused in the walls of the church of
Agios Dimitrios.
Archaeological Museum of Dion, ΜΔ 5701

Originally used in the northern cemetery of Dion, this fragment of the upper part of a grave stele depicts a young girl in left-facing profile. She has wavy hair, bound in a fillet, and wears a peplos with overfall and false sleeves. The young woman was probably holding something in her right hand. When whole, the stele had a gabled pediment, and its sides were framed by plain, narrow bands. The coarse-grained marble is off-white with gray veining.

The type of monument and the sculptural characteristics of the figure connect this provincial work with island models of the mid-fifth-century BC. As the earliest example of sculpture from ancient Dion, the stele is of particular interest because it attests Ionian influence on the artistic production of the area.

Selected bibliography
Stefanidou-Tiveriou 1975: 35–43; Pandermalis 2000: 14.

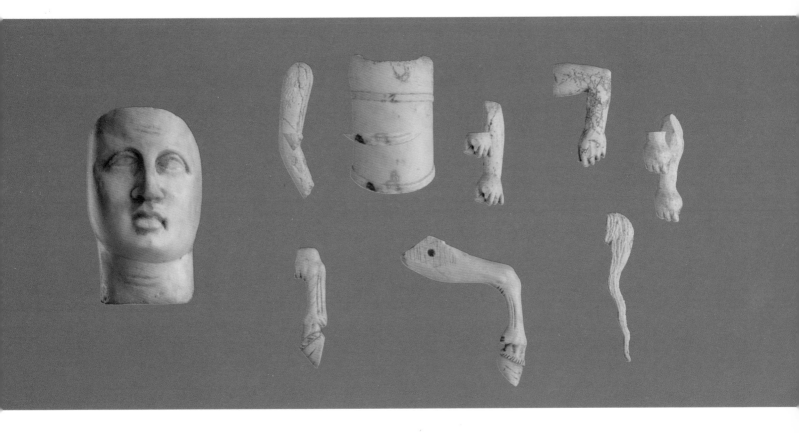

61

NINE DECORATIVE INLAYS FOR A FUNERARY *KLINE* (COUCH)

Late 3rd century BC
Bone
Head of youth (MΔ 2060): H. 3.5 cm
Arms (MΔ 2061–2063, 2072): L. 5–5.3 cm
Breastplate (MΔ 2067): H. 7 cm; W. 4 cm
Horse limbs (MΔ 2065, 2066, 2069): L. 6–7.5 cm
Karitsa. Macedonian Tomb IV.
Archaeological Museum of Dion, MΔ 2060–2063, 2065–2067, 2069, 2072

A number of small, bone decorative elements from a wooden couch, similar to those from the royal tombs at Vergina, were found in the burial chamber known as Macedonian Tomb IV. Originally the figures were fitted onto a frieze depicting the scene of an equestrian battle, on the long, front side of the couch. The group includes two small male heads, a warrior's breastplate, human arms, and horses' limbs. The inlays are in good condition, but the remaining parts of the figures must have been made of perishable materials.

Selected bibliography
Pandermalis 1985: 12; Pfrommer 1990: 247; Sismanides 1997: 148ff.; Pandermalis 2000: 266, 270; Tsiafis 2009: 84ff.

  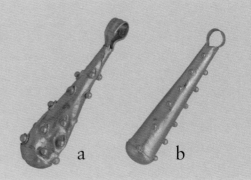

62–64

FUNERARY GOODS FROM FEMALE BURIALS

A signet ring (cat. no. 62) was discovered inside a vase that contained the bones of a small girl. The vase was placed, as secondary burial, in front of the threshold of the marble doors closing the entrance to Macedonian Tomb IV, located beneath a high tumulus west of the modern village of Karitsa. Two additional female cist graves with gold grave goods—including a bracelet with lion-head finials (cat. no. 63), another bracelet with snake-head finials, two diadems, and amulets in the shape of clubs (cat. no. 64)—were also unearthed in the proximity of this tomb, on either side of the road leading to it. The riches and quality of the grave goods in these burials bear witness to the prosperity enjoyed by the Macedonians of Dion in the period after Alexander the Great's campaign in the East.

62. RING WITH EROS SITTING ON AN ALTAR

4th–3rd century BC
Gold
Diam. hoop 2 cm
Bezel: L. 1.8 cm; W. 1.5 cm
Karitsa. Vase burial at the entrance to Macedonian Tomb IV.
Archaeological Museum of Dion, MΔ 2041, MΔ 2042

Intact and in excellent condition, this ring has a hoop that is flat on the inside and rounded on the outside, and that flares out at the top, widening into an oval receptacle in which the freestanding bezel can be set. The bezel has an image of the infant Eros in relief. The winged god is sitting astride a rectangular altar decorated with molding and a festoon. He looks down slightly, and his arms are folded in front of his body. His left hand holds a slim, barely discernible wand (or perhaps a flower stalk).

The choice of the decorative motif on the ring is related to its funerary use. The depiction of Eros would have recalled how the girl met an untimely death, but at the same time it offered comfort by placing the child under the god's protection.

Selected bibliography

Pfrommer 1990: 247; Pandermalis 2000: 271; Jackson 2006: 220; Tsiafis 2009: 100–102. Cf. Marshall 1968: 12 no. 54, 20 no. 99; Boardman 1970: 214 types VIII–IX, 299 nos. 734, 738; Spier 1992: 35 no. 54.

63. BRACELET WITH LION-HEAD FINIALS

Late 3rd century BC
Gold
Circum. 14 cm; Diam. 5 cm
Karitsa. Cist grave II near Macedonian Tomb IV.
Archaeological Museum of Dion, MΔ 2036

This bracelet is made of three interwoven strands of gold fitted into cylindrical finials ending in lions' heads. The surface of the finials is shaped like a collar and decorated with foliate scroll, twisted wire work, and spherules, while the point at which the finial is attached to the bracelet is covered with a wreath of tongue-shaped leaves. The finely worked lions' heads originally had inlaid eyes, now lost. The bracelet, in excellent condition, was made using a variety of techniques: the heads were mold cast, the band was hammered, and the other decoration was achieved with filigree and granulation.

Selected bibliography

Pandermalis 1985: 12; Pfrommer 1990: 337; Tsiafis 2009: 99. Cf. Deppert-Lippitz 1985: 223 fig. 158, 233 fig. 169.

64 a–b. TWO AMULETS IN THE FORM OF CLUBS

3rd century BC
Gold
a (left): MΔ 2037: H. 3.2 cm
b (right): MΔ 2031: H. 3.5 cm
Karitsa. Cist graves I and II near Macedonian Tomb IV.
Archaeological Museum of Dion, MΔ 2031, MΔ 2037

These two intact amulets are in the form of clubs with small granulated spheres. Cat. no. 64a is dented toward the bottom. The club is a reference to Heracles, a demigod with protective and apotropaic qualities. His image, symbols, and name were common talismans for protecting people or homes in Hellenistic times. Club-shaped amulets are found in the cemeteries of ancient cities in Macedonia and Thrace, sometimes alone, sometimes as pendants on necklaces along with other apotropaic symbols.

Selected bibliography

Pandermalis 1985: 12; Tsiafis 2009, 96, 100. Cf. Bruneau 1964; Marshall 1969: 227 nos. 2036–39; Trakosopoulou 2004: 130 no. 18; Faraone 2013: 85–88.

  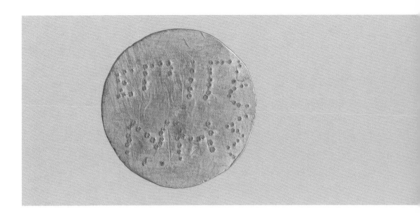

65–66

GRAVE GOOD FROM MACEDONIAN TOMB V

Tomb V, found in the vicinity of another tomb known as Macedonian Tomb II, was part of a group of monumental tombs that constituted one of the ancient necropoleis of the city of Dion, located near the modern village of Karitsa. The tomb yielded very few grave goods, among which are a coin of Alexander the Great (cat. no. 65) and a disc inscribed with the name of the deceased (cat. no. 66).

65. COIN OF ALEXANDER THE GREAT

319–310 BC
Silver
Diam. 1.6 cm
Karitsa. Macedonian Tomb V. Found in the burial chamber.
Archaeological Museum of Dion, ΜΔ 8909

The obverse of this Macedonian silver drachm depicts the profile head of a beardless Heracles with his lion-skin headdress, encircled by a series of dots. On the reverse, Zeus is depicted seated on a curule chair with a scepter in his left hand and an eagle on his right. The inscription on the obverse, ΑΛΕΞΑΝΔΡΟΥ (of Alexander), is partially preserved. Two symbols in the field allow us to identify the mint: the letters ΕΛΙ on the left and a lion's head below the chair. The coin is in good condition.

The coin was minted after Alexander's death (323 BC) in Asia Minor, at a mint that was probably located in Colophon. For some years after the death of the great commander, his successors continued to mint coinage in his name for political reasons. The Colophon mint began operating after Alexander the Great had ended his campaign in Asia, when he needed to produce large quantities of coins to pay the disbanded troops. The presence of a number of drachms from the Colophon mint in Dion must be linked with the return home of Macedonian veterans.

Selected bibliography
Pandermalis 2000: 271; Tsiafis 2009: 103. Cf. Price 1991: no. 1776; Kremydi-Sicilianou 1996: 76.

66. INSCRIBED DISC

325–250 BC
Gold
Diam. 1.2 cm
Karitsa. Macedonian Tomb V. Found in the burial chamber.
Archaeological Museum of Dion, ΜΔ 8910

This is a rare example of a "Charon's obol," or viaticum, associated with the practice of placing a coin on the mouth of the deceased or leaving a metal token with directions for the underworld journey in the context of the Bacchic and Orphic cults. The name Epigenes (ΕΠΙΓΕΝΗΣ) is inscribed on this intact beaten-gold disc in letters made up of punched dots. The inscription of the name of the deceased distinguishes the disc from the usual gold viaticum, imprinted with the face of a coin. Similar examples of Orphic or Dionysiac tokens with a short text, or just the name of the deceased, have been found in other cemeteries in Macedonia, usually in the form of gold leaves inscribed with the name of the deceased initiate.

Selected bibliography
Pandermalis 2000: 271; Tzifopoulos 2011: 231ff.; Tzifopoulos 2012: 544.

67

GRAVE STELE WITH SCENE OF *DEXTRARUM IUNCTIO* (HANDCLASP)

Early Imperial period
Marble
H. 75 cm; L. 57 cm; W. 15 cm
Dion. West cemetery.
Archaeological Museum of Dion, MΔ 7836

This funerary stele takes the form of a shrine with a gabled pediment and a tenon at the bottom to insert the stele into a base. The upper part of the relief depicts a handclasp (*dextrarum iunctio*). Below the woman's hand is a stringed instrument, a kind of harp known as a nabla (Lat. *nabilium*), while under the man's hand are a key, a pen, and an inkwell. Two Latin verse inscriptions above the joined hands note that in her lifetime the woman was devoted to the Muses, and that the man faithfully performed the duties of an archivist (*tabularius*). At bottom right, eight verses, inscribed on an open papyrus scroll, speak of the couple's mutual fidelity and love. The white marble of the stele is in good condition, with some damage to the lower part.

The stele is of particular interest because of its depiction of the nabla, which was known only from written sources prior to discovery of the Dion relief. The nabla was a musical instrument of Phoenician provenance that was familiar to the Jews, who used it in religious ceremonies; the Greeks, who used it at banquets; and the Romans, who used it at festivals. The iconographic composition here is unusual in every respect as it lacks images or names of the deceased, while it depicts a handclasp and objects associated with the activities, social status, and personal relationship of the married couple. The imagery together with the inscriptions constitute a rare example of the shifting of the semiological balance from individuals to the moral and cultural values of society in the Roman period through the metaphorical use of symbols and concepts.

Selected bibliography

Pandermalis 1994: 131–33; Pandermalis 2000: 240–41; Busch 2001: 297–304; Vendries 2004–5: 469–502; Pingiatoglou 2011: 617 no. 389.

68–70

68. PALETTE

Roman period
Stone
H. 8 cm; L. 13.7 cm; D.1 cm
Karitsa. Northern cemetery. Kalamboukas field, grave 58.
Archaeological Museum of Dion, MΔ 8911

A palette such as this stone slab was used for mixing ingredients to produce cosmetics or medicaments. Its discovery among the grave goods of a female burial indicates that it was employed for cosmetics. Small quantities of pigments were placed on the surface, using a copper-alloy spatula (see cat. no. 69), and mixed with water or gum. The beauty preparations were then applied to the face in the form of powder or lotion. This palette is grayish brown stone with patches of dark gray and veining. It is parallelepipedal in shape, with chamfered sides. The condition is good, with some small chips along the bottom edge. The underside has a smooth surface, while the top shows signs of use and staining.

In the Roman period, the beauty regime played an important part in women's everyday lives, as it was a sign of their social status. To paint their faces they used a variety of pigments made from plants or more usually minerals, despite their toxicity. Lead carbonate (or white lead) gave the desired pallor to face and hands, minium (red lead) and cinnabar put a blush on cheeks, and kohl—made from antimony sulphide or lead sulphide (galena)—was used as eyeliner or to color eyebrows. Less expensive cosmetics were made from chalk, ochre, soot, and coal.

Selected bibliography
Cf. Milne 1907: 171; Olson 2008: 60–66.

69. SPATULA

Roman period
Copper alloy
L. 17 cm
Karitsa. Northern cemetery. Kalamboukas field, grave 58.
Archaeological Museum of Dion, MΔ 8912

This copper-alloy instrument consists of a long, tapering handle, terminating at one end in a rectangular "spoon," angular in cross-section, and at the other end in a spherical knop. The handle is decorated with three metal beads at the point where it joins the spoon, and reinforced with three rings where it begins to taper. The spatula was cast in a mold and is in fair condition, with green patina. Part of the spoon-shaped end is missing.

The Dion example is a type of spatula usually known as a *kyathiskomele* (spatula-cum-spoon) to distinguish it from the *spathomele* (a flat probe). It was used in medicine as a catheter or curette and in pharmaceutical contexts for measuring ingredients, mixing substances in powder or unguent form, and for stirring liquid preparations. This instrument was found with a stone palette (cat. no. 68) in a female burial, indicating that it was a domestic implement used for mixing pigments in the preparation of cosmetics.

Selected bibliography
Cf. Milne 1907: 61–63; Jackson 1990: 17; Bliquez 2015: 125ff.

70. MIRROR

Roman period
Copper alloy
Diam. 10.4 cm
Karitsa. Northern cemetery. Kalamboukas field, grave 79.
Archaeological Museum of Dion, MΔ 8913

The slightly curved reflective surface of this undecorated, circular mirror has been preserved in excellent condition. There are traces of iron oxidation (rust) on the back where a strap handle, now missing, was once attached. Greek and Roman mirrors were made of copper alloys with a high tin content and were burnished, as is this cast copper example, to give a satisfactory reflection of their owners. The back is corroded, with a green patina.

A symbol of womanhood, and at the same time a functional object required for a woman's daily toilette, the mirror was a typical grave good in female burials along with jewelry and other cosmetic implements.

Selected bibliography
Pandermalis 2001: 350, 354 fig. 14. Cf. Richter 1915: 251ff.

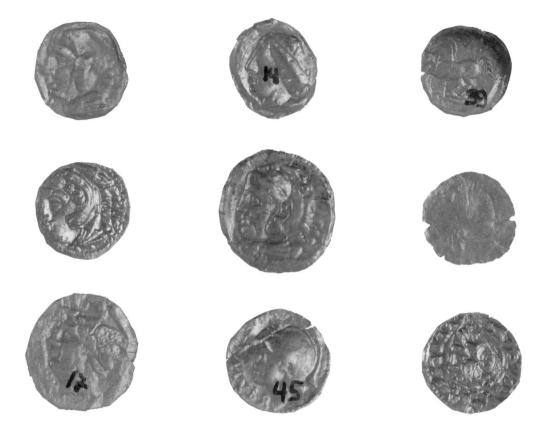

71

NINE IMPRESSIONS OF COINS ("GHOST COINS")

4th–3rd century BC
Gold
Diam. 1.5–2.1 cm; Weight 0.1–0.2 gr
Karitsa. Northern cemetery.
Kalamboukas field: MΔ 8920: grave 90; MΔ 8930: grave 70;
    MΔ 8931: grave 34; MΔ 8932: grave 49.
Dion. Northern cemetery: MΔ 8914: grave 72;
    MΔ 8916: grave 84; MΔ 8917: grave 5; MΔ 8933: grave 78.
Dion. Southern cemetery: MΔ 8915: grave II.
Archaeological Museum of Dion, MΔ 8914–8917, 8920,
8930–8933

The term *danakē* originally referred to a Persian unit of weight for silver bullion with a value of slightly more than an obol. Greeks used the term for the so-called ghost coins made from thin sheets of gold leaf that were stamped with the faces of genuine coins. The tokens were placed on or in the mouths of the deceased as "Charon's obols" (*viatica*), to be used for paying the ferryman who transported souls to Hades. These examples are intact and in good condition. In the excavation of ancient Dion's extensive northern cemetery, numerous gold *viatica* in the form of ghost coins from various periods were found. The following images (from top to bottom, left to right) have been identified:

(top)

MΔ 8914: Head of Heracles with a lion's skin, from a coin of Alexander the Great (r. 336–323 BC).

MΔ 8931: Head of a youth or the god Apollo with a fillet in his hair, from a coin of Alexander the Great.

MΔ 8930: Horse; inscribed: ΑΛΕΞ[ΑΝΔΡΟΥ] (of Alex[ander]), from a coin of Alexander the Great.

(center)

MΔ 8915: Head of Heracles with a lion's skin, from a coin of Cassander (r. 305–297 BC).

MΔ 8916: Head of Heracles with a lion's skin, from a coin of Cassander.

MΔ 8917: Head of Athena, from a coin of Antigonos II (r. 277–274, 272–239 BC).

(bottom)

MΔ 8932: Head of a youth with attributes of Apollo, Hermes, and Poseidon, also interpretable as a Genius or Apollo Vejovis, from a denarius of the Roman Republic (ca. 2nd–1st century BC).

MΔ 8920: Head of Alexander the Great wearing a helmet, inscribed [Α]ΛΕΞΑΝΔΡΟΥ (of [A]lexander), from a coin of the Macedonian state.

MΔ 8933: Head of Alexander the Great with a lion's skin, inscribed [Α]ΛΕΞΑΝΔΡΟΥ (of [A]lexander), from a coin of the Macedonian state.

Selected bibliography
Cf. Gaebler 1935: 454–58, 489–91, 818–25; Kurtz and Boardman 1971: 166; Crawford 1974: 352; Melville-Jones 1986: 65; Stevens 1991: 223–29; SNG 2000: 746–79, 876–88, 900–936, 1103–6, 1143–46.

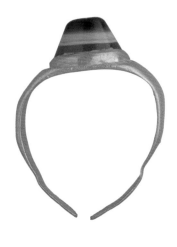

72

73

PAIR OF EARRINGS WITH PENDANTS

3rd–4th century AD
Gold, emeralds, garnets, pearls
H. 4 cm; W. 1.5 cm
Karitsa. Northern cemetery. Kalamboukas field, grave 79.
Archaeological Museum of Dion, ΜΔ 8923α, ΜΔ 8923β

Each of these earrings consists of a square, openwork plaque decorated with palmettes in the corners and decorative forms in between. A polyhedral emerald is set in the center of each plaque, while at the bottom is a long, thin strip of gold that covers the suspensions rings to which the pendants are attached. Each pendant consists of a chain on which are hung red gemstones set in a gold mount with a pearl hung at the bottom. On the back of each earring, a suspension hook has been preserved, attached above two narrow bands set diagonally. This type of earring was very common in the Late Roman period. The earrings were created using the openwork technique and beaten gold. The main stones have not survived intact. The middle pendant on one of the earrings and two pearls are missing.

Selected bibliography
Cf. Deppert-Lippitz 1985: 23–24 no. 75; Geroulanou 1999: 275–77 nos. 447–57.

RING WITH SEMIPRECIOUS STONE BEZEL

1st–2nd century AD
Gold, semiprecious stone
Hoop: Diam. 3 cm
Bezel: Diam. base 1.3 cm
Karitsa. Northern cemetery. Kalamboukas field, grave 87.
Archaeological Museum of Dion, ΜΔ 8924

The flat hoop of this ring splays out to the shoulders and then narrows on either side where it meets the integral, parallelogram-shaped bezel. A raised, semiprecious stone with an insect, possibly a grasshopper, in relief is set in the center of the bezel. The beaten gold of this ring is in good condition, although the hoop is broken at the bottom.

The form taken by the stone, with its bands of color, shows that this was a talismanic ring. In the Roman period, stones destined for rings were shaped and polished rather than faceted (a technique known as the cabochon cut), or they were cut in the shape of a truncated cone with an elliptical base parallel to the bands on the gem, to give the impression of an eye as protection against the "evil eye."

Selected bibliography
Cf. Greifenhagen 1970: 48 no. 14.24; Deppert-Lippitz 1985: 30 no. 123.

74

75

TWO ALABASTRA (PERFUME BOTTLES)
Late 3rd–early 5th century AD
Glass
H. 16.2 cm; Diam. max. 4 cm
From Dion. Northern cemetery.
Archaeological Museum of Dion, ΜΔ 8925α, ΜΔ 8925β

Made in the shape of miniature amphorae with cylindrical bodies, these alabastra have horizontal shoulders, cylindrical necks, and funnel-shaped mouths with annular rims. Two vertical strap-handles spring from the shoulders and are bent back under the rim and attached to the sides of the neck. This type of glass vessel originated in the late third century AD and survived into the fifth century. These examples are mold-blown opaque white glass.

Products of a single workshop, these two identical alabastra were found in a female burial with other grave goods (see cat. no. 75). Unlike the dead woman's personal possessions, the perfume bottles were probably intended from the start to be used at the grave, either as containers of scented oils or as offerings from relatives of the deceased.

Selected bibliography
Pandermalis 2001: 350 fig. 13. Cf. Isings 1957: 157–58 type 127; Antonaras 2009: 224 type 74.

DIPSTICK
1st–2nd century AD
Glass
L. 22 cm; Diam. max. 2 cm
From Dion. Northern cemetery.
Archaeological Museum of Dion, ΜΔ 8926

Rods of this type originated in the Hellenistic period but later became widespread, above all in Roman times. This example is made of semi-opaque, greenish glass. The top of the twisted, tapering rod has a cone-shaped head, while the end tapers to a sharp point. These rods were often placed in the aperture in the glass spindle weights that served as stoppers for glass vessels. The "dipsticks" were used as stirrers and as droppers for applying perfumes and are mostly found as grave goods in female burials. The bottom tip and the very top of the head are missing from this example.

Selected bibliography
Pandermalis 2001: 350 fig. 12. Cf. Isings 1957: 94–95 type 79; Antonaras 2009: 330–32 type 148.

76

MINIATURIZED VESSEL WITH INCISED INSCRIPTION

Mid-2nd–4th century AD

Glass

H. 9 cm; Diam. 7.5 cm

Karitsa. Northern cemetery. Kalamboukas field, grave 48.

Archaeological Museum of Dion, MΔ 8927

This free-blown spherical vessel is made of transparent, plain glass. The body is decorated with four vertically aligned groups of concentric circles. Another two groups of circles are arranged horizontally to decorate the shoulders, creating between them a band in which a woman's name is inscribed in angular lettering: ΦΙΛΗΤΗϹ (of Filete).

Vessels of this type originated in the mid-second-century AD and remained in use up to the fourth century. The larger examples were mainly used as tableware, while the smaller ones were perfume bottles. This vessel from the Roman cemetery in Dion must have been one of Filete's personal possessions in her lifetime, and after her death was placed in her grave as a perfume bottle (*alabastron*), in accordance with the funerary customs of the day.

Selected bibliography

Pandermalis 2001: 349 fig. 3. Cf. Isings 1957: 121–22 type 103; Weinberg and McClellan 1992: 131–32; Whitehouse 1997: 177 nos. 310–11; Antonaras 2009: 190–92 type 50, 322–23 type 145, 350.

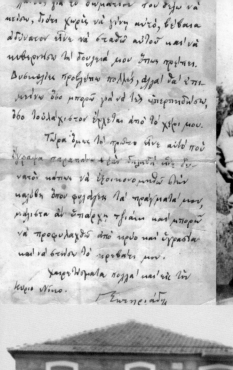

ΟΞΙΟΝΑ ΠΡΟΤΟΥ ΝΑΟΥ ΤΗ

ΝΔΕΕΙΚΟΝΑΣΤΗΣΑ ΕΝΠ

Ω ΤΕΜΕ Ξ ΡΤΟΥ ΔΙΟΣ ΤΟΥ

Ο ΛΥΜΠΟ ΟΥΕΛΕΣΟ ΑΙ ΔΕΚΑ

ΑΝΔΡΑΣ ΜΕΤΑΤΩΝ ΑΡΧΟΝΤ

BIBLIOGRAPHY

Adam-Veleni 2012: P. Adam-Veleni, ed. *Από τον Πλάτωνα στον Βολταίρο και τον Κοραή: Η Αρχαία Ελληνική Φιλοσοφία και ο Διαφωτισμός* [From Plato to Voltaire and Korais: The ancient Greek philosophy and the Enlightenment; Artworks from the Louvre Museum in Thessaloniki]. Thessaloniki, 2012.

Alexander 1965: J. Alexander. "The Spectacle Fibulae of Southern Europe." *American Journal of Archaeology* 69 (1965): 7–23.

Amandry 1998: M. Amandry. "Le monnayage de la Res Publica Coloniae Philippensium." *Stephanos nomismatikos: Edith Schönert-Geiss zum 65; Geburtstag*, ed. U. Peter, 23–31. Berlin, 1998.

Amandry 2015: M. Amandry. "Le monnayage de la Res Publica Coloniae Philippiensium: Nouvelles données." In *Fides: Contributions to Numismatics in Honor of Richard B. Witschonke*, ed. P. van Alfen, G. Bransbourg, and M. Amandry, 495–507. New York, 2015.

Andronikos 1969: M. Andronikos. *Βεργίνα I: Το Νεκροταφείον των Τύμβων* [Vergina I: The cemetery of tombs]. Βιβλιοθήκη της εν Αθήναις Αρχαιολογικής Εταιρείας [Library of the Archaeological Society in Athens] 62. Athens, 1969.

Antonaras 2009: A. Antonaras. *Ρωμαϊκή και παλαιοχριστιανική υαλουργία: 1ος αι. π.Χ.–6ος αι. μ.Χ.; Παραγωγή και προϊόντα; Τα αγγεία από τη Θεσσαλονίκη και την περιοχή της* [Roman and Early Christian glass working: Vessels from Thessaloniki and its region]. Athens, 2009.

Arvanitaki 2013: A. Arvanitaki. "Αρχαιότητες ρωμαϊκών χρόνων από την κεντρική Πιερία [Antiquities of Roman times in central Pieria]." *Το Αρχαιολογικό Έργο στη Μακεδονία και Θράκη* [Archaeological Work in Macedonia and Thrace Series] 23 (2009): 178–80.

Athanassiadi and Frede 1999: P. Athanassiadi and M. Frede, eds. *Pagan Monotheism in Late Antiquity*. Oxford, 1999.

Bailey 1988: D. Bailey. *A Catalogue of the Lamps in the British Museum*. Vol. 3, *Roman Provincial Lamps*. London, 1988.

Bailey 1996: D. Bailey. *Lamps of Metal and Stone, and Lampstands*. London, 1996.

Bakalakis 1964: G. Bakalakis. "Ανασκαφή Δίου [Excavations at Dion]." *Αρχαιολογικό Δελτίο: Χρονικά* [Archaeological Bulletin] 19 (1964).

Bakalakis 1966: G. Bakalakis. "Ανασκαφή Δίου [Excavations at Dion]." *Αρχαιολογικό Δελτίο: Χρονικά* [Archaeological Bulletin] 21 (1966).

Bakalakis 1968: G. Bakalakis. "Ανασκαφή Δίου [Excavations at Dion]." *Αρχαιολογικό Δελτίο: Χρονικά* [Archaeological Bulletin] 23 (1968).

Bakalakis 1969: G. Bakalakis. "Ανασκαφή Δίου [Excavations at Dion]." *Αρχαιολογικό Δελτίο: Χρονικά* [Archaeological Bulletin] 24 (1969).

Bakalakis 1971: G. Bakalakis. "Ανασκαφή Δίου [Excavations at Dion]." *Αρχαιολογικό Δελτίο: Χρονικά* [Archaeological Bulletin] 26 (1971).

Bakalakis 1982: G. Bakalakis. "Baphyras." In *Pro arte antiqua: Festschrift für Hedwig Kenner*, ed. E. Alföldi-Rosenbaum. Sonderschriften vom Österreichischen Archäologischen Institut in Wien 18, pt. 1, 28ff. Vienna, 1982.

Baumer 1997: L. E. Baumer. *Vorbilder und Vorlagen: Studien zu klassischen Frauenstatuen und ihrer Verwendung für Reliefs und Statuetten des 5. und 4. Jahrhunderts vor Christus*. Bern, 1997.

Beschi 1988: L. Beschi. "Demeter." In *Lexicon Iconographicum Mythologiae Classicae* (*LIMC*), vol. 4, 844–92. Zurich, 1988.

Bielfeldt 2014: R. Bielfeldt. "The Lure and Lore of Light: Roman Lamps in the Harvard Art Museums." In *Ancient Bronzes through a Modern Lens: Introductory Essays on the Study of Ancient Mediterranean and Near Eastern Bronzes*, ed. S. Ebbinghaus, 171–91. New Haven, 2014.

Bliquez 2015: L. Bliquez. *The Tools of Asclepius: Surgical Instruments in Greek and Roman Times*. Leiden, 2015.

Blümel 1931: C. Blümel. *Römische Kopien griechischer Skulpturen des fünften Jahrhunderts v. Chr.* Berlin, 1931.

Boardman 1970: J. Boardman. *Greek Gems and Finger Rings: Early Bronze Age to Late Classical*. London, 1970.

Boucher 1980: S. Boucher, ed. *Bronzes Antiques du Musée de la Civilisation Gallo-Romaine à Lyon*. Vol. 2, *Instrumentum-Aegyptiaca*. Lyon, 1980.

Bouzakis et al. 2008: K. D. Bouzakis et al. "Design and Manufacturing Aspects of a Vaginal Speculum of Antiquity, as Investigated by Computer Tomographies." *Journal of Archaeological Science* 35 (2008): 633–42.

Bouzek 1974: J. Bouzek. *The Attic Dark Age Incised Ware*. Prague, 1974.

Bouzek 1997: J. Bouzek. *Greece, Anatolia and Europe: Cultural Interrelations During the Early Iron Age*. Studies in Mediterranean Archaeology 122. Jonsered, 1997.

Bremmer 1987: J. N. Bremmer. "Myth and Ritual in Ancient Rome: The Nonae Capratinae." In *Roman Myth and Mythography*, ed. J. N. Bremmer and N. M. Horsfall, 76–88. Bulletin of the Institute of Classical Studies, supp. 52 (1987).

Bruneau 1964: P. Bruneau. "Apotropaia déliens: La massue d'Héraclès." *Bulletin de correspondance hellénique* 88 (1964): 159–68.

Bruneau 1965: P. Bruneau. *Exploration archéologique de Délos: Les Lampes*. Paris, 1965.

Burkert 1993: W. Burkert. *Αρχαία Ελληνική Θρησκεία*. Athens, 1993. Originally published as *Greek Religion*. Oxford, 1985.

Busch 2001: S. Busch. "Leider keine Göttin: Übersehene Senare aus Dion." *Zeitschrift für Papyrologie und Epigraphik* 137 (2001): 247–304.

de Callataÿ 2011: F. de Callataÿ. "More than It Would Seem: The Use of Coinage by the Romans in Late Hellenistic Asia Minor (133–63 BC)." *American Journal of Numismatics* 23 (2011): 55–86.

de Caro 1987: S. de Caro. "The Sculptures of the Villa of Poppaea at Oplontis: A Preliminary Report." In *Ancient Roman Villa Gardens*, ed. E. B. MacDougal, 77–133. Dumbarton Oaks Colloquium on the History of Landscape Architecture 10. Washington, DC, 1987.

Chaniotis 2010: A. Chaniotis. "Megatheism: The Search for the Almighty God and the Competition of Cults." In *One God: Pagan Monotheism in the Roman Empire*, ed. S. Mitchell and P. van Nuffelen, 112–40. Cambridge, 2010.

Christodoulou 2011: P. Christodoulou. "Les reliefs votifs du sanctuaire d'Isis à Dion." In *Bibliotheca Isiaca II*, ed. L. Bricault and R. Veymiers, 11–22. Bordeaux, 2011.

Christodoulou forthcoming: P. Christodoulou. "Δύο προτομές αγοριών με σκόλλυν από το Δίον [Two statues of boys with tufts from Dion]." In *Γλυπτική και κοινωνία στη Ρωμαϊκή Ελλάδα: Καλλιτεχνικά προϊόντα, κοινωνικές προβολές; Διεθνές Αρχαιολογικό Συνέδριο, Ρέθυμνο* [Sculpture and society in Roman Greece: Artistic production, social projections]. International Archaeological Congress, Rethymnon, 2014. Forthcoming.

Chrysostomou 2003: P. Chrysostomou. "Συνεισφορές σε λατρείες θεο τή των και ηρώων από την Βοττιαία και την Πιερία της Μακεδονίας [Studies on the worship of deities and heroes from Boeotia and Pieria, Macedonia]." *Ευλιμένη* 4 (2003): 135–52.

Clairmont 1993: C. Clairmont. *Classical Attic Tombstones*. Supp. vol. Kilchberg, 1993.

Claridge 1990: A. Claridge. "Ancient Techniques of Making Joins in Marble Statuary." In *Marble: Art Historical and Scientific Perspectives on Ancient Sculpture*, ed. M. True and J. Podany, 135–62. Malibu, CA, 1990.

Clinton 1992: K. Clinton. *Myth and Cult: The Iconography of the Eleusinian Mysteries; The Martin P. Nilsson Lectures on Greek Religion.* Swedish Institute at Athens, 1990. Stockholm, 1992.

Conticello de Spagnolis and de Carolis 1988: M. Conticello de Spagnolis and E. de Carolis. *Le lucerne di bronzo di Ercolano e Pompei.* Rome, 1988.

Cormack 1970: J. M. R. Cormack. "Inscriptions from Pieria." *Klio* 52 (1970): 49–66.

Crawford 1974: M. H. Crawford. *Roman Republican Coinage.* London, 1974.

Davison 2009: C. C. Davison. *Pheidias: The Sculptures and Ancient Sources.* Bulletin of the Institute of Classical Studies, supp. 105. London, 2009.

Demaille 2008: J. Demaille. "Les P. Anthestii: Une famille d'affranchis dans l'élite municipale de la colonie romaine de Dion." In *La fin du statut servile? (affranchissement, libération, abolition)*, ed. A. Gonzales, 183–202. Actes du XXXème colloque du GIREA, Besançon, 2005. Besançon, 2008.

Demaille 2015: J. Demaille 2015. "Esclaves et affranchis sur le territoire de la colonie romaine de Dion (Piérie, Macédoine)." In *Los espacios de la esclavitud y la dependencia desde antigüedad*, ed. A. Beltrán, I. Sastre, and M. Valdés, 537–59. Actas del XXXV colloquio de GIREA, 2015. Besançon, 2015.

Deonna 1908: W. Deonna. "Les lampes antiques trouvées à Délos." *Bulletin de Correspondance Hellénique* 32 (1908): 133–36.

Deppert-Lippitz 1985: B. Deppert-Lippitz. *Griechischer Goldschmuck.* Mainz am Rhein, 1985.

Despinis 1997: G. Despinis. *Κατάλογος Γλυπτών του Αρχαιολογικού Μουσείου Θεσσαλονίκης* [Catalogue of sculpture in the Archaeological Museum of Thessaloniki]. Vol. 1. Thessaloniki, 1997.

Despinis, Stefanidou-Tiveriou, and Voutiras 1997: G. Despinis, T. Stefanidou-Tiveriou, and E. Voutiras. *Κατάλογος Γλυπτών του Αρχαιολογικού Μουσείου Θεσσαλονίκης, I* [Catalogue of sculptures from the Archaeological Museum of Thessaloniki, I]. Thessaloniki, 1987.

Dowden 2006: K. Dowden. *Zeus.* London, 2006.

Droste 2001: M. Droste. *Die Asklepiaden: Untersuchungen zur Ikonographie und Bedeutung.* Aachen, 2001.

Dunand 1973: F. Dunand. *Le culte d'Isis dans le bassin oriental de la Méditerranée.* Vol. 2, *Le culte d'Isis en Grèce.* Leiden, 1973.

Edelstein and Edelstein 1945: E. J. L. Edelstein and L. Edelstein. *Asclepius: A Collection and Interpretation of the Testimonies.* 1945; Baltimore, 1998.

Faraone 2013: C. A. Faraone. *Vanishing Acts: Deletio Morbi as Speech Act and Visual Design on Ancient Greek Amulets.* Bulletin of the Institute of Classical Studies, supp. 115. London, 2013.

Farnoux 1992: A. Farnoux. "Lykourgos I." In *Lexicon Iconographicum Mythologiae Classicae (LIMC)*, vol. 6, pt. 1, 309–19. Zurich, 1992.

Farraguna 1998: M. Farraguna. "Aspetti amministrativi e finanziari della monarchia macedone tra IVe III secolo a.C." *Athenaeum* 86 (1998): 375–78.

Gaebler 1935: H. Gaebler. *Die antiken Münzen von Makedonia und Paionia.* Die antiken Münzen Nord-Griechenlands 3. Berlin, 1935.

Geroulanou 1999: A. Geroulanou. *Διάτρητα: Τα διάτρητα χρυσά κοσμήματα από τον 3ο έως τον 7ο αιώνα μ.Χ* [Diatrita: Gold pierced-work jewelry from the 3rd to the 7th century]. Athens, 1999.

Giuman 1999a: M. Giuman. *La dea, la vergine, il sangue: Archeologia di un culto femminile.* Milan, 1999.

Giuman 1999b: M. Giuman. "Metamorfosi di una dea: da Artemide ad Iside in un Santuario di Dion." *Ostraka* 8 (1999): 427–46.

Goulaki 1981: A. Goulaki. "Klassische und klassizistische Nikedarstellungen." Diss., University of Bonn, 1981.

Graf 1984: F. Graf. *Nordionische Kulte: Religionsgeschichtliche und epigraphische Untersuchungen zu den Kulten von Chios, Erythrai, Klazomenai und Phokaia.* Rome, 1984.

Greifenhagen 1970: A. Greifenhagen. *Schmuckarbeiten in Edelmetall.* Vol. 1, *Fundgruppen.* Staatliche Museen Preussischer Kulturbesitz, Antikenabteilung 1. Berlin, 1970.

Hatzopoulos 2000: M. Hatzopoulos. "Le lac Pyrrolia en Macedoine." *Τεκμήρια* 5 (2000): 65–70.

Hatzopoulos 2013: M. Hatzopoulos. "Was Dion Macedonia's Religious Centre?" In *Greek Federal States and Their Sanctuaries: Identity and Integration*, ed. P. Funke and M. Haake, 163–72. Proceedings of an International Conference of the Cluster of Excellence "Religion and Politics," Münster, 2010. Stuttgart, 2013.

Havela 2012: K. Havela. "Τα ταφικά έθιμα ως δείκτης διακοινοτικών και διαπολιτισμικών επαφών στο χώρο της Κεντρικής Μακεδονίας κατά την Εποχή του Σιδήρου [Iron Age burial customs as markers of intercommunal and intercultural contacts in Central Macedonia]." In *Athanasia: The Earthly, the Celestial and the Underworld in the Mediterranean from the Late Bronze and the Early Iron Age*, ed. N. Stampolides, 305–22. International Archaeological Conference, Rhodes, 2009. Heraklion, 2012.

Heyob 1975: S. K. Heyob. *The Cult of Isis among Women in the Graeco-Roman World*. Leiden, 1975.

Heuzey and Daumet 1876: L. Heuzey and H. Daumet. *Mission archéologique de Macédoine*. Paris, 1876.

Higgins 1967: R. A. Higgins. *Greek Terracottas*. London, 1967.

Horsley 1994: G. H. R. Horsley. "A Bilingual Funerary Monument in *kionedon* Form from Dion in Northern Greece." *Chiron* 24 (1994): 209–19.

Howgego, Heuchert, and Burnett 2005: C. Howgego, V. Heuchert, and A. Burnett, eds. *Coinage and Identity in the Roman Provinces*. Oxford, 2005.

Howland 1958: R. H. Howland. *The Athenian Agora: Results of Excavations Conducted by the American School of Classical Studies at Athens*. Vol. 4, *Greek Lamps and Their Survivals*. Princeton, 1958.

Hurst and Schachter 1996: A. Hurst and A. Schachter, eds. *La montagne des Muses*. Geneva, 1996.

Isings 1957: C. Isings. *Roman Glass from Dated Finds*. Groningen, 1957.

Jackson 2006: M. M. Jackson. *Hellenistic Gold Eros Jewellery: Technique, Style and Chronology*. BAR International Series 1510. Oxford, 2006.

Jackson 1990: R. Jackson. "Roman Doctors and Their Instruments: Recent Research into Ancient Practice." *Journal of Roman Archaeology* 3 (1990): 5–27.

Jones 1935: W. H. S. Jones, trans. *Pausanias: Description of Greece*. Vol. 4. London, 1935.

Josifovski 2001: P. Josifovski. *Rimskata monetarnica vo Stobi* [Roman mint of Stobi]. Skopje, 2001.

Kabus-Preisshofen 1989: R. Kabus-Preisshofen. *Die hellenistische Plastik der Insel Kos*. Mitteilungen des Deutschen Archäologischen Instituts, Athenische Abteilung 14. Berlin, 1989.

Kagan 2006: J. Kagan. "Small Change and the Beginning of Coinage at Abdera." In *Agoranomia: Studies in Money and Exchange Presented to John H. Kroll*, ed. P. van Alfen, 49–60. New York, 2006.

Kakrides 1986a: I. Th. Kakrides. Ελληνική μυθολογία [Greek mythology]. Vol. 2, *Hoi theoi* [The gods]. Athens, 1986.

Kakrides 1986b: I. Th. Kakrides. Ελληνική μυθολογία [Greek mythology]. Vol. 3, *Hoi heroes* [The heroes]. Athens, 1986.

Käppel 1992: L. Käppel. *Paian: Studien zur Geschichte einer Gattung*. Berlin, 1992.

Karaghiorga-Stathakopoulou 1986: T. Karaghiorga-Stathakopoulou. "Demeter." In *Lexicon Iconographicum Mythologiae Classicae* (*LIMC*), vol. 3, 88. Zurich, 1986.

Karasmanis 2005: B. Karasmanis. "Η αρχαία ύδραυλις και η ανακατασκευή της" [The ancient hydraulis and its reconstruction]. Αρχαιολογία και Τέχνες [Archaeology and Arts] 95 (2005): 61–67.

Karadedos 1983: G. Karadedos. "Το ελληνιστικό θέατρο του Δίου" [The Hellenistic theater at Dion]. Αρχαία Μακεδονία [Ancient Macedonia] *IV*, 1983, 235f.

Karadedos 1991: G. Karadedos. Τελευταία στοιχεία για τη σκηνή του ελληνιστικού θεάτρου του Δίου [Latest figures for the scene of the Hellenistic theater at Dion]. Το Αρχαιολογικό Έργο στη Μακεδονία και Θράκη [Archaeological Work in Macedonia and Thrace Series] 5 (1991), 157ff.

Kondoleon 1994: C. Kondoleon. *Domestic and Divine: Roman Mosaics in the House of Dionysos*. Ithaca, 1994.

Kremydi 1996: S. Kremydi. *Η νομισματοκοπία της ρωμαϊκής αποικίας του Δίου* [The coinage from the Roman colony of Dion]. Athens, 1996.

Kremydi 2002: S. Kremydi. "Οι κοπές των πόλεων στους αυτοκρατορικούς χρόνους. το παράδειγμα της Μακεδονίας [Civic issues during imperial times: The case of Macedonia]." Η ιστορική διαδρομή της νομισματικής μονάδας στην Ελλάδα, Εθνικό Ίδρυμα Ερευνών [Studies in the history of numismatic units in Greece, National Hellenic Research Foundation], 47–62. Athens, 2002.

Kremydi 2011: S. Kremydi. "Coinage and Finance." In *Brill's Companion to Ancient Macedon: Studies in the Archaeology and History of Macedon, 650 BC–300 AD*, ed. R. J. Lane Fox, 159–78. Leiden, 2011.

Kremydi and Marcellesi forthcoming: S. Kremydi and M.-C. Marcellesi, eds. *Les Alexandres après Alexandre: Histoire d'une monnaie commune, Athens*. Meletemata Series, Institute of Historical Research. Athens, forthcoming.

Kremydi-Sicilianou 1996: S. Kremydi-Sicilianou. *Η νομισματοκοπία της ρωμαϊκής αποικίας του Δίου* [The coinage from the Roman colony of Dion]. Bibliotheca of the Hellenic Numismatic Society 4. Athens, 1996.

Kremydi-Sicilianou 2002: S. Kremydi-Sicilianou. "Victoria Augusta on Macedonian Coins: Remarks on Dating and Interpretation." *Tekmeria* 7 (2002): 63–84.

Kurtz and Boardman 1971: D. Kurtz and J. Boardman. *Greek Burial Customs*. Ithaca, 1971.

Langdon 1976: M. K. Langdon. *A Sanctuary of Zeus on Mount Hymettos*. Hesperia, supp. 16. Princeton, 1976.

Lattimore 2011: R. Lattimore, trans. *The Iliad of Homer*. Chicago, 2011.

Leake 1967: W. M. Leake. *Travels in Northern Greece*. Vol. 3. 1835. London, 1967.

Lesky 2008: A. Lesky. Ιστορία της αρχαίας ελληνικής λογοτεχνίας [History of ancient Greek literature]. Thessaloniki, 2008.

Mallwitz 1972: A. Mallwitz. *Olympia und seine Bauten*. Darmstadt, 1972.

Mallwitz 1988: A. Mallwitz. "Cult and Competition Locations at Olympia." In *The Archaeology of the Olympics: The Olympics and Other Festivals in Antiquity*, ed. W. Raschke, 79–109. Madison, 1988.

Marcadé 1984: J. Marcadé. "La lampe au nègre de Bordeneuve-de-Bory." In *Alessandria e il mondo ellenistico romano: Studi in onore di Achille Adriani*, ed. G. Barone et al., vol. 3, 445–48. Rome, 1984.

Mari 1988: M. Mari. "Le Olimpie Macedoni di Dion tra Archelao e l'età Romana." *Rivista difilologia ed istruzione classica* 126 (1988): 137–69.

Mari 2002: M. Mari. "Al di là dell'Olimpo: Macedoni e grandi santuari della Grecia dall'età arcaica al primo ellenismo." *Melethemata* 34. Paris, 2002.

Markovits 2003: Michael Markovits. *Die Orgel im Altertum*. Leiden, 2003.

Marshall 1968: F. H. Marshall. *Catalogue of the Finger Rings, Greek, Etruscan, and Roman, in the Departments of Antiquities, British Museum*. London, 1968.

Marshall 1969: F. H. Marshall. *Catalogue of the Jewellery, Greek, Etruscan, and Roman, in the Departments of Antiquities, British Museum*. London, 1969.

Meijer 2007: P. A. Meijer. *Stoic Theology: Proofs for the Existence of the Cosmic God and of the Traditional Gods; Including a Commentary on Cleanthes' Hymn on Zeus*. Delft, 2007.

Melville-Jones 1986: J. R. Melville-Jones. *A Dictionary of Ancient Greek Coins*. London, 1986.

Milne 1907: J. S. Milne. *Surgical Instruments in Greek and Roman Times*. London, 1907.

Most 2006: G. W. Most, ed. and trans. *Hesiod: Theogony; Works and Days; Testimonia*. Cambridge, MA, 2006.

Nigdelis 2010: P. Nigdelis. "Voluntary Associations in Roman Thessaloniki." In *From Roman to Early Christian Thessalonike*, ed. L. Nasrallah, Ch. Bakirtzis, and S. J. Friesen, 333–59. Harvard Theological Studies 64. Cambridge, MA, 2010.

Nilsson 1955: M. Nilsson. *Geschichte der griecbichen Religion: In systematischer Darstellung mit besonderer Rücksicht auf Geschichte und Methodik der einzelnen Disziplinen*. Vol. 1, *Die Religion Griechenlands bis auf die griechische Weltherrschaft*. Munich, 1955.

Nowicki 2001: K. Nowicki. "Minoan Peak Sanctuaries: Reassessing Their Origins." In *Potnia: Deities and Religion in the Aegean Bronze Age*, ed. R. Laffineur and R. Hägg, 31–38. Proceedings of the 8th International Aegean Conference/8e Rencontre égéenne internationale, Göteborg University, 2000. Liege and Austin, TX, 2001.

Oikonomos 1915: G. P. Oikonomos. Επιγραφαί της Μακεδονίας [Inscriptions of Macedonia]. Athens, 1915.

Olson 2008: K. Olson. *Dress and the Roman Woman: Self-Presentation and Society*. London, 2008.

Orlandos 1958: A. Orlandos. Τα υλικά δομής των αρχαίων Ελλήνων [The building materials of the ancient Greeks]. Vol. 2. Athens, 1958.

Pandermalis 1973: D. Pandermalis. "Λατρείες και ιερά του Δίου Πιερίας [Cults and temples at Dion, Pieria]." In Αρχαία Μακεδονία [Ancient Macedonia], vol. 2, 331ff. Thessaloniki, 1973.

Pandermalis 1977: D. Pandermalis. "Λατρείες και ιερά του Δίου Πιερίας [Cults and temples at Dion, Pieria]." In Αρχαία Μακεδονία: Διεθνές Συμπόσιο II [Ancient Macedonia, International Symposium II], 331–42. Papers delivered at the Second International Symposium, Institute for Balkan Studies, Thessaloniki, 1977. Thessaloniki, 1977.

Pandermalis 1981: D. Pandermalis. "Inscriptions from Dion: Addenda et corrigenda." In *Ancient Macedonian Studies in Honour of Charles F. Edson*, ed. H. Dell, 283–94. Thessaloniki, 1981.

Pandermalis 1982: D. Pandermalis. "Ein neues Heiligtum in Dion." *Archäologischer Anzeiger* (1982): 727–35.

Pandermalis 1984a: D. Pandermalis. Δίον Η ιερή πόλη των Μακεδόνων στους πρόποδες του Ολύμπου [Dion: The sacred city of the Macedonians at the foot of Mount Olympus]. Thessaloniki, 1984.

Pandermalis 1984b: D. Pandermalis. "Οι επιγραφές του Δίου [The inscriptions from Dion]." Πρακτικά του Η΄ Διεθνούς Συνεδρίου Ελληνικής και Λατινικής Επιγραφικής [Proceedings of the International Congress of Greek and Latin Epigraphy], Athens, 1982, 271–77. Athens, 1984.

Pandermalis 1985: D. Pandermalis. "Οι μακεδονικοί τάφοι της Πιερίας [The Macedonian tombs of Pieria]." In Οι Αρχαιολόγοι μιλούν για την Πιερία [Archaeologists talk about Pieria], 9–13. Thessaloniki, 1985.

Pandermalis 1987: D. Pandermalis. "Η ανασκαφή μιας αίθουσας συμποσίων στο Δίον [The excavation of a banqueting hall at Dion]." Το Αρχαιολογικό Έργο στη Μακεδονία και Θράκη [Archaeological Work in Macedonia and Thrace series] 1 (1987): 181–88.

Pandermalis 1988a: D. Pandermalis. "Η ανασκαφή του Δίου [Excavations at Dion]." Το Αρχαιολογικό Έργο στη Μακεδονία και στη Θράκη [Archaeological Work in Macedonia and Thrace Series] 2: (1988): 147–50.

Pandermalis 1988b: D. Pandermalis. "Αντίγραφα των αυτοκρατορικών χρόνων στη Μακεδονία [Copies of the imperial period in Macedonia]." In *Πρακτικά του XII Διεθνούς Συνεδρίου Κλασικής Αρχαιολογίας* [Proceedings of the XII International Congress of Classical Archaeology], Athens, 1983, vol. 3, 213–16. Athens, 1988.

Pandermalis 1989a: D. Pandermalis. "Δίον: Ο τομέας της έπαυλης του Διονύσου το 1989 [Dion: The sector of the Dionysus Villa 1989]." *To Αρχαιολογικό Έργο στη Μακεδονία και στη Θράκη* [Archaeological Work in Macedonia and Thrace Series] 3, no. 1 (1989): 141–48.

Pandermalis 1989b: D. Pandermalis. "Το νεκροταφείο των τύμβων [The cemetery of the tumuli]." *Αρχαιολογία* [Archaeology] 33 (1989): 4–53.

Pandermalis 1990: D. Pandermalis. "Στους δρόμους και τα εργαστήρια του Δίου [The streets and workshops of Dion]." In *Οι αρχαιολόγοι μιλούν για την Πιερία* [Archaeologists talk about Pieria] (1986), 10–15. NELE Pieria, 1990.

Pandermalis 1992: D. Pandermalis. "Η ύδραυλις του Δίου [The hydraulis of Dion]." *To Αρχαιολογικό Έργο στη Μακεδονία και στη Θράκη* [Archaeological Work in Macedonia and Thrace Series] 6, no. 1 (1992): 217–22.

Pandermalis 1993: D. Pandermalis. "Η ανασκαφή του Δίου κατά το 1993 και η χάλκινη διόπτρα [The excavation of Dion in 1993 and the bronze speculum]." *To Αρχαιολογικό Έργο στη Μακεδονία και στη Θράκη* [Archaeological Work in Macedonia and Thrace Series] 7, no. 1 (1993): 195–99.

Pandermalis 1994: D. Pandermalis. "Ανασκαφή του Δίου κατά το 1994 και το ανάγλυφο της νάβλας [The excavations at Dion in 1994 and the relief with the nabla]." *To Αρχαιολογικό Έργο στη Μακεδονία και στη Θράκη* [Archaeological Work in Macedonia and Thrace Series] 8, no. 1 (1994): 131–36.

Pandermalis 1995: D. Pandermalis. "Ανασκαφή Δίου 1995 [Dion excavation, 1995]." *To Αρχαιολογικό Έργο στη Μακεδονία και στη Θράκη* [Archaeological Work in Macedonia and Thrace Series] 9, no. 1 (1995): 167–72.

Pandermalis 1996: D. Pandermalis. "Δίον: Η δεκαετία των ανασκαφών [Dion: Ten years' excavation], 1987–1997." *To Αρχαιολογικό Έργο στη Μακεδονία και στη Θράκη* [Archaeological Work in Macedonia and Thrace Series] 10, no. A (1996): 205–14.

Pandermalis 1997a: D. Pandermalis. Δίον: Αρχαιολογικός χώρος και Μουσείο [Dion: The archaeological site and the museum]. Athens, 1997.

Pandermalis 1997b: D. Pandermalis. "Δίον 1997: Ο επιστάτης, οι Πελειγάνες και οι λοιποί πολίτες [Dion 1997: The epistates, the peleiganes, and other citizens]. *To Αρχαιολογικό Έργο στη Μακεδονία και στη Θράκη* [Archaeological Work in Macedonia and Thrace Series] 11 (1997): 233–40.

Pandermalis 1998: D. Pandermalis. "Δίον 1998: Εκατόμβες και Σωτήρια [Dion 1998: Hecatombs and mysteries]." *To Αρχαιολογικό Έργο στη Μακεδονία και στη Θράκη* [Archaeological Work in Macedonia and Thrace Series] 12 (1998): 291–98.

Pandermalis 1999a: D. Pandermalis. *Δίον: Η ανακάλυψη* [Dion: The discovery]. Athens, 1999.

Pandermalis 1999b: D. Pandermalis. "Δίον 1999: Μουσαϊσταί—Βασιλεύς Δημήτριος [Dion 1999: The Mousaïstaí and King Demetrius]." *To Αρχαιολογικό Έργο στη Μακεδονία και στη Θράκη* [Archaeological Work in Macedonia and Thrace series] 13, no. 1 (1999): 415–23.

Pandermalis 2000: D. Pandermalis. *Discovering Dion*. Athens, 2000.

Pandermalis 2001: D. Pandermalis. "Δίέων ύαλα σκεύη [Glass vessels of Dion]." *To Αρχαιολογικό Έργο στη Μακεδονία και στη Θράκη* [Archaeological Work in Macedonia and Thrace Series] 15, no. 1 (2001): 347–54.

Pandermalis 2002: D. Pandermalis. "Δίον 2000 [Dion 2000]." *To Αρχαιολογικό Έργο στη Μακεδονία και στη Θράκη* [Archaeo-logical work in Macedonia and Thrace series] 14 (2002): 381f.

Pandermalis 2003: D. Pandermalis. "Ζεύς ύψιστος και άλλα [Zeus Hypsistos and others]." *To Αρχαιολογικό Έργο στη Μακεδονία και στη Θράκη* [Archaeological Work in Macedonia and Thrace Series] 17, no. 1 (2003): 417–24.

Pandermalis 2006: D. Pandermalis. "Δίον 2006 [Dion 2006]." *To Αρχαιολογικό Έργο στη Μακεδονία και στη Θράκη* [Archaeological Work in Macedonia and Thrace Series] 20, no. 1 (2006): 567–75.

Pandermalis 2009: D. Pandermalis. "Δίον, Ιστορικά και Λατρευτικά " [Dion, history and worship]. In *To Αρχαιολογικό Έργο στη Μακεδονία και στη Θράκη 20 χρόνια* [Archaeological Work in Macedonia and Thrace Series, Twenty Years], 261–71. Thessaloniki, 2009.

Papaefthymiou 2002: E. Papaefthymiou. *Édessa de Macedoine: Étude historique et numismatique*. Athens, 2002.

Papageorgiou 2011: P. Papageorgiou. "Μια ξακουστή γιατρός στο αρχαίο Δίον [A famous doctor in ancient Dion]." In *Νάματα: τιμητικός τόμος για τον καθηγητή Δημήτριο Παντερμαλή* [Namata: Volume in honor of Dimitrios Pandermalis], ed. S. Pingiatoglou and T. Stefanidou-Tiveriou, 249–56. Thessaloniki, 2011.

Papazoglou 1988: F. Papazoglou. *Les villes de Macédoine l'epoque romaine*. Paris, 1988.

Parker 2011: R. Parker. "The Thessalian Olympia." *Zeitschrift für Papyrologie und Epigraphik* 177 (2011): 111–18.

Peatfield 1990: A. A. D. Peatfield. "Minoan Peak Sanctuaries: History and Society." *Opuscula Atheniensia* 18 (1990): 117–31.

Pfrommer 1990: M. Pfrommer. *Untersuchungen zur Chronologie friihund hochhellenistischen Goldschmucks*. Istanbuler Forschungen 37. Tubingen, 1990.

Picard 2006: O. Picard. "Mines, monnaies et impérialisme: Conflits autour du Pangée (478–413 av. J.-Chr.)." In *Rois, cités, nécropoles: Institutions, rites et monuments en Macédoine*, ed. M. B. Hatzopoulos et al. Actes des colloques de Nanterre, 2002, et d'Athènes, 2004. Meletemata 45, 269–82. Athens, 2006.

Picard 2010: O. Picard. "Rome et la Grèce à la basse époque hellénistique: Monnaies et impérialisme." *Journal des Savants* 2010: 161–92.

Pingiatoglou 1981: S. Pingiatoglou. *Eileithyia*. Wurzburg, 1981.

Pingiatoglou 1990: S. Pingiatoglou. "Το ιερό της Δήμητρας στο Δίον: Ανασκαφή 1990 [The sanctuary of Demeter at Dion: 1990 excavations]." Το *Αρχαιολογικό Έργο στη Μακεδονία και στη Θράκη* [Archaeological Work in Macedonia and Thrace Series] 4 (1990): 205–15.

Pingiatoglou 1999: S. Pingiatoglou. "Η λατρεία της θεάς Δήμητρας στην Αρχαία Μακεδονία [The cult of the goddess Demeter in ancient Macedonia." In *Αρχαία Μακεδονία VI: Διεθνές Συμπόσιο* 1996 [Ancient Macedonia VI: International Symposium, 1996], vol. 2, 911–19. Thessaloniki, 1999.

Pingiatoglou 2005: S. Pingiatoglou. *Δίον: Το ιερό της Δήμητρος; Οι λύχνοι* [Dion: The sanctuary of Demeter; Lamps]. Thessaloniki, 2005.

Pingiatoglou 2010a: S. Pingiatoglou. "Cults of Female Deities at Dion." *Kernos* 23 (2010): 179–92.

Pingiatoglou 2010b: S. Pingiatoglou. "Το ιερό της Δήμητρος στο Δίον [The sanctuary of Demeter at Dion]." In *Ιερά και λατρείες της Δήμητρας στον αρχαίο ελληνικό κόσμο* (Πρακτικά Επιστημονικού Συμποσίου, Πανεπιστήμιο Θεσσαλίας, Βόλος) [Sanctuaries and cults of Demeter in the ancient Greek world], 201–24. Proceedings of the Scientific Symposium, University of Thessaly, 2005. Bolos, 2010.

Pingiatoglou 2011: S. Pingiatoglou. Catalogue entries. In *Au royaume d'Alexandre le Grand: La Macédoine antique*, ed. S. Descamps-Lequime et al. Exhibition catalogue, Musée du Louvre, Paris, 2011–12. Paris, 2011.

Pingiatoglou 2014: S. Pingiatoglou. "Das religiöse Leben in Dion von den Anfängen bis in augusteische Zeit." In *Marburger Winckelmann-Programm 2014*, ed. R. Amedick, H. Froning, and W. Held, 49–56. Marburg, 2014.

Pingiatoglou 2015: S. Pingiatoglou. *Δίον: Το ιερό της Δήμητρος* [Dion: The sanctuary of Demeter]. Thessaloniki, 2015.

Pingiatoglou et al. 2009: S. Pingiatoglou, K. Vasteli, E. Pavlopoulou, and D. Tsiafis. "Δίον 2007–2009: Ανασκαφικές έρευνες στο οικοδομικό τετράγωνο της αρχαίας αγοράς [Dion 2007–2009: Excavations in the block of the ancient agora]." Το *Αρχαιολογικό Έργο στη Μακεδονία και στη Θράκη* [Archaeological Work in Macedonia and Thrace Series] 23 (2009): 141ff.

Polacco 1989: L. Polacco. "Transe non-dionysiaque dans le théâtre grec." In *Transe et théâtre*, 55–62. Actes de la table ronde internationale, Montpellier, 1988. Montpellier, 1989.

Polacco 1990: L. Polacco. *Il teatro antico di Siracusa*. Padua, 1990.

Poulaki-Pandermali 1997: E. Poulaki-Pandermali. "Μακεδονίς Γη [The land of Macedonia]." In *Αφιέρωμα στον N. Hammond* Παράρτημα Μακεδονικών αρ. 7 [Tribute to N. Hammond; Macedonian Supplement, no. 7], 365–87. Thessaloniki, 1997.

Poulaki-Pandermali 2013: E. Poulaki-Pandermali. *Μακεδονικός Όλυμπος: Μύθος—Ιστορία—Αρχαιολογία, Θεσσαλονίκη; ΚΖ' Εφορεία Προϊστορικών και Κλασικών Αρχαιοτήτων* [Macedonian Olympus: Myth—History—Archaeology; Thessaloniki, 27th Ephorate of Prehistoric and Classical Antiquities]. Thessaloniki, 2013.

Price 1991: M. J. Price. *The Coinage in the Name of Alexander the Great and Philip Arrhidaeus: A British Museum Catalogue*. London, 1991.

Rhomiopoulou and Kilian-Dirlmeier 1989: K. Rhomiopoulou and I. Kilian-Dirlmeier. "Neue Funde aus der eisenzeitlichen Hügelnekropole von Vergina, Griechisch Makedonien." *Prähistorische Zeitschrift* 64 (1989): 86–145.

Richardson 1974: N. Richardson. *The Homeric Hymn to Demeter*. Oxford, 1974.

Richter 1915: G. M. A. Richter. *Greek, Etruscan and Roman Bronzes*. New York, 1915.

Richter 1966: G. M. A. Richter. *The Furniture of the Greeks, Etruscans and Romans*. London, 1966.

Rigsby 1994: K. J. Rigsby. "Graecolatina." *Zeitschrift für Papyrologie und Epigraphik* 102 (1994): 191–93.

Robens et al. 2014: E. Robens et al. *Balances: Instruments, Manufacturers, History*. Heidelberg, 2014.

Robert 1949: L. Robert. *Hellenica* 7 (1949): 126–28.

Robinson 1933: D. M. Robinson. *Excavations at Olynthus*. Vol. 7, *The Terra-cottas of Olynthus Found in 1931*. Baltimore, 1933.

Romano and Voyatzis 2010: D. G. Romano and M. E. Voyatzis. "Excavating at the Birthplace of Zeus." *Expedition* 52 (2010): 9–21.

Rubensohn 1895: O. Rubensohn. "Demeter als Heilgottheit." *MDAI(A)* 20 (1895): 360–67.

Sakellarakis 1976: J. A. Sakellarakis. "Kretisch-mykenische Siegel in griechischen Heiligtümern." In *Neue Forschungen in griechischen Heiligtümern*, ed. U. Jantzen, 283–308. Internationales Symposion in Olympia, 1974. Tübingen, 1976.

Samana 2003: É. Samama. *Les médecins dans le monde grec: Sources épigraphiques sur la naissance d'un corps médical*. Geneva, 2003.

Šašel Kos 1979: M. Šašel Kos. *Inscriptiones Latinae in Graecia repertae: Additamenta ad CIL III*. Faenza, 1979.

Scheibler 1976: I. Scheibler. *Griechische Lampen*. Kerameikos: Ergebnisse der Ausgrabungen 11. Berlin, 1976.

Schrader 1941: H. Schrader. *Das Zeusbild des Pheidias in Olympia*. Berlin, 1941.

Seaford 2006: R. Seaford. *Dionysos*. London, 2006.

Simon 1996: E. Simon. *Οι θεοί των αρχαίων Ελλήνων*. Thessaloniki, 1996. Originally published as *Die Götter der Griechen*. Zurich, 1969.

Sismanides 1997: K. Sismanides. *Κλίνες και κλινοειδείς κατασκευές των μακεδονικών τάφων* [Beds and funerary klinai of Macedonian tombs]. Athens, 1997.

SNG 2000: Sylloge Nummorum Graecorum, Greece 2. *The Alpha Bank Collection* (Macedonia 1: Alexander 1– Perseus). Athens, 2000.

Snowden 1970: F. M. Snowden. *Blacks in Antiquity: Ethiopians in the Greco-Roman Experience*. Cambridge, MA, 1970.

Soteriades 1928: G. Soteriades. "Ανασκαφή Δίου (Excavations at Dion)." *Πρακτικά Αρχαιολογικής Εταιρείας* [Proceedings of the Archaeological Society] 83 (1928): 59–85.

Soteriades 1929: G. Soteriades. "Ανασκαφή Δίου (Excavations at Dion)." *Πρακτικά Αρχαιολογικής Εταιρείας* [Proceedings of the Archaeological Society] 84 (1929): 69–82.

Soteriades 1930: G. Soteriades. "Ανασκαφή Δίου (Excavations at Dion)." *Πρακτικά Αρχαιολογικής Εταιρείας* [Proceedings of the Archaeological Society] 85 (1930): 36–51.

Soteriades 1931: G. Soteriades. "Ανασκαφή Δίου (Excavations at Dion)." *Πρακτικά Αρχαιολογικής Εταιρείας* [Proceedings of the Archaeological Society] 86 (1931): 43–55.

Sourvinou-Inwood 1988: C. Sourvinou-Inwood. *Studies in Girls' Transitions: Aspects of the Arkteia and Age Representation in Attic Iconography*. Athens, 1988.

de Spagnolis and de Carolis 1983: M. de Spagnolis and E. de Carolis. *Museo nazionale romano: 4, 1, bronzi; 1, Le lucerne*. Rome, 1983.

Spier 1992: J. Spier. *Ancient Gems and Finger Rings: Catalogue of the Collection*. Malibu, CA, 1992.

Stefanidou-Tiveriou 1975: T. Stefanidou-Tiveriou. "Επιτύμβια στήλη από το Δίον Πιερίας [Tombstone from Dion, Pieria]." *Αρχαιολογικό Δελτίο: Μελέτα* [Archaeological Bulletin: Studies] 30 (1975): 35–44.

Stefanidou-Tiveriou 1993: T. Stefanidou-Tiveriou. *Τραπεζοφόρα με πλαστική διακόσμηση: Η Αττική Ομάδα* [Trapezoforos with plastic decoration: Attica Group]. Athens, 1993.

Stefanidou-Tiveriou 1998: T. Stefanidou-Tiveriou. *Ανασκαφή Δίου: 1, Η οχύρωση* [Dion excavations: 1, The fortifications]. Thessaloniki, 1998.

Steiner 2010: H. Steiner, ed. *Alpine Brandopferplätze: Archäologische und naturwissenschaftliche Untersuchungen=Roghi votivi alpini: Archeologia e scienze naturali*. Trento, 2010.

Stevens 1991: S. T. Stevens. "Charon's Obol and Other Coins in Ancient Funerary Practice." *Phoenix* 45 (1991): 215–29.

Stewart 2012: A. Stewart. "Hellenistic Freestanding Sculpture from the Athenian Agora: Part 1, Aphrodite." *Hesperia* 81, no. 2 (2012): 267–342.

Stroux 2009: C. Stroux. "Appendice: Caratteristiche musicali dell'hydraulis di Dion." In *La Musa dimenticata: Aspetti dell'esperienza musicale greca in età ellenistica*, ed. M. C. Martinelli, F. Pelosi, and C. Pernigotti, 267–69. Convengo di studio Pisa, Scuola Normale Superiore, 2006. Pisa, 2009.

Tataki 2006: A. B. Tataki. *The Roman Presence in Macedonia: Evidence from Personal Names*. Athens, 2006.

Thomas 1981: E. Thomas. "Zu stilistischen Gruppen und zu Werkstätten neupalastzeitlicher Glyptik." In *Studien zur minoischen und helladischen Glyptik: Beiträge zum 2*, ed. I. Pini and W.-D. Niemeier, 225–40. Marburger Siegel-Symposium, September 1978. Corpus der minoischen und mykenischen Siegel 1. Berlin, 1981.

Thonemann 2010: P. Thonemann. "The Women of Akmoneia." *Journal of Roman Studies* 100 (2010): 163–78.

Touratsoglou 1988: I. Touratsoglou. *Die Münzstätte von Thessaloniki in der römischen Kaiserzeit (32/31 v. Chr. bis 268 n. Chr.)*. Berlin, 1988.

Trakosopoulou 2004: E. Trakosopoulou. "Jewelry in Macedonia." In *Alexander the Great: Treasures from an Epic Era of Hellenism*, ed. D. Pandermalis, 115–37. New York, 2004.

Tsiafis 2009: I. D. Tsiafis. *Οι Μακεδονικοί τάφοι του Δίου* [The Macedonian tombs of Dion]. Thessaloniki, 2009.

Turner 1967: V. Turner. *The Forest of Symbols: Aspects of Ndembu Ritual*. Ithaca, NY, 1967.

Tzanavari 2012: K. Tzanavari. "Αναθηματικός κιονίσκος στον Δία Ύψιστο από τα Πλανά Χαλκιδικής [Votive kioniskos to Zeus Hypsistos from "Plana," Chalcidice]." In *Δινήεσσα: Τιμητικός τόμος για την Κατερίνα Ρωμιοπούλου* [Dinessa: Volume in honor of Katerina Romiopoulou], 587–600. Thessaloniki, 2012.

Tzifopoulos 2011: Y. Tzifopoulos. "37. Ad OF 496." In *Tracing Orpheus: Studies of Orphic Fragments; In Honour of Alberto Bernabé*, ed. M. H. de Jáuregui et al., 231–35. Sozomena 10. Berlin, 2011.

Tzifopoulos 2012: Y. Tzifopoulos. "Από το σύνταγμα (corpus) των επιγραφών της βορείου Πιερίας. οι μεταθανάτιες δοξασίες στη Μακεδονία και τα βακχικά-ορφικά ελάσματα [Since the constitution (corpus) of inscriptions in northern Pieria: Postmortem beliefs in Macedonia, and Bacchic-Orphic lamellae]." In *Θρεπτήρια: Μελέτες για την αρχαία Μακεδονία* [Threptiria: Studies on ancient Macedonia], ed. M. Tiberios, P. Nigdelis, and P. Adam-Veleni, 544–63. Thessaloniki, 2012.

Vasileiadou 2011: I. Vasileiadou. *Η αγροτική ζωή στην αρχαία Πιερία: Αρχαιολογικά τεκμήρια* [Rural life in ancient Pieria: Archaeological evidence]. Thessaloniki, 2011.

Vendries 2004–5: C. Vendries. "Une musicienne et son instrument à cordes sur une stèle funéraire de Dion en Macédoine: Enfin le *nablium*?" *Bulletin de correspondance hellénique* 128–29 (2004–5): 469–502.

Vermeule and von Bothmer 1959: C. C. Vermeule and D. von Bothmer. "Notes on a New Edition of Michaelis: Ancient Marbles in Great Britain; Part 3: 2." *American Journal of Archaeology* 63 (1959): 329–48.

Versnel 2011: H. S. Versnel. *Coping with the Gods: Wayward Readings in Greek Theology.* Leiden, 2011.

Voutiras 1998: E. Voutiras. "Athéna dans les cités de Macédoine." *Kernos* 11 (1998): 111–29.

Voutiras 2006: E. Voutiras. "Le culte de Zeus en Macédoine avant la conquête romaine." In *Rois, cités, nécropoles: Institutions, rites et monuments en Macédoine,* ed. A.-M. Guimier-Sorbets, M. B. Chatzopoulos, and Y. Morizot, 333–46. Actes des colloques de Nanterre, 2002, et d'Athènes, 2004. Athens, 2006.

Weinberg and McClellan 1992: G. D. Weinberg and M. C. McClellan. *Glass Vessels in Ancient Greece: Their History Illustrated from the Collection of the National Archaeological Museum, Athens.* Athens, 1992.

Whitehouse 1997: D. Whitehouse. *Roman Glass in the Corning Museum of Glass.* Vol. 1. Corning, NY, 1997.

Wörrle 1988: M. Wörrle. *Stadt und Fest im kaiserzeitlichen Kleinasien: Studien zu einer agonistischen Stiftung aus Oinoanda.* Munich, 1988.

Zimmer 2002: F. Zimmer. *Die griechische Klassik—Idee oder Wirklichkeit.* Eine Ausstellung im Martin-Gropius-Bau, Berlin, 2002, und in der Kunst- und Ausstellungshalle der Bundesrepublik Deutschland, Bonn, 2002. Mainz, 2002.

From left to right and from top to bottom:

1. Letter from George Soteriades to Mr. N. Zavadias, the guard of the archaeological site of Dion (1930).

2. Mr. N. Zavadias at Dion posing with some visitors. At the center, a funerary stele found during the excavations.

3. List of antiquities transferred from Dion to the Thessaloniki Museum. Written on an accounting ledger sheet by Mr. N. Zavadias.

4. The first Museum at Dion (ca. 1931).

5. Mr. G. Zavadias (the new guard of the site), the village postman, and two visitors posing by the ruins of the Christian Basilica (1956).

6. Transcription of an inscription by G. Zavadias (1964).

7. Beginning of excavations at the South wall under the direction of George Bakalakis.

8. Two of the village's elders seated by the Roman Theater.

9. Transcription of an inscription by G. Zavadias (May 1964).

10. "Uncle" Lazos Sykiotis, in traditional dress, visits the excavations of the Hellenistic Theater (Summer 1973).

Drawings and Photography Credits

Hellenic Ministry of Culture and Sports

Dion Excavations Archive

Additional Photography

MOUNT OLYMPUS